Seasons of the
TROUT

Seasons of the TROUT

Strategies for the Year-Round Western Angler

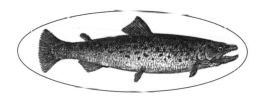

BY NEALE STREEKS

ILLUSTRATIONS BY ROD WALINCHUS

PRUETT PUBLISHING COMPANY
BOULDER, COLORADO

Printed in the United States
10 9 8 7 6 5 4 3 2 1

Library of Congress Cataloging-in-Publication Data

Streeks, Neale.
    Seasons of the trout : strategies for the year-round western
angler / by Neale Streeks.
        p.   cm.
    Includes bibliographical references (p. 251) and index.
    ISBN 0-87108-895-9 (hc)
    1. Trout fishing—West (U.S.) 2. Trout—Behavior—West (U.S.)
I. Title.
    SH688.U6S76   1998
    799.1'757'0978—dc21   98-39450
                                                            CIP

Cover and interior design by Julie Long
Book composition by Lyn Chaffee
Cover and interior photographs by Neale Streeks
Illustrations by Rod Walinchus

CONTENTS

CONTENTS

LIST OF COLOR PLATES

Color plates found after page 120

INTRODUCTION

By NATURE, TROUT are curious creatures. Their behavior and feeding habits are shaped by the particular river or lake habitat they inhabit. Their preference for certain food items at certain times of day or of the year is a reflection of that habitat. Fishing pressure, too, tends to increase their gastronomic refinement. They get picky and can prefer realistic fly patterns over general attractor patterns.

When a beginner sorts through all the books available on the subject of fly fishing for trout, the number of titles and their super specialization can be overwhelming. The variety and proliferation of books bear testimony to the infinite angles of the sport as well as the many ways it can consume an angler's psyche. In the past, beginning anglers who wanted to read about the complexities of trout fishing had to sift through a confusing array of hatch books. Western anglers faced an even tougher time since most fly fishing books focused on eastern and midwestern waters and hatches. Material on western water was sketchy and incomplete. That's all changed today, as the major focus on trout fishing has shifted westward. Even so, reading an intricate hatch book tends to leave beginner and intermediate anglers a little stunned by the end. Insects are covered categorically in a heavy "information overload" format. The accessible, practical information one really looks for is often lost in a vast display of scientific jargon and detail. Not all hatches are important to all anglers. There are bugs and there are bugs. Beginning anglers want and need simple, straightforward information about bugs that will help them catch fish and learn about trout behavior. The more complex material can be digested later!

Seasons of the Trout presents insect hatch and other applicable trout fishing information in a more user friendly way: a season by season approach that covers what anglers are most likely to encounter along western rivers. If you're fishing in May, for example, you can read the Early Summer chapter for an overview of that season. River conditions, trout behavior, hatches, and fishing advice are presented simply, clearly, and interestingly to help ease a beginner onto the path of knowledge and understanding. Over one hundred photos and illustrations provide the important visual detail one needs to learn about and identify the aquatic insects that are critical for success in the sport.

The trout's world will always be a complex one, as complex as your personality, time, and determination allow it to be. You can fish successfully using a handful of general patterns to catch an acceptable number of fish. But the complexity of the sport has its own appeal, and it offers the interested angler greater challenges and deeper rewards. When you develop an appreciation and understanding of the intricacies of fly fishing, you gain a deeper, more enduring knowledge of the river environment as a whole. This ultimately leads to more fish caught and bigger stories to tell. It's a "win-win" situation for the studious angler.

Seasons of the Trout will help you learn how to look at a river, expect certain hatches, identify corresponding trout behavior, and anticipate your way to success. You'll actually learn how to see and catch those large trout sipping flies in shallow edge waters rather than wading through and spooking them. You'll learn how to analyze river conditions to deduce what the trout's undetectable food sources are so you can present the proper nymphs in such a way as to routinely fool the trout. And you'll learn to consider those difficult-to-catch trout that target emergers *before* you head to the water so the right flies will be in the tackle box when those ultimate moments of truth come.

I have written *Seasons of the Trout* with the hope that it makes this learning path a little easier to follow (easier than it was for me!) for those who are relatively new to the sport, for trout fishing is always an interesting and absorbing game.

1

MOUNTAIN SPRING
March and April

Almost imper-
ceptibly, winter
begins to roll back
north into the Canadian provinces whence it came. One day you realize it
is really gone. The feel of the warming sun and the windborne scents of
the earth's richness tell you that the best is yet to come.

Winter leaves behind a stark yet dramatic scene of endless mountain ranges, deep-worn valleys, and wandering waters. Snow still buries
high peaks and fills the contours of north-facing coulees, gulches, and
slopes. West-flowing drainages bristle with the promising greens of fir,
spruce, and pine forests through the long winter. Blue sky east-slope landscapes are more bare. Bleak gray-brown grasslands seem to roll on forever.
They are highlighted by the last holdouts of snow in sunless folds that
define their great windswept vastness. Distant mountain ranges, lonely
highways, and cottonwood bottoms help frame such scenes, cutting down
the overwhelming immensity of the West into a portion humans can better comprehend.

Along creeks and rivers, leafless willow thickets glow in shades of
vermillion, russet, and gold. This bit of brightness immediately draws the

eye streamside, where the cold water flows. Ice may still glaze the water along banks in shaded eddies. Lakes are still frozen, but most moving waters are once again running free, either muddied or clear. Unseasonably warm temperatures can raise the silt-laden water. There's a lot of snow yet to be melted in the high country. The high point of daily activity in the valley floor at this season might be when the ranch pickup dumps another morning load of hay for the appreciative herd of winter-range cattle.

Clear spring water calls to anglers, too. And though water temperatures may perhaps be 34–40 degrees Fahrenheit, life is beginning to stir in rivers and streams across the West. Both aquatic insects and trout are becoming more active with the increased daylight and its warming effects. An annual cycle is beginning, one that may be well known (or at least known in part) to the old and experienced yet seems an insurmountable riddle to a newcomer to the stream.

The shapes of trout become visible now, holding and flitting about in the elbow pools of small meadow streams. The riseforms of surface-feeding trout become more common on rich tailwater rivers and spring creeks, where spring comes a little sooner than it does on other types of water. Midges proliferate, and *Baetis* mayflies will soon be hatching. Small winter and spring stoneflies cavort along the edges of swifter mountain streams, especially on sunny days when warming rays bathe riverside boulders. Trout rise to these, too. Yes, there's much to look forward to when winter rolls back and spring greets the Rockies.

Effects of Spring Weather

Because the Rocky Mountain West includes such vast north-to-south, Pacific-to-prairie, and zero-to-10,000-foot altitude differences, it's impossible to make vast generalizations stick, especially when it comes to weather! Spring weather plays a multifaceted role in fishing, and especially fly fishing. Increasing daylight and warming temperatures stimulate fish and insect activity as spring progresses. A sudden downward plunge in air and water temperatures can put fish off for a time (it would invigorate the fish during a hot summer period). Large-volume, dam-controlled, and spring-fed rivers keep more constant temperatures. In these places a cold snap might not have too noticeable an effect on trout behavior, especially if it was accompanied by cloudy, humid weather. It could increase midge- and mayfly-hatch activity and thus bring up more risers. Smaller shallow creeks and rivers change temperatures more quickly. Cold fronts chill streams and can slow down hatches and fish—not immediately, perhaps, but before too long. Low-pressure fronts seem to activate trout in most cases, even if only for a brief (minutes or hours) period of time.

How well a body of water maintains its temperature can indicate how dependable the fishing there will be. Trout adjust somewhat to various temperatures; it's sudden change they don't like. I see trout happily rising in different rivers with stable water temperatures ranging from 38–70 degrees. Carrying and using a thermometer, recording water temperatures of your local stream, and noting how the trout react to it will advance your local knowledge. Noting the temperature and date when a certain hatch first starts and ends will help you define the hatch limits for your home waters. Once you know these, your catch rate should increase. (Or, if nothing else, perhaps your less-productive onstream time can decrease.)

Other facets of weather and temperature come into play in spring-time. Though rising air temperatures increase both water temperatures and insect and trout activity, they also melt snow! Too much warmth too soon can trigger big snowmelts, or runoffs. A quick-rising muddying river will do little for your dry-fly potential (though nymph and streamer fishing along the edges could be productive). If the river warmed to the right temperature, that could get stonefly nymphs migrating toward the banks for upcoming emergences. Early-season heat waves that muddy rivers send serious anglers in search of dam-controlled rivers or spring creeks, where waters continue to flow clear. These water types tend to have more consistent hatches, too, and steadier-rising fish. Some lakes could be ice-free, though not the ones at higher elevations.

Another aspect of spring weather can factor in when it comes to insect hatches and rising-trout behavior. This is sunshine and arid conditions as compared to overcast and humid ones, including rain and snow. Some aquatic insects prefer the former, others the latter. Barometric pressure might play a role, too, at least in part.

A prime example here is the *Baetis* mayfly's general preference for overcast conditions. This very important family of mayflies hatches best when the sun is obscured. It's an afternoon hatch that can really boom on

Snowmelt triggers rising rivers. Here, a muddying tributary enters a dam-controlled river. Runoff occurs periodically from winter through spring, but the biggest one starts sometime in May and continues through most of June.

cloudy, drizzly, and snowy days. No weather seems too foul once this seasonal emergence has begun. (*Baetis* hatches begin showing as early as March on some waters, more typically in late April on Montana rivers.)

The trout, too, seem to rise better on overcast days in spring, perhaps because they've spent a winter in deeper, darker conditions. One often sees good examples of this on partly cloudy days, particularly on mellow-flowing rivers with good *Baetis* mayfly and midge hatches. When the sun is behind a cloud, bugs hatch and fish rise. When a bright ray of sun beams down and hits the water, all bug-hatching and fish-rising activity can cease, as if a switch had been flipped. Tailwater and spring-creek waters, where *Baetis* and fish populations are highest, can show this effect most clearly. Because mayflies can neither eat nor drink and must shed their delicate covering, humid conditions and low light suit them best. Sunny arid conditions could cause dehydration. This may be the reason many (but not all) mayfly species avoid hatching on the sunniest days.

Midges, too, are very important in spring. They seem to hatch best in humid conditions, whether sunny or overcast. They're not sun-shy, as *Baetis* are, but they do hatch better when there's more humidity hovering about the river valley. Spring *Baetis* mayflies mixed with midges paint a splendid fishing scene on many western waters, as good as it gets at times. If overcast, humid, and windless conditions prevail, it's time to hit the river! The bugs and spring trout don't mind windy inclement weather as much as many anglers do!

On the other side of the sunshine spectrum are little winter and spring stoneflies. These are more active on sunny warm days. They are most populous on a different water type—swifter-flowing rocky mountain streams. I've seen instances on partly cloudy days when bugs and rising fish only showed up when the sun came out and warmed the earth. The trout tend to rush up and grab the fly with a quick swirl or splash, perhaps being a little suspicious of sun and surface so early in the year. Tailwater and spring-creek trout get in a slower, surer rising groove on overcast days, presenting steadier targets as they repeatedly rise to thicker hatches. Each scenario has its own appeal.

Spring hatches mostly occur in the afternoons, with the exception of the midges, which hatch well then or at any other time of day. Afternoon and early evening usually show the most rising fish, when air and water temperatures have reached their high for the day and bugs are most numerous. There is seldom a need to get on the water early in spring. Even trout taking streamers and nymphs seem to hit best from late morning on. And no doubt much of your time on a spring river will be spent fishing the water blind with wet flies. A good session with rising fish will be a luxury in many quarters, one to capitalize on while you can and to enjoy.

On the whole, a steady-warming spring is better for fishing than is one of great temperature fluctuation. Snow melts slowly and steadily. Rivers stay clearer and more stable. Hatches and fish activity increase. Fishing opportunities are maximized, and trip conditions are more dependable. Quickly alternating hot and cold snaps muddy and chill rivers, making a good trip hard to time.

A low-snowpack winter in the mountains can make for very good spring and early-summer fishing, with low, clear water conditions and hatch-oriented trout. Unfortunately, it can also cause severe drought conditions in midsummer and fall, which can kill quite a few fish. Many mountain rivers depend on a steady-melting snowpack, not on rainfall, for their water in the summer. Without a good snowpack, fisheries managers and concerned anglers always worry a bit about the trout's welfare.

EARLY-SPRING RIVER CONDITIONS

Early spring in the Rockies finds most river flows low and clear. The high-water period occurs when high-elevation snowmelt takes place, often with the addition of early-summer rains. This high-water or runoff period occurs from April to early July, depending on location, altitude, and yearly weather patterns. This is different from the East and West Coasts, where rain generally causes the highest water flows, which come in winter and spring. Some visitors from the East Coast are sadly surprised when they come out to Montana in June expecting summer conditions and dry-fly thrills, only to find that most rivers are at their seasonal highs. Big, muddy water often greets them. The chance of a salmonfly hatch and throwing big wet flies will be their best freestone hope. Drainages toward the West Coast, to the south, and at lower elevations can, naturally, experience snowmelt high-water periods earlier than those experienced nearer the crest of the northern Rockies.

The March-through-April period in the Rockies is usually one of excellent fishing conditions, with low, clear water and some rising fish. Productive fishing periods are certainly shorter now than they will be in summer, and are often confined to afternoons. Good fishing is had, though, including some banner days for all techniques.

If premature heat waves (temperatures in the seventies) and heavy rain don't show too soon, rivers stay clear. In Montana, we anticipate the high muddy river period to begin some time in May. It will last through most of June and possibly into early July during a big snowpack year. Higher than average rainfall can push rivers to flood stages. Much of the West receives scant rainfall by East and Northwest Coast standards. In Great Falls, we average 13–14 inches of total precipitation a year. We often get only 11–12 inches. It doesn't take too much extra rain to push June rivers over their banks! We plan to capitalize on as much good fishing as possible before that time period begins! "Mini runoffs," or unseasonably warm temperatures, can muddy rivers in April, too. Smaller rivers with small drainages often clear sooner than large rivers like the Yellowstone, with its massive snowfed drainage.

Some drainages stay clearer than others, too, and show better or different hatches. As early spring blooms into summer, keen anglers will pursue trout in clear-flowing drainages, dam-controlled rivers, spring creeks, and lakes (big-fish water!), wherever better fishing conditions prevail. It's not impossible to experience good fishing on a rising muddy river, either, if a stonefly hatch is about to happen or is underway. The fish can be aggressive and easy to catch for a while, but this is a chancier scenario, where alternating success and abject failure can take you on a roller coaster ride of angling experiences. Fishing the edge waters with large flies is likely to be the order of the day. There's an awful lot of good water to explore out there, literally thousands of productive miles of every description. River and stream fishing seasons vary from state to state, though. Here in Montana, most rivers are open year-round. Most streams and creeks are closed from November to the third week in May. Most lakes are open year-round too but are governed by the ice. Many are heavily ice-fished in the winter. When the ice is first going off, some big fish are caught in what open water there is. From then on, it's "big fish fever" through spring and into summer.

The Trout, the River, and Feeding Behavior

Come spring, trout start fanning out into their traditional feeding lies in a river. Winter found some of them pooled up. Their greatly reduced metabolic rate caused by the cold water made them feed less often, with less vigor, and generally in slower, deeper water. This is perhaps more true in smaller rivers, which are more temperature sensitive, than it is in large dam-controlled rivers and spring creeks, where water temperatures are more stable.

As waters warm into the upper thirties, then forties, hatches gain the trout's attention. Fish move back into edge waters (the shallow, slower edges of the river), riffle drop-offs, eddies, and other feeding locations where their rising metabolic rate (including the rate at which they digest food) can find gastronomic satisfaction. On the Bighorn, for instance, trout can be found rising consistently to midges when water temperatures are in the upper thirties. The browns and rainbows there jump and fight hard at this temperature, too. It's something they have adapted to in this cold-flowing tailwater.

Because riffles carry the largest number of available nymphs and spring nymph populations are approaching their peaks, trout will move into these productive areas, where currents are thwarted. Riffles sometimes look like faster water to the casual observer. They are, however, tailout zones, where the river loses much of its velocity while sifting over and through cobble and gravel. Trout can hold easily in gravel bar drop-offs and riffles and let the food come to them. Prespawning rainbows and cutthroats begin to gang up in pools below riffle areas that they will soon spawn in. Both prefer smaller tributaries for spawning, many of which are closed to fishing in spring. When limited to main trunk rivers, however, big prespawn rainbows can be found near their spawning-areas-to-be.

Favorite trout hangouts on midge-rich rivers (especially tailwaters) include quieter waters of varying depths, from several inches to several feet. A trout can't afford to burn a lot of energy while filling up on midges. It has to rise and "bulge" (take pupae just under the surface—something that may look like a rise but actually is not) so many times that it will choose places where it doesn't have to fight much current to do so. This is especially true with larger fish. Rather featureless edge waters, eddies, the calm zone behind a point or inside bend—anywhere out of the main force

Rising fish can be found in some spring creeks and tailwaters in early spring. Fewer are likely to be seen in the swifter freestone rivers.

of the current where midges collect is where spring trout might be found rising. Large trout can be found in surprisingly shallow slow waters.

In swifter freestone rivers trout will be pushing up into the drop-off at the heads of pools. Stonefly, caddis, and mayfly nymphs will be getting bigger and more active as hatch dates approach. Fish will haunt eddy lines, cut banks, and boulder-littered bellies of pools, too. During a hatch, some fish will move over to the quieter edge waters or drop back toward the tail of a pool, where currents are weaker, water is shallower, and rising is easier. Look for risers *before* wading in!

The shallow slow-water zone known to some as the eye of the pool is a favorite trout spot, too. The spring sun warms slow shallow water just a bit. Sometimes a careful, stealthy coverage of this water (don't walk right up in plain view and wade into it—sneak up, stay back, and cast quietly) with a small streamer or swimming nymph can produce the best results on a cold spring day. The trout still might not be very aggressive, so a slower retrieve can work better.

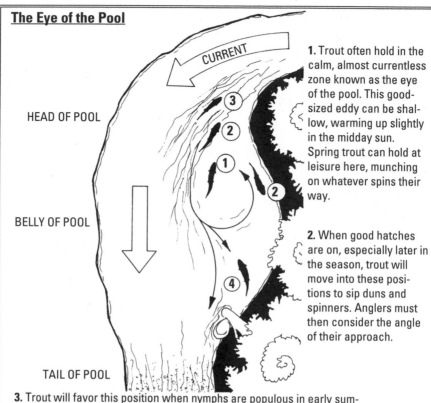

The Eye of the Pool

HEAD OF POOL

BELLY OF POOL

TAIL OF POOL

CURRENT

1. Trout often hold in the calm, almost currentless zone known as the eye of the pool. This good-sized eddy can be shallow, warming up slightly in the midday sun. Spring trout can hold at leisure here, munching on whatever spins their way.

2. When good hatches are on, especially later in the season, trout will move into these positions to sip duns and spinners. Anglers must then consider the angle of their approach.

3. Trout will favor this position when nymphs are populous in early summer, and in late summer and fall. In these later periods, trout find nymphs and also use the riffle for its increased oxygen level in the heated summer water. The rippling eddy lines also provide overhead camouflage from predators, a benefit brown trout seem especially aware of.

4. Where the eddying current splits and glides right into the bank is a productive spot. So much the better if a little foam is collected there, or if some sort of bank cover is available to the fish.

I'll often start the day streamer fishing with a normal midpaced retrieve. If no action is forthcoming, I'll slow it down. Should takes be few and far between, I'll dead-drift the streamer, giving it the occasional twitch so that lethargic cold-water fish don't have to chase it. I do this a lot when I'm float fishing. You just want to bounce it off their noses. This allows streamers to sink deeper, too, which can be very important in near-frigid waters. Trout will hover just above the bottom and along deeper edges, eat at a more limited pace, and be more reluctant to chase food. (Summer trout often hang just under the surface, because so much of their food is carried upon it.) And no matter how long you dead-drift a streamer, the river's currents always impart some action to it, whether you want them to or not.

I might also experiment with hanging a smaller nymph as a dropper off a dead-drifted streamer. Most trout subsist on smaller fare, especially through winter and early spring. The larger streamer catches a trout's eye, but the smaller (#14–18) nymph is often the fly it will take.

Another fly I like in spring is a crayfish pattern. The naturals are plentiful in many rivers, and trout love them. One Pennsylvania study showed that trout took crayfish in preference to small fish and sculpin, or at least ate them more often. Perhaps this is because they're easier to catch. A trout will attack a crayfish, blow it out, take it in its mouth again, and work it 'til it's easy to swallow. It might break a big one up before swallowing it. Hits on crayfish flies and streamers in general are of the violent sort, something that appeals to my primitive instincts. (Trout taking dead-drifted streamers can be quite subtle, though, just picking them out of the flow.) A hard, quick hook set should follow. When spring trout are working, usually at midday, when the water's warmed the most, a spring crayfishing session can be quite productive and exciting. Nymphing may work better overall, but I like the active stripping that is necessary and the savage takes. There's nothing subtle about it! Brown Woolly Buggers work well for this, too.

I once caught a 13-inch brown that got a streamer caught in its gills. It was doomed, and I quickly killed it. Upon inspecting its stomach contents I found twelve medium-size crayfish, one sculpin, plus a good number of sowbugs and midge larvae. Although every fish can have its own feeding and food preferences, this is not an unusual diet for river-bred browns. This one took food items on both ends of the spectrum, from the tiny and numerous midge larvae to midsize crayfish. There is no doubt that most big brown trout (and many large rainbows) prefer large food items when they can easily procure them. The only limiting factor is the size of their mouths. The colder the water is, though, the longer it takes them to digest their food, and the less often they eat.

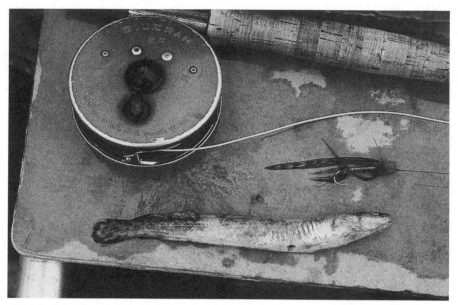

A 14-inch brown already had this 7-inch burbot sticking out of its throat when it ate my #4 streamer. Such gluttony is not uncommon when trout are in a feeding mood.

In shallower rocky rivers, large stonefly nymphs might be the most common large food item taken in spring, followed by sculpins. Stonefly nymphs (at .5 to 2.5 inches) are always available to some degree but especially as the first hatches of larger spring and summer species draw nearer. These big nymphs crawl to the banks or to objects protruding from the river, including boulders and bridge pilings, to hatch. Trout really get on these migrations of nymphs when they occur. The many species of stoneflies found on most western rivers give them repeated opportunities.

For the most part, trout in early spring will hold nearer the bottom than they will in summer. A good hatch will bring them briefly to the surface, but they're not likely to linger there when it's over. Trout on midge-rich tailwaters are an exception. These fish are "looking up" and are surface-oriented much earlier in the year.

Many trout seem surface-shy in spring, and sun-shy, too. It's been a long time since they feasted steadily from the river's surface, so they're a little leery of it at first. The trip to the ceiling of their world does expose them to predators, be they bird, mammal, or larger fish. In any case, quick, splashy rises are often seen during spring hatches. Later in the year the same fish will make slow tilting glides up to engulf hatches as part of their daily routine.

SPRING SPAWNING

Spawning affects river systems in several ways. First, the spawning fish themselves quit feeding and move out, thus removing themselves from the general fishing scene. One does catch them occasionally on a variety of wet flies if they spawn in the main stem river where one is fishing. Most rainbows and cutthroats, the spring spawners of greatest concern to most fishermen, seek smaller tributaries to spawn in. Many of these are seasonally closed to fishing to protect the spawning fish.

In some cases, rivers that are predominantly rainbow fisheries see an outflow of fish to tributaries in spring. The river's fishable population might drop by half between late March and late May. In other cases, where browns dominate, the effect is less noticeable.

Rivers that feed lakes usually act as spawning grounds for the resident lake fish. Long rivers that come out below dams can see big rainbows stack up. In both cases an influx of larger than average trout move in for one to two months. In some lake-river systems, such as Yellowstone Lake, a percentage of the trout swim downstream a bit to gravelly sections of river that flow out of the lake, as well as to stretches feeding into it. In any case, a seasonal influx and concentration of big spawning rainbows or cutts can provide trophy opportunities in certain locales. Some lake-feeding rivers become known for big rainbows in the spring and big browns in the fall.

Many cutthroat populations occur at high-enough elevations or in smaller closed-season waters so that fishing them in spawning season is less common. Fish and game departments today are desirous of protecting the remaining races of native cutthroats. The increased or decreased availability of rainbows and cutthroats in spring is one consequence of the spawning season. With the lessened numbers of rainbows in some of my area rivers, this means a greater percentage of brown trout are caught. These are the larger fish, on average. I find spring to be one of the best times to catch big browns, and they hit in the middle of the day!

Because egg patterns work so well from fall through spring, when most fish spawn, one might wonder if browns and nonspawning fish move up into rainbow beds to enjoy a nutritious meal. Suckers and some other small fish spawn in spring, too. Do trout eat many of these eggs? If so, how far will trout follow spawning fish up to feed on their eggs? Do they become selective to eggs? I can't remember ever seeing a study that analyzed these questions or the stomach contents of fish close to spawning beds. Such questions might be shrugged off, or found offensive to pure match-the-hatch anglers, but as the saying goes, inquiring minds want to know! It's just another facet of river life to explore, understand, and capitalize on when fishing.

EARLY-SPRING HATCHES AND FLY PATTERNS

Spring hatches are few, and they lack the diversity seen later on in summer. This makes things easier for anglers to figure out. What hatches there are can be very important to fishing success, especially if you like the sight of rising fish. There are spring days, though, when a hatch is on the water but nothing seems to be feeding on it, at least on top of the water. Perhaps it's good that we're starting out on an easy footing. It will help prepare you for the bonanza of hatches that blossom in early summer.

For the angler who prefers above all else to find rising fish, the following spring hatches will be those most likely to bring trout to the surface. Nothing animates a river scene or fires the imagination of an angler like the rings of rising trout spreading across a river's surface.

Midges

Midges hatch year-round and are of great importance from late fall through winter and into spring. Often they'll be the only hatch in these periods. As spring blossoms into early summer, many more aquatic insects become active and hatch. These are often mixed with midges. The trout will feed on both.

Freestone rivers (snow- and rain-fed rivers without dams or much spring water) will eventually rise and become muddy in late spring. Midges will be of little importance then. With the swift murky water and

This spring stomach sample features numerous midge larvae, pupae, and adults; free-roaming caddis larvae; sowbugs, and a few Baetis *mayfly nymphs. It's a typical diet, especially on tailwaters and spring creeks. These items range in fly size from #16–24.*

the larger aquatic insects present, larger fly patterns will be better producers at this time.

On spring creeks, tailwater rivers, and other slow-paced low-gradient streams, midges can dominate dry-fly fishing from late winter through spring. Some excellent experiences of casting to rising fish can be had around the West then.

Most spring midges are gray to black in color. Some may show a tinge of olive. Trout can eat the larvae but tend to eat more ascending and hatching pupae and adults when they are available. On swifter mountain streams midges can be of less importance, sharing the trout's attention with the little winter stoneflies, which we'll discuss in a moment.

Although beginning anglers often look at midge fishing initially as some terrible thing to pursue, with small flies and picky fish, it often turns out that midge fishing is the simplest thing possible. There are often no other hatches to confuse matters. Fly pattern choices are few and easy. A few midge adult and pupa patterns and you're set. If your eyesight is bad, make sure you have some magnifying glasses to help you tie on flies.

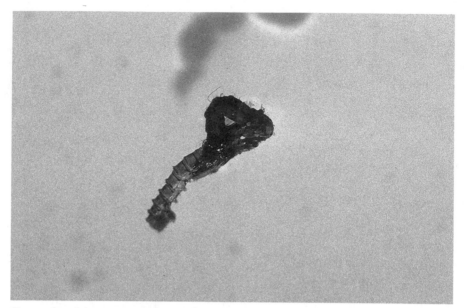

Trout often intercept ascending midge pupae just under the surface. This can look like a rising fish, because a surface disturbance and swirl are created.

You can also use a small strike indicator, even when fishing the dry fly. I usually use a more visible dry fly for a strike indicator, something like a #14–18 Parachute Adams. Some midging trout take this as well.

If your viewing conditions are good (your fly contrasts well with and is visible against its background), using a #18–20 Griffith's Gnat with a #18–22 midge pupa as a dropper is an excellent start. I like to fish the dropper 10–12 inches below the dry fly. In this way, both flies are within range of the fish. The dropper leader (5–7X) is tied to the bend of the dry-fly's hook.

Even if the trout appear to be rising, some may be targeting ascending pupae just beneath the surface. This can produce a swirl on the surface that looks just like a rise. In this case, the pupa pattern will most likely be taken. If it turns out the fish are taking the dry fly most of the time, I cut off the dropper and fish the dry fly alone. This eliminates a few tangles, as dropper rigs occasionally create. Often, however, the fish will take either the dry or dropper. That makes the two-fly rig more productive.

By casting smoothly in slight under-and-over ovals, you'll eliminate some tangles with multiple fly rigs. By insuring that your back and

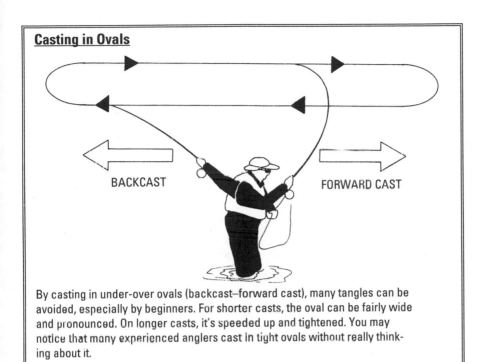

Casting in Ovals

BACKCAST

FORWARD CAST

By casting in under-over ovals (backcast–forward cast), many tangles can be avoided, especially by beginners. For shorter casts, the oval can be fairly wide and pronounced. On longer casts, it's speeded up and tightened. You may notice that many experienced anglers cast in tight ovals without really thinking about it.

forward casts are traveling on slightly different planes, you'll have many fewer tangles. It seems to me that traditional fly-casting instruction advocates back and forward casts on exactly the same plane. No wonder tangles can be so frequent!

For picky *and* wary fish, casting at about a 45-degree downstream angle can be advisable, especially on expansive waters where you have room to move around the fish. This way, the fish sees the fly before it sees the leader. This is the key to fooling many larger spooky trout. The trick is to master an easy ploy known as the reach cast.

Position yourself even with or slightly upstream of the fish, not downstream, as is traditionally done. Make a normal straight-overhead forward cast, but as it unfurls in front of you and is still airborne, point, or "reach," your rod upstream as far as you comfortably can. You can even lean your whole body upstream to do so. The farther upstream you reach and lean, the longer the subsequent drag-free drift of the dry fly will be. You must cast beyond the drift lane you're aiming for, because reaching

The Downstream Reach Cast

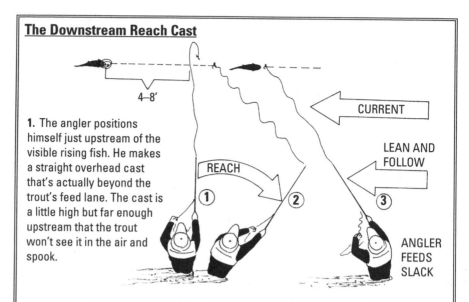

1. The angler positions himself just upstream of the visible rising fish. He makes a straight overhead cast that's actually beyond the trout's feed lane. The cast is a little high but far enough upstream that the trout won't see it in the air and spook.

2. While the fly line is still going forward and is high up in the air, the angler smoothly leans his rod and body upstream as far as he can comfortably reach. While doing this, his fly is eventually brought back across the trout's feed lane. When it's judged to be over the feed lane (and this takes a little practice), the rod tip and line are dropped to the water. Now the fly will go over the fish before the leader will. It's a good idea to feed out some additional slack line as soon as the fly lands. This further extends the upcoming drift of your fly. (Trying to feed out slack at the last second, just as it comes to the fish, usually causes drag.)

If the fly has landed beyond the trout's feed lane, simply lift the rod tip upstream and back until it skids the fly into place. Then drop the rod tip and carry on. If it's too short, recast, but only if it's still far enough upstream to be out of the trout's field of vision; otherwise, let it drift by him first.

3. Now that the fly is in the fish's feed lane, pay out slack and follow the fly's progress with your rod tip and body. At the end of the drift you'll be leaning and pointing the rod downstream. This technique is commonly used on larger flat-water rivers where anglers can move into desired positions to cast to picky fish.

If a large, steady-, and slow-rising trout is your quarry, pause half a second before setting the hook. Otherwise, you'll pull the fly out of his still unclosed mouth. Wait until his head goes back under before snugging up (not jerking) on the line. Then be ready for a run!

tends to pull some line and the fly back toward you. You should also be letting line slide through the guides of your rod while you are reaching. This lessens the pull-back effect on your fly and gains longer drag-free drifts.

This casting adaptation is useful in most casting situations, with the exception of the directly upstream presentations one most commonly makes on small swift streams. It will come in handy all season, especially when picky steady-rising trout are taking numbers of small midges, mayflies, and caddis. It also allows nymphs and streamers to sink deeper and drift longer. The reach cast is an absolute necessity when one is fishing from a boat, allowing much longer drag-free drifts along eddying banks.

When you are midging, absolute dead-drift floats of the fly are not always necessary. A little observation will show that midges often hover, buzz, and move across the surface. A twitch of your fly or the slightest drag sometimes solicits a take from midging trout. Slight movement in a midge pupa dropper isn't fatal either, because the naturals are rising to the surface from the bottom, wriggling and struggling in preparation for escaping their pupal shucks. I aim to achieve dead-drift presentations but allow a slightly dragging fly to go over a fish anyway. And more often than not, even if you think your fly is floating perfectly, the river's current will be creating subtle drag on leader and fly, something you can never totally eliminate, only reduce by using the lightest and thinnest-diameter tippets.

SPRING MIDGES

MATCHING FLY PATTERN SIZES: #16–24

COLOR: LARVA—OLIVES, BROWNS, REDDISH BROWNS, BLACK

PUPA—GRAYS, OLIVES, REDDISH BROWNS, SOME WITH WHITISH ANTENNAE

ADULT—IN SPRING, MOST GRAYS, OLIVES, AND BLACK WITH CLEAR WINGS AND LIGHT GRAY ANTENNAE

Habitat: All waters; particularly important to fish in slow rich waters, where both small-insect and trout populations are high.

Little Winter and Spring Stoneflies

Several genera of small winter-to-spring stoneflies are widespread across western waters. *Capnia* stoneflies hatch through the winter. More genera and species start in February to April and carry on into June. By that time, larger stonefly species overshadow them.

Little winter and spring stoneflies are black and brown. In fact, many anglers call them little black and brown stones. Regardless of what they are called, they are numerous in rocky, swift rivers. Their demand for well-oxygenated water is high. Many feed on decaying leaves and sticks and the organisms that flourish among them. Before hatching, most crawl toward shore or protruding rocks (or bridge abutments) along the river's bottom. Unlike their larger cousins the salmonflies and golden stones, which emerge at night, little black and brown stoneflies emerge afternoons, at the warmest time of day. A few species hatch at the river's surface while

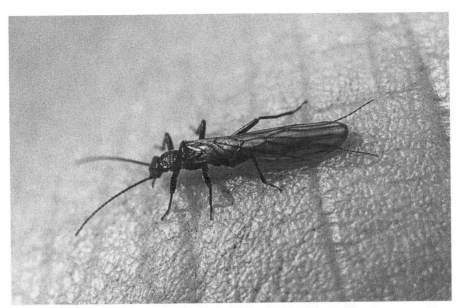

Little winter stoneflies can be found on-stream from February through April or May. They're most active on warmer days. Freestone trout like to rise to them when populations and conditions are right. They're never as numerous as midges or Baetis *mayflies, but there can be just enough of them to bring some trout up.*

drifting downstream, in mayfly and caddis fashion. Fishing little stonefly nymphs should turn up some fish in spring waters. A midge-pupa or green caddis-worm dropper wouldn't be a bad idea, either.

Adult spring stoneflies are most active on sunny warm days, unlike *Baetis* mayflies and some other spring hatches. It is then that the stoneflies fly about and lay eggs, making themselves most available to trout. I was on the Bitterroot River one blustery March day. Snow squalls and cloud-ripping winds kept spring stonefly activity down. As soon as a warming beam of sunlight illuminated the winter-browned earth, little #16 black stoneflies took to the air and water. Trout immediately rose to them until the short-lived sunshine again flickered out beneath quick-moving eastbound clouds.

You can often see at least three species of little stoneflies on or around the water in spring. (See color plate no. 1.) As the year moves through March, April, and heads toward May, more species and higher numbers of flies tend to be seen. They range in hook size from #18–8.

SPRING STONEFLIES

MATCHING FLY PATTERN SIZES: #18–8
COLOR (NYMPH AND ADULT): BLACK AND DARK BROWN

Habitat: Swifter rivers and streams that are clean and well oxygenated.

Most are black or shades of dark brown or gray. Toward early summer, lighter and colored undersides become prominent, with pale to bright orange or a tannish coloration, along with medium to dark gray-brown wings on top. In early spring, though, black will predominate. For the entomologically minded, these include the genus *Capnia*, the little winter stonefly (the smallest to hatch all winter and into spring); *Nemoura*, the little brown stonefly (the most common in spring, slightly larger); and *Leuctra*, the needle fly (with wings that roll around the top of the body when the insect is at rest, rather than lying flat). There are many more species of each than most anglers realize; well over one hundred combined species can be found scrambling along North American stream shores. Their similar shape and coloring makes exacting imitations of particular species unnecessary. Thank goodness for small favors!

On swift mountain rivers these little stoneflies can be the biggest attraction to trout in early spring. Midges and *Baetis* mayflies could rank second. Caddis larvae (worms and cased caddis) figure frequently in stomach samples, too. Days of fair to good dry-fly fishing could be encountered, especially on sunny afternoons. Expect to spend more time nymphing and using streamers, though.

On spring creeks and tailwater rivers, and on reaches of river where slower meandering currents flow, midges and then *Baetis* mayflies could be more important, with fewer little stoneflies around. There will probably be some, though, and these just add to the surface fare and the possibility of rising spring fish. Because many fly shops don't carry much in the way of little winter and spring stonefly imitations, you might have to look around a bit or tie up some of your own. The naturals won't necessarily give you rising-fish action to depend on, but there often are places where they bring up fish with at least some regularity. Ask around, especially with the most experienced anglers you can find. In many cases fish may be rising to them but no one's around to notice. Some pieces of the western hatch puzzle are still being squared away by anglers who push both extremes of the season.

As the stonefly season enters early summer, look for larger species along western rivers. Salmonfly hatches begin as early as May on some rivers, drawing anglers from all over the country. This is something we'll look at in Chapter 2.

Baetis Mayflies

This is an extremely widespread mayfly genus, and one that is very important to anglers. These mayflies commonly have two generations a season, hatching in spring and then again in fall. They are found in both the western and eastern United States, and in Europe, too. This is one group of mayflies whose Latin name has become widely used by the angling public. They are also called blue-winged olives, or just olives. In the eastern United States and England, other species are called blue-winged olive, so *Baetis* is a more reliable term. Many other mayfly species are known by their common names rather than the Latin.

Baetis mayflies feature olive-gray to olive-brown bodies and medium gray wings. They often appear dark gray on the water. They're rather small, #16–20, but they hatch in big numbers for long seasonal

CHAPTER ONE

durations when few other hatches are on the water. (See color plate no. 2.)

Baetis hatch from about noon to late afternoon or early evening in spring. This is the warmest time of day then. Despite that, they prefer overcast, humid conditions to hatch in. Cloudy, rainy, even snowy days bring out the best hatches. This is a hatch you can depend on. Foul weather doesn't lessen it a bit; in fact, these are just the days you want to be on the river, looking for good hatches and rising fish!

Baetis mayflies begin hatching as early as March on some lower-elevation rivers and spring creeks. I've heard of some hatching even earlier than that. Where I live in Montana, *Baetis* show up about the third week of April on most rivers. They'll hatch predictably from then into June. This gives about two months of rising-fish potential on spring and early-summer afternoons before waters rise too high, making possible a leisurely approach to some of the season's best dry-fly fishing! An afternoon session on the river, a thermos of hot coffee, a dependable hatch, and numerous rising fish—what could be better? When an overcast, drizzly day is forecast in late spring, it's time to close up shop and head for the stream!

In the first part of the spring, midges will be the only other major hatch, with the addition of little winter and spring stoneflies on swifter rivers. Midges prefer humid conditions to hatch in, too, but care less about sunshine than *Baetis* do. Spring *Baetis* don't like bright, sunny, and arid spring days. Some will hatch, but not nearly as many as on cloudy, damp afternoons.

A typical scenario sees some trout rising to midges in the morning, more and more fish rising to *Baetis* mixed with midges in the afternoon, and some fish rising in the evening to crippled *Baetis* duns and more midges. *Baetis* hatches usually end in early evening, say 4:00 to 5:00 P.M., but there can be so many flies that fail to emerge properly that dead duns mixed with midges, and perhaps some *Baetis* spinners, can keep some trout rising 'til dark. This situation will be best on tailwater rivers and spring creeks, whose slower low-gradient flows and rich waters favor profuse daily hatches of these smaller flies. Freestone rivers will have *Baetis*, too, and sometimes in impressive numbers. One stretch may show more bugs and rising fish than another, so it's best to cover some ground and look for bugs and risers. Swift, bouldered rivers will show less steady-rising fish activity. Hatches come and go more quickly and don't tend to last as

Baetis nymphs are numerous, active, and available to trout through much of the season. The naturals, which inspired the Pheasant Tail Nymph, range in size from #16–24.

long. Bugs don't linger in the flows as long as they do on slower-paced rivers, where trout can sip them at leisure. Swift rivers often fish better in spring with nymphs.

Baetis nymphs are numerous in most rivers and can be quite active, swimming about frequently in search of food and cover. Trout have plenty of opportunities to eat them, and do so. *Baetis* nymphs show up routinely in stomach samples. They range in hook size from #18–24, though nymph imitations in #16 and even #14 catch plenty of fish.

The Pheasant Tail Nymph, a British pattern tied to imitate *Baetis* nymphs of Britain, has become the standard *Baetis* pattern here, too. The addition of a bead head has made it even more effective in many cases. Before, during, and after the daily *Baetis* hatch, these nymph imitations will catch a lot of fish. Fishing one or two Beadhead Pheasant Tail Nymphs beneath a strike indicator is a sure way to catch at least some fish (and maybe a lot) in most clear spring waters, as well as during the rest of the season.

Some trout may focus on emergers when a hatch is on. These are

The Beadhead Pheasant Tail Nymph has become a classic, routinely duping thousands of trout across the West. The most commonly used sizes are #14–18.

the nymphs that hang just below the surface as the dun (adult winged fly) crawls up and out of the nymphal shuck before emerging on the river's surface. There are patterns tied to imitate this process known variously as floating nymphs, emergers, or cripples. Cripples imitate duns that fail to escape the nymphal shuck completely and die. In some mayfly species, *Baetis* included, the percentage of cripples is fairly high. But the overall number of hatching flies is much higher yet, so the species has no trouble carrying on.

Where I fish *Baetis* hatches, it seems that dun imitations work well enough most of the time. I rarely fish emerger patterns, just dry flies to imitate duns. *Baetis* do ride the currents a long time before flying off, a very long time. One sees flotillas of *Baetis* duns drifting downstream, getting blown by wind into trout feed lanes, whirling in eddies, and giving trout every opportunity to feed on them. Spring and especially fall *Baetis* mayflies provide some of the season's best dry-fly fishing on certain waters.

My favorite dry-fly pattern for the *Baetis* hatch continues to be the Parachute Adams. It works well on my area trout, and from what I hear,

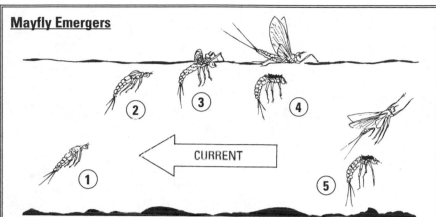

Mayfly Emergers

CURRENT

1. Trout may focus on mayfly nymphs as they swim to the surface prior to hatching. Subtle boils and flashes in the water, combined with a few duns or freshly hatched mayflies on the surface, should alert anglers to this.

2. Nymphs can have a difficult time breaking through the surface to hatch. Some will pause and rest just beneath it, recouping their strength. This is when a floating or sub-surface nymph (which can be fished as a dropper) can work best. If swirls but no trout noses are seen, or if trout backs and fins but not heads are seen, the fish are probably focusing on these.

3. Some trout may focus on mayfly emergers just as they struggle out of their nymphal shucks. This varies from fish to fish and hatch to hatch. Fishing pressure affects trout behavior, too. Many emergent patterns are offered by shops and catalogues these days. Most are designed to be partly on top of and partly beneath the water.

4. The dun finally gets out of its shuck and steps up onto the water's surface. How long this takes, and how long the dun rides serenely on the surface (if long at all), varies from species to species.

5. A few species of swift-water mayflies leave their nymphal shucks before reaching the surface. These can be imitated by traditional wet flies and soft hackles as well as with more modern designs.

on trout all over the country. Most *Baetis*-feeding trout here will take a well cast and controlled Parachute Adams. I tie some with black wings, too, which show up better in situations where the sun produces a lot of glare. Trout seem to like the bold wing silhouette, too.

Other popular and effective patterns include Baetis (often listed as Olive) Sparkle Duns, Thorax patterns, and the traditional Adams. Even little

Baetis are among the few mayfly species that like to crawl under water to lay their eggs. The rolled-back wings capture air beneath them, creating a shimmering, reflective highlight. Do trout key in on these easy-to-see morsels as hundreds of them crawl down logs and rocks?

BAETIS Mayflies

MATCHING FLY PATTERN SIZE: #16–20

COLOR: NYMPH—AMBER BROWNS TO OLIVE BROWNS, THREE TAILS

DUN—MEDIUM GRAY WINGS, OLIVE GRAY BODY, TWO WISPY TAILS

SPINNER—CLEAR WINGS, TANNISH TO REDDISH BROWN BODY, TWO TAILS

Note: Baetis duns have a shrunken, barely noticeable hind wing. This helps in telling them from some other similar-looking mayflies, which have smaller but well-developed hind wings.

Habitat: Most rivers and streams; particularly important on flatter tailwater rivers and spring creeks, but also on spring freestone rivers when they are low and clear.

BAETIS Fly Patterns

NYMPH:

      PHEASANT TAIL #14–22

      BEADHEAD PHEASANT TAIL #14–18

      FLOATING OLIVE NYMPH #16–20

DUN:

      PARACHUTE ADAMS #14–22

      OLIVE SPARKLE DUN #16–20

      OLIVE THORAX #14–22

      ADAMS #14–20

      H & L VARIANT #14–20

Note: #14s are larger than the naturals, but many fish will take them, especially in riffle lines, wind chop, and where fishing pressure is low. *Baetis* mayflies begin their seasonal emergence close to a size #16–18. As the hatch continues toward midsummer, the naturals get smaller, more like a #20 or even #22. This is true of mayflies in general. Early-summer and fall mayflies tend to be larger than midsummer ones. The smaller size and lighter color of midsummer mayflies is thought to be a way for these noneating and nondrinking insects to avoid dehydration. Many spring and fall mayflies, including *Baetis*, are dark colored, so their bodies absorb heat at those cooler times of year.

#16–20 Royal Wulffs and H & L Variants work well at times. These attractor patterns are easy to see on the water and catch fish, too. There are many times when just getting your fly small enough to suit the fish will be enough to catch a good percentage of them. Solid casting skills, using the reach cast, and dead-drifting exacting presentations will add up to catching fish. Casting skills are most important.

    Baetis spinners are of less importance than the profuse hatches of duns would lead you to believe. This is because many of them crawl under water to lay their eggs rather than depositing them on the river's surface and dying, as most mayflies do. You will see them on the water, often mixed with larger numbers of duns, and trout do take them. It would be interesting to know how many of the underwater crawling adults trout eat, for after they die, many must break loose and wash downstream.

When *Baetis* spinners crawl under water to lay eggs, they carefully roll their wings over their backs, capturing some air underneath. This trapped air glistens brightly as they begin their crawling descent. Perhaps trout pick off these visible targets. At least I can pretend that my Bead-head Pheasant Tail Nymph is being taken for a dislodged *Baetis* spinner! Fishing below a riffle when *Baetis* spinners are seen in the air (and are crawling down your waders) could be productive.

March Browns (*Rhithrogena morrisoni*)

"March brown" is a term that started in England, migrated to the East Coast of the United States, and was then carried West on stage-coaches and 747s. In each place it refers to a different mayfly. To clear things up a bit, anglers often call the Rocky Mountain–Pacific Northwest variety the western march brown. (See color plate no. 3.)

This is a common and widespread genus of mayflies across the West, with the one species known as the march brown (*R. morrisoni*) being an important spring mayfly. It requires clean swift-flowing rivers. The duns have light gray wings with strong brown mottling. The wings look large on the water and rake back to near a 45-degree angle. The body varies in color a bit (which is true with many mayflies), from shades of olive to brown. The undersides are lighter. There are two sturdy tails.

These flies are noticeably larger than *Baetis* when both are seen side by side. The taller, raked-back wings are obvious, too. March browns hatch late mornings to early afternoons. Spinner falls take place at the same time. The spinners have clear wings, two long, sturdy tails, and bodies that are reddish brown on top and tan underneath. Both dun and spinner are imitated on #14–16 hooks.

March brown nymphs are of the clinger variety, holding tight to rocks in swift currents. They remain hidden from trout more than the swimming *Baetis* nymphs do. It is when they emerge that they become of interest. They are thought to leave their nymphal shucks on the way to the surface, making the last bit of the upward trip through the water as winged adults. Most mayflies emerge at the surface, rather than under it. Due to this hatching procedure, wet flies, emergers, and soft hackles come into play. These are fished both dead drift beneath the surface and with the traditional wet-fly swing. Takes can be bold and can break light tippets. You can get away with fishing these on 4X leaders in most cases, whereas you would probably want to use 5X when fishing march brown dry flies.

Western march browns hatch as early as late February in some lower West Coast drainages. They become more widespread in March and April. They don't show up in higher-altitude Rocky Mountain rivers until late April or May, a couple weeks after the *Baetis* mayflies start. When they do, some good dry-fly action can be had if rivers haven't risen and become muddy yet. There is usually a clear-water period in this time frame, but spring river levels vary from year to year.

One can run into a mixed hatch bag on many spring rivers, especially by late April. The morning could start with midges, especially if a humid day is on hand. March browns can hatch well from late morning to just past noon. Spinners could be mixed in or might just follow the duns. Little spring stoneflies could materialize as the day warms, becoming active and possibly numerous depending on the water type. *Baetis* could show up after lunch and carry on 'til 4:00 P.M. or so. On richer waters the *Baetis* could provide the best action of the day. Midges can continue to be mixed in all day until evening. The importance of an aquatic insect can vary from river to river and stretch to stretch, because each species has its own niche in a river's ecology.

March browns are a substantial hatch on many rivers. It seems to me that this has traditionally been ignored by many anglers around the Rocky Mountain West. I know of many stretches of different rivers where march brown duns will be drifting on the currents, fish will be rising, but few if any anglers will be seen capitalizing on the situation. There are no tourist anglers around, and even resident anglers seem to be waiting for summer. As western angling and its literature grow to explore every possibility across this huge landscape, such fishing opportunities are becoming better understood. Find some stretches of river where this hatch is good and where fish rise to it, then mark it down in your angling calendar. Explore its perimeter dates (by fishing, of course) and note the seasonal hatch niche. By compiling such information, then checking the same hatch out on other, and perhaps less popular rivers, you can discover some excellent seasonal opportunities and solitude. Then, if all else fails, you can still slam a Woolly Bugger out there or dredge with nymphs.

CHAPTER ONE

March Brown Mayflies

MATCHING FLY PATTERN SIZE: #14–16

COLOR: NYMPH—DARK GRAYS TO BROWNS AND REDDISH BROWNS, THREE TAILS

DUN—MOTTLED GRAY-BROWN WINGS RAKED BACK, OLIVE-BROWN BODY, TANNISH UNDERNEATH, TWO TAILS

SPINNER—CLEAR WINGS, REDDISH BROWN BODY, TANNISH UNDERNEATH, TWO STURDY TAILS

Habitat: Medium to swift clean rivers

March Brown Fly Patterns

NYMPH:

BEADHEAD HARE'S EAR, DARK #12–16

EMERGER:

MARCH BROWN SOFT HACKLE #14–16

PARTRIDGE AND PEACOCK SOFT HACKLE #14–16

MARCH BROWN (TRADITIONAL WET FLY) #14–16

ADULT, DRY FLY:

MARCH BROWN HAIRWING DUN #14–16

TRADITIONAL MARCH BROWN #14–16

PARACHUTE ADAMS #14–16 (CAN BE TIED WITH DARKER BODY AND WING)

BROWN WULFF #12–16

Note: Fast water may allow the use of larger patterns. Try soft hackles if flies are on the surface but few risers are seen. If spring waters are high and murky, concentrate on stream edges, or fish deep. A heavy black Woolly Bugger is always a reasonable high-water choice. A nymph can be fished below it as a dropper.

Caddis—The Mother's Day Hatch

The first major caddis hatch of the Rocky Mountain year begins as early as mid- to late April on some rivers. In others it may be delayed until May or even June. It perhaps occurs earlier in some low-elevation West Coast rivers. It has become known as the Mother's Day hatch around Montana because it sometimes peaks around that holiday in the first half of May.

This #14–16 dark gray-brown caddis (with gray and olive body) hatches in amazing numbers as a rule, but for a short period of time, from a few days to perhaps two weeks. On more stable flows, where water temperatures are more constant, it can go on longer. As with most aquatic insects, the hatch dates are thought to be triggered by increasing water temperature and lengthening daylight; each species has developed its own requirements. When the temperature and daylight get to the right point, it's just like the pistol going off at a track meet—the hatch starts its seasonal emergence.

Grannom caddisflies are among the season's first caddis arrivals, and can be super-abundant where they are found. In the Rockies, late April to early May is the usual arrival time.

Grannoms are among the caddisfly species that have cased larvae. This #12–16 Bead-head imitation can work well as a searching pattern most of the year.

The Latin name for this spring caddis is *Brachycentrus occiden-talis*. It and other caddis similar to it have been known to older generations as the grannom (which is a name of British origin). Afternoon and evening is the time to be on the water for this hatch, though one could run into march brown mayflies on the same river a little earlier in the day. Other drainages might see this bug showing up in the next chapter's time frame—early summer.

This caddis can hatch in staggering numbers. Thousands emerge and can form rafts on the water and pile up like foam in eddies. There can be too many to contend with. Both emerging-pupa patterns and dry flies catch fish. Sometimes not matching the hatch but showing the fish something a little different might work best.

Earlier in spring, one can fish the larval imitation, a Beadhead Cased Caddis. The naturals are obviously very numerous on the streambed. There are other species that hatch later in summer, too, with similar-looking cases. Consequently, cased caddis and the free-crawling green and tan caddis-worm imitations are worth bouncing along the bottom all season.

Early caddis hatches can be prolific enough to really turn fish on. If the hatch and low water conditions coincide, it's time to be on-stream!

This potentially awesome hatch occurs in a transition period. Late April to early May can see quick-rising and muddying waters if a warm spell hits, melting tons of mountain snow. One year the fishing can be hot. The next, zippo. The Yellowstone River, just one of the many places where this hatch occurs, is particularly noted for how fast it can blow out from runoff or snowmelt water. This quickly brings the fishing to a halt.

Ask and fish around to find caddis-hatch hot spots in your locale. As summer progresses, many more species of caddis will hatch, many of which look quite a bit like this one. The same caddis patterns, plus some lighter-colored and smaller models, should keep producing for you all season. On many rivers, caddis dominate the overall hatch scene. Although I prefer the way mayflies float downstream and bring up steadier-rising fish, I cannot deny that there are many times when caddisflies are the bugs to be imitating.

The blessing of a new spring primes anglers for another season of promise. Earth and air smell fresh, greens are exploding everywhere. There

Spring Grannom, or Mother's Day Hatch

MATCHING FLY PATTERN SIZE: #14–18
COLOR: LARVA—CASED CADDIS, MEDIUM BROWNS WITH BLACK HEAD
         PUPA—DARK GRAY THORAX, OLIVE ABDOMEN
         ADULT—DARK GRAY TO GRAY-BROWN WINGS, OLIVE BODY

Habitat: Most river types

Spring Caddis Fly Patterns

NYMPH:
         BEADHEAD CASED CADDIS #12–16

EMERGER, PUPA:
         LAFONTAINE SPARKLE PUPA IN GRAY AND OLIVE #14–16
         PARTRIDGE AND PEACOCK SOFT HACKLE (DARKER HACKLE) #14–16

ADULT, DRY FLY
         X CADDIS #14–16
         PARACHUTE CADDIS, OLIVE #14–16
         ELKHAIR CADDIS, DARK #14–16
         ROYAL TRUDE #12–16

are new rivers and hatches to explore, old hot spots to revisit, and a list of "want to's" a mile long. For the beginner, there are few hatches that need be considered. It's an easy time to figure out and to capitalize on, especially compared to what comes next. Early summer offers a proliferation of hatches and river life that can be daunting initially.

Remember that different river types will show different spring hatches. On some, midges and *Baetis* mayflies will provide most of the surface action. Other, swifter rivers may favor spring stoneflies and march

Spring Hatch Chart—February through May

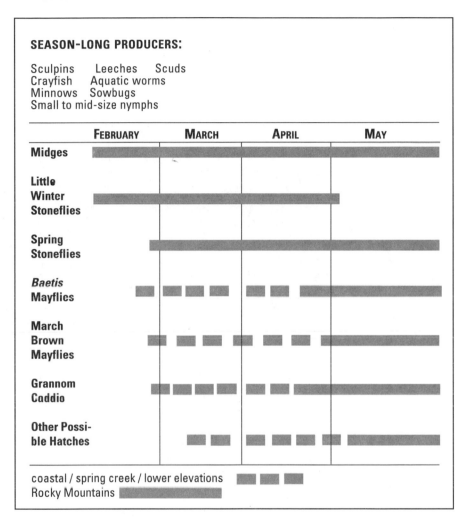

SEASON-LONG PRODUCERS:

Sculpins   Leeches   Scuds
Crayfish   Aquatic worms
Minnows   Sowbugs
Small to mid-size nymphs

	FEBRUARY	MARCH	APRIL	MAY
Midges				
Little Winter Stoneflies				
Spring Stoneflies				
Baetis Mayflies				
March Brown Mayflies				
Grannom Caddio				
Other Possible Hatches				

coastal / spring creek / lower elevations
Rocky Mountains

browns. The Mother's Day caddis hatch could dominate action while it lasts. Some rivers have all these hatches. In any case, all anglers will be hoping that spring rivers stay low and clear just a little longer, maximizing the dry-fly possibilities before the inevitable snowmelt and spring rain muddy them up. Then it will be time to hunt down the clear-water prospects and hot hatches of early summer.

2

EARLY SUMMER
May and June

Although the flowering greens of spring have already bloomed in coastal California, Oregon, and Washington, it's not until mid-May that the interior labyrinth of the Rockies emerges from its winter tans and browns. This sudden greening brings an overdose of spring fever to anglers who haven't been out capitalizing on the early season's clear-water fishing, and even to those that have. For now the allure of the outdoors, of living rivers and plentiful hatches is offset by the nagging knowledge that the runoff will soon commence. Snow melting off peaks and high ranges will soon raise and muddy rivers. Every year is different, but it's only a matter of time.

Mini runoffs have already occurred, even in midwinter. Snow-storms come and go. Chinook winds bring warm air, melting lower-elevation snows quickly. Runoff, floods, and ice jams can happen any time over the winter, and can kill and strand trout. In January of 1997 temperatures in Great Falls went from a snowy minus 30 degrees to 50 degrees. That's an 80-degree temperature change in a matter of days! This may melt low-elevation snow rapidly, but the main summer runoff is yet to come.

Many western anglers try to balance the fishing possibilities with the realities of the early-summer season. What rivers are still in shape? Where are the hot hatches or productive nonhatch fishing? Road trips are eagerly made. *Baetis* here, grannom there. Many salmon fly hatches commence in this time period, too. A carnival atmosphere can pervade some valleys now. Cowhands can only shake their heads. It's a time for Bitch Creeks, Woolly Buggers, and Sofa Pillows, words that easily separate anglers from ranchers in mountain-town saloons come evening.

For the more serious rising-fish addict, there are spring creeks, tailwaters, and perhaps some still-clear mellow rivers where the salmon fly isn't king. (Lakes are losing their ice, too, which presents some big-fish opportunities.) Here one hopes for steadier rising fish and profuse hatches. Good *Baetis* and midge hatches linger on. March browns and caddis mix in. Pale morning dun mayflies and numerous caddis species begin hatching toward the end of this time period in many places. Some big mayflies, including green and brown drakes, might be found, too.

This is a time when river temperatures rise steadily. Many hatches occur. Mature nymph populations are reaching yearly peaks, and the trout's metabolism is in full swing. Deep-nymphing tactics hold great promise now. As rivers rise, dry-fly sessions decrease.

Novices may find the array of hatches a little confusing at this time. There are many rivers, however, where only a few hatches will be important at any one time and a handful of generic patterns should bring some success. Casting skills and proper presentation are every bit as important. For instance, having the weights and right line setup to fish deep nymphs can be important on freestone rivers at times. Controlling the line during the fly's drift so it has time to sink and bounce along the streambed can be more critical than the fly pattern itself. Trout are now seeing and eating many species of nymphs in a seasonal time of plenty. Most are sticking to the bottom or in bankside pockets in order to stay out of strengthening currents. An unweighted and poorly controlled nymph that quickly skids across the river just under the surface can give poor results. One can make many a favorite fly pattern work at this time of year *if* it's in the trout's face.

EFFECTS OF EARLY-SUMMER WEATHER

Early-summer weather in the mountains can be rather fickle. Hot bluebird days can alternate with bone-chilling rain or snowstorms. This is the West's rainiest time of year. At times rain triggers good hatches and feeding fish. Heavy rains just add to mountain snowmelt, though, increasing the rising-river potential. Peak water flows of the year usually occur in these months, when rain and runoff combine. It's no time to be without good rain gear, waders, and sunscreen.

Now one keeps a close eye on freestone river levels when planning some fishing. A hot spell will likely raise and muddy rivers. Tailwaters can remain good, though even these go up in water volume, sometimes doubling or tripling as feeder streams peak, especially in years of high snowpack. Many remain clear, but tailwater fishing suffers when water volumes rise. Lakes with oversized trout can be of particular interest to fly fishers now, as can spring creeks. Get your scud and leech patterns ready. The uppermost reaches of some rivers stay fairly clear, too, as lower sections gather tributaries and funnel runoff waters into impressive flows. These can be worth searching out.

One also begins paying special attention to the banks of rivers at

Pounding the banks becomes a high-water tactic, especially when the larger stonefly species are hatching.

this time. Rising river flows push many trout into calmer, less turbid edge waters. Adding to the impetus are numerous bank-migrating pre-emergent stonefly species. (One Montana study showed sixty-seven species of stonefly in the Gallatin River alone!) Some mayfly and caddis nymphs migrate to calmer edge waters before hatching, too. Terrestrial foods are washed in from the inundated banks. Though many consider terrestrials to be a late-summer game, they start figuring into trout diets from spring on. Beetles and ants are quickly activated by the earth's warmth. Worms, both aquatic and terrestrial, wash free. Early summer really presents trout with a glut of food that is varied and features many larger morsels. From giant salmon fly nymphs to midges, crayfish to snails, the subsurface food base is approaching its peak.

The effect of varying light levels on rising fish is still to be seen. Many hatches are beginning to pop, especially toward late June. Most prefer overcast days for hatching. Trout prefer it, too. A prolonged cool spell can slow snowmelt and potentially lower and clear river levels a bit. A cool cloudy day, and especially a calm humid one, can set off some excellent hatch and rising-fish action. Trout can take nymphs and streamers better, too.

Sunny days won't necessarily be devoid of rising fish, though. Some insect species are more tolerant of sunshine: Egg-laying stoneflies might be seen. A concentrated egg-laying exhibition by large stoneflies is just what you want for big fly, big fish action. This can certainly happen on sunny afternoons and evenings. Some mayflies will be seen, too, often provoking quick swirling or splashy rises on freestone rivers in early-season sunshine. There probably won't be as many steadily rising fish as there would be on the perfect overcast day, but you'll just have to be out there to find out!

EARLY-SUMMER RIVER CONDITIONS

As we've been discussing, May through June is the runoff season in the Rockies. One expects most rivers to go out at some point in this time. Early May can remain very good, with intensifying hatches livening up the fishing scene. It's too bad doom is on the horizon. In years with low snowpack, runoff can be minimized, with continued good to excellent fishing. Many rivers will start coming down in late June. Some bigger ones might stay up into early July. Each year will be a bit different.

Pending high water signals a pivotal point in early-summer decision making. Typical choices include fishing any river that's reasonably clear, or targeting a due or continuing hatch. Some rivers may have more big rainbows than usual, because fish that have spawned are still about. Of course, you might just hit the closest river at hand and take what it dishes out. In murky conditions, larger black or bright-colored (yellow, white, pink, chartreuse) flies are the choice of many anglers, because fish can see them more easily. In any case, choices are a hard part of the early-summer game. Time is fleeting and conditions could get worse.

For instance, one might choose to fish the *Baetis* hatch in a clear tailwater river. This hatch has been going on for some time and is quite dependable. It should still be out in force in the first half of early summer, probably mixed with midges. The flies are small but numerous. On quality rivers the trout get into a good daily afternoon groove feeding on them. They rise repeatedly and for several hours, making good targets. The fishing can be challenging at times, but the challenges are there for the taking.

Or one could choose to hit the famous salmon fly hatch. This type of fishing is a chancier affair. You might know the usual hatch date and have made a few phone calls to keep current. The river is likely a bit high and could either be rising or coming down. Any sudden heat wave can start a snowmelt going depending on the snowpack. By the time you hear the hatch is hot, it could already be sputtering out. Hatches of larger insects, while dramatic, are generally short-lived. It's exciting if you hit it right, and at times spectacular. A quick salmon fly road trip often results in high water and mediocre fishing, though. It's the lure of hitting the hatch just right that keeps people coming back. And who can blame them? The actual fishing and conditions are frequently second-rate, but have fun anyway.

Another choice is just to hit any river that's reasonably clear and hope for the best. Hatches to anticipate include spring stoneflies, march browns, *Baetis* mayflies, grannom caddis, and midges, especially in the first half of this time period. You might chance onto a salmon fly hatch, too. By late June, pale morning duns, green drakes, golden stones, and several caddis species are likely to be out. Even if you don't know much about hatches, some success is likely to come.

Fishing a streamer usually yields results and occasionally bigger than average fish. Slow down the retrieve and sink the fly deeper if success isn't forthcoming. Deep nymphs fished systematically along edge-water pockets and riffle dropoffs can produce steadier results at times.

Early-season fish can be less picky than late-summer ones, but don't depend on it. Understanding seasonal hatches will increase the odds that you have the right fly for the right job. Always keep your eyes open for rising fish, even when fishing wet flies. Slow foam-ladened eddies, inside bends, and edge waters are likely places to see them, as well as wherever a hatch might be piled up by wind or water.

It's not unusual to see an early-summer hatch going on and little or nothing rising to it, especially in rising or high flows. Imitating the nymph or emerger of a hatch can produce better results. Multiple-nymph rigs are an excellent idea. Having one large, heavily weighted salmon fly nymph with a smaller "match the current hatch" nymph as a dropper can catch plenty of fish.

As I mentioned in the first chapter, I find spring to be a good time to catch larger river browns on streamers. This continues from the March through April period into May, with fish still hitting hard in the warmth of midday. As summer progresses and waters drop and begin to clear, larger browns push their feeding activities into the low-light periods—dusk, night, and dawn. I catch quite a few 18–23-inch browns in midday in summer, and on dry flies. From this size up, they're sticking to more of a big-food-item diet in most rivers.

Although tailwater anglers have come to expect clear water, it's not unusual for dam releases to increase at this time, especially if a big runoff is looming in the forecast. In such rising tailwater conditions, trout tend to rise less and less. Food items such as aquatic worms, sowbugs, and mayfly and caddis nymphs must be imitated, with weight added to the leader and strike indicators used. Most tailwaters lack large stoneflies due to the nature of the water (too slow), but many have crayfish and minnows as big-fly options.

Early summer can be prime time for lake fishing, for many mountain lakes have become or are becoming ice-free. The ice-out period in particular can produce some trophies. Rainbows can haunt edges, looking for spawning sites. Most rainbows don't succeed without in- or out-flowing tributaries, and many lakes are stocked with them. Lakes first become ice-free from March to May, or even June, depending on location and altitude.

Altitude is a major factor in determining when lakes become ice-free. Just after ice-out can be a prime time to catch extra-large trout.

Spring creeks and tailwater rivers can present the best running-water options. Tailwaters include both natural lake outflows and dam releases. The hatching insects will be smaller, but profuse. The trout tend to be steady risers. Nymphing is usually dependable, too. Scuds, leeches, midges, *Callibaetis* mayflies, damselfly nymphs, and giant caddis are among a lake trout's favorite fare.

Big dam releases will thwart fishing success to some degree, so it's wise to check on current and scheduled releases before traveling. The runoff accumulation of water that comes out of dam-controlled rivers can continue longer than the runoff on their upstream tributaries. It can take a while to drain a big lake in a year of high snowpack. High clear flows often continue into early July. As long as water levels don't fluctuate a lot, the fish will settle in and moderate fishing results can be had. When the water drops for the summer, though, the hatches and trout can really turn on.

THE TROUT, THE RIVER, AND FEEDING BEHAVIOR

By early summer, water temperatures have risen enough to increase the trout's metabolism significantly. This means they're more active and can eat and digest food at a faster rate than in winter and early spring. Trout will begin putting on weight now, as hatches proliferate and subsurface food items become plentiful. Many rainbows and cutthroats will be coming back from spawning grounds, too, eager to eat and regain their condition after the rigors of breeding.

By now, trout are filling their usual niches in the river as nymphs become very abundant. It is a time when the banks can be of added interest to anglers. In high flows, banks are easier to fish and easier for a lot of fish to maintain themselves along. Float-fishing tactics at this time of year generally target the banks. Stonefly hatches, triggered by rising water temperatures and increasing daylight, lead trout bankside, too. One should pay special attention to large eddies and slower-water areas such as at inside bends and in the eyes of pools. Here the trout can stay out of forceful currents and capitalize on the growing seasonal food glut. In cold rivers, big shallow eddies can warm a bit in midday sunshine, too. These should be fished systematically with slow-retrieved streamers and nymphs. If a good stonefly hatch and egg laying are in evidence, a twitched dry could be tried, perhaps with a nymph dropper.

On swift freestone rivers there can be so many hatches about to pop, of so many different species, that trout get to eat an abundance of activating and growing nymphs. It is along the bottom, in eddy lines, beside banks, and in pockets that trout will be holding. They can have little interest in rising due to the proliferation of nymphs and the rising water. Small mayflies and caddis may go untouched on the surface, but trout could be targeting their nymphs and emergers near the bottom.

In murky flows it might take bigger bugs to bring fish up, and even then only when they're numerous enough for the trout to get used to. If rivers remain clear, more risers are likely to be seen, especially in calmer edge waters, eddies, and tailouts. Freestone rivers feature larger insect species, too, and a greater diversity of them. Therefore, attractor patterns like Stimulators, Trudes, Wulffs, and Humpies fool many a fish. Medium-to-large scruffy nymphs make good droppers. Hitting a freestoner when trout are smashing attractor patterns is one of the real joys of fly fishing.

Attractor patterns can work best from early summer to midsummer. Bountiful big-fly hatches combined with clearing water can make for exciting surface action. These artificials make good strike indicators, too.

On spring creeks and tailwaters the hatches are less diverse and feature smaller insects. They feature greater insect numbers, though, and for long seasonal and daily durations. This generally adds up to more steadily rising trout, some of which are quite large. Trout populations are higher in tailwaters, too, so the rising-fish potential is greater yet.

Most spring creeks and tailwaters lack the big stonefly species. (There are exceptions, such as the natural lake outflows of the Henrys Fork's Box Canyon and the Madison below Quake Lake.) The best fishable hatches include smaller midges, *Baetis* and pale morning dun mayflies, and numerous caddis. Some larger flies like green and brown drakes are seen, but even these are poorly represented in many tailwaters. Here one gets used to picky fish that see enough of one hatch (and enough of anglers) to figure the game out. Attractor patterns are less likely to work routinely, though they're not out of the question, especially in smaller sizes. Tailwater trout can get just as jaded by the latest high-tech emerger

Tailwater and spring creek trout can be very consistent risers. Profuse hatches of small-fly species means that a lot of flies will have to be eaten in order for these fish to fill up. The result is a steady-rising but picky target for the angler.

pattern that everybody is using as they can by a small attractor that nobody is. Tiny H & L Variants, Wulffs, and Humpies work quite well in sizes #16–20. Some days big fish smash larger versions, too. In any case, expect to see spring creek and tailwater trout more focused on a particular hatch than freestone trout are likely to be, sometimes to an antagonizing degree! These clear-water hatches last for weeks and months, so trout know what to look for and what to avoid.

Tailwater trout will feed in very shallow weed-laced flats and edge waters, places where the inexperienced angler wouldn't think big trout would hold. When a hatch is on, it's often better to walk and look for rising fish before making a cast. Any slow water out of the main force of the current is a likely hunting ground. Just off the edges of the main current, in transitional-water zones, widening eddy lines, weed-bed breaks, and around gravel bars are some of the places big rising trout might be seen. They'll also rise along the shallowest, most nondescript banks you can imagine. They care little about depth or traditional cover. It's mellow water flows with a supply of currentborne food they desire. Hunting visible trout on tailwaters and spring creeks is a major angling tactic.

Back on the swifter freestone rivers, which are likely to be murky, one can go straight to a "fishing the water" strategy. You should look for rising fish, but there might be few or none to be seen much of the time. Freestone hatch opportunities come and go more quickly, in part due to the speed of the water. Few flies are left lingering around. (Thousands of flies, cripples, and spentwings can linger on slower tailwater rivers.) Also, many freestone insect species have ecological niches that restrict them to particular water types. This often means that flies are hatching here but not there, and for brief periods of time. In any case, one can blind-fish deep nymphs right off the bat on freestoners and be in a good position to catch fish. A larger dry with a nymph dropper is a viable option. Deep, dead-drifted Woolly Buggers are good early-summer flies,

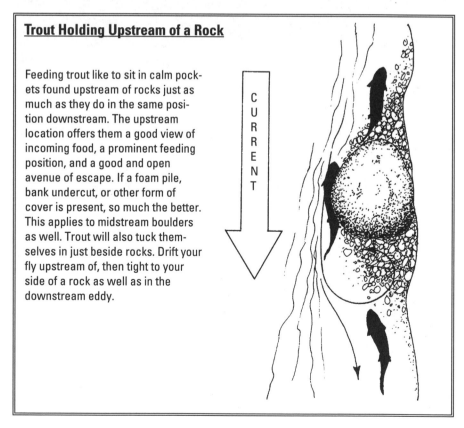

Trout Holding Upstream of a Rock

Feeding trout like to sit in calm pockets found upstream of rocks just as much as they do in the same position downstream. The upstream location offers them a good view of incoming food, a prominent feeding position, and a good and open avenue of escape. If a foam pile, bank undercut, or other form of cover is present, so much the better. This applies to midstream boulders as well. Trout will also tuck themselves in just beside rocks. Drift your fly upstream of, then tight to your side of a rock as well as in the downstream eddy.

CURRENT

too. Upon swinging downstream, they can be slow-stripped back up parallel to the banks. Trout take them for stonefly nymphs or sculpin (or just because they're hungry). Here, too, it's the edges of the main current, protected pockets, eddies, and banks that deserve special attention. Dropoffs at the heads of pools are very productive for deep nymphing. Large feeding trout like to sit upstream of and along the sides of boulders, too, not just behind them. Where the main current moderates along edge waters and tailouts are favorite boulder lies. Dominant fish take dominant positions. Such locations become obvious to the angler with experience on-stream.

EARLY-SUMMER HATCHES AND FLY PATTERNS

This can be a confusing time of year for a beginner trying to grasp the hatch scene. It starts out easy enough, but the number and diversity of hatches grow. Some are important, some are not. Fortunately, on any one river the noteworthy hatches will be fewer than the whole slate.

This is also a transitional time. Most of the spring hatches continue into May. The midges, *Baetis*, winter and spring stoneflies, march browns, and grannom caddis are still around. Some of these can continue into June, depending on the river's location. When they end, there can be high water and other hatches to take their place.

On some tailwater rivers there's a gap between when the best spring *Baetis* hatches end and when the summer pale morning duns and caddis begin. This can prove to be a mediocre period of dry-fly fishing and rising water, with midges, nymphs, San Juan Worms, and streamers carrying it through. The trout still have to eat something.

On freestone rivers, a wider variety of niche hatches begin overlapping. In many cases the larger stonefly species will dominate fishing success overall, even though there are plenty of smaller mayflies and caddis around. In other times and places, freestone trout will capitalize on prolific hatches of smaller fare, especially in years with low runoff. A variety of #10–16 stonefly, mayfly, and caddis species can be mixed together, along with the larger #2–8 stoneflies. What this can mean is that a #8 Stimulator or Royal Trude will catch just as many and bigger fish than attempts to more closely match smaller hatches might. The profusion of seasonal hatches, especially in late June to mid-July, often draws trout that aren't as particular as they are hungry.

It's casting skill now that can count most. Being able to quickly figure (in the duration of a backcast) where the best but unseen trout will be holding is step one. Placing your fly accurately and achieving long drag-free drifts with the reach cast is step two (especially from a boat). Cast quickly and accurately. Keep your fly on productive water. That's the name of the attractor pattern game. You want your fly to cover miles of water nonstop. The efficient caster usually wins the freestone blind-fishing day.

When it comes to the abundant nymphs of early summer, some generalities can be made. Faster water will favor medium to large nymphs (#16–2). From a tying standpoint, these are scruffy and somewhat thick. Swift-water nymphs tend to be more widely built, with strong gripping legs to help hold on in heavy flows, and prominent gills. One exception would be the free-roaming caddis larvae, or caddis worms as they're sometimes called. These are slimmer and often green. Most other swift-water

Fast-water nymphs generally feature a wider look, prominent gills and gripping legs, and a slightly larger size. Barring the larger stoneflies, #12–18 is the most common size.

nymphs are graying tan to brown to black. The classic Hare's Ear (and now the Beadhead Hare's Ear) is a great generic imitation. The simple Montana Nymph is still a good producer. At this time of year I'd feel confident fishing these two nymphs in tandem. It's getting them deep and controlling the drift that counts. Long drag-free drifts (or at least the illusion thereof, for currents always move your fly around more than you think) take practice to master. The right accessories are needed, too, like split shot and strike indicators, or buoyant dry flies.

Slow-water nymphs, on the other hand, such as the majority of those found in tailwater rivers, spring creeks, and big eddies, are smaller and slimmer. Many are swimmers, as opposed to clingers and crawlers. They are streamlined and somewhat insignificant-looking. Many are imitated on #16–20 hooks rather than on the #2–16 models you can get away with in swift rivers. There are exceptions, but this is generally true. Important here are *Baetis* and pale morning dun mayfly nymphs. Midge larvae are numerous too, along with sowbugs and snails (trout favorites). Cased caddis can be very plentiful (some, like the October caddis larvae, are quite large, #6–8, though most are #12–18). Trout eat a lot of these.

Many slow-water nymphs are small and streamlined. Most are active swimmers rather than clingers. There are some large, #10–14 naturals, but the majority of slow-water mayfly nymphs are #16–22.

Stoneflies

Because stoneflies include the largest and most dramatic aquatic insects of early summer, we'll begin with them. As you'll recall, there were #16 little winter stoneflies hatching from late winter into spring. From March to July, #14–8 spring or little brown stoneflies mix in. As temperatures and waters rise in April and May, more stoneflies appear in the #10–6 range. One species known as the Skwala (*Skwala parallela*) has become a local happening in the last decade. It hatches with some other stonefly species in March through April. On freestone rivers at that time, stoneflies can command the trout's attention as much as midges and *Baetis* do on tailwaters and spring creeks.

As waters continue to rise and warm into the fifties, larger stonefly species emerge, including the biggest, the giant salmon fly (so called because of the salmon orange coloration that accents its thorax). What we see is many of the season's largest aquatic insects hatching at the season's highest water-flow levels, or just at the point where they begin to come down. Perhaps this helps hide them from finned predators, for waters tend to be murky and the increased volume spreads fish around a bit. In years of low water the big flies we're about to discuss hatch out in more confined clear flows. This can bring on some memorable fishing episodes because fish and big flies are in such close and visible proximity.

I can remember such years when the golden stonefly hatch was as good as it ever gets. Once, two other anglers and I landed 144 fish to 23 inches and had twice that many boiling hits, all by early afternoon on dry flies. I may never see such a day again, but this is what a low-water early summer has the potential to dish out. Last May I had a day when several smaller stonefly species were hatching just before high water kicked in. These ranged in size from #16–8, which is a common spring–early summer situation. We landed more than forty fish on Stimulators, had at least seven doubles, and many more misses. *Baetis* figured into the afternoon action, too, and were thick along eddying banks, but there was no need to switch flies. Such are the experiences possible when you hit stonefly action right. It's hard to beat!

Salmon Fly (*Pteronarcys californica*)

This giant stonefly measures a full 2 to 2.5 inches long. The salmon-colored thorax and abdomen highlights are in bright contrast to an otherwise drab gray appearance. It's significantly bigger than any of the spring stoneflies that precede it. Salmon flies are so big that fish can shy away from the adults at first. But if the hatch is profuse, trout will soon be on them. (See color plate no. 4.)

Salmon flies start hatching as early as late April in some coastal California drainages. Mid- to late May sees many more hatching around the West. Many Montana rivers have late-June emergences. In the higher elevations of Yellowstone Park, the hatch continues into mid-July. Those wishing to fish the biggest dry flies possible to big lunging fish could travel and follow this hatch around for two full months.

Salmon fly nymphs take two to four years to mature, so there are always some large ones in the water (Come mid- to late summer many of these seem to burrow down into streambed cobble and not be particularly available to fish except perhaps at night.) Even during the hatch, nymph fishing is often the most consistent. There are years when the dry-fly fishing never gets very good. High water and mediocre hatch years do provide hit-or-miss fishing experiences.

Unlike most mayflies and caddis, salmon flies crawl toward the banks, then up and out of the water on riverside rocks to hatch. This hatch is triggered when water temperatures first reach 50–55 degrees. A migration of nymphs begins from midriver toward the banks (or protruding boulders and bridge pilings). This occurs in the afternoon through the evening. The nymphs generally crawl out of the water after dark, which is a good thing, because predators of every description relish them. Trout can follow the multitude of #4–6 nymphs toward the shore during these concentrated migrations, taking up feeding positions there. As with most of the largest aquatic insects, these hatches are short-lived. Being at the right place at the right time is required for fishing success. (See color plate no. 5.)

Deep-fishing black and dark brown stonefly nymphs is a ritual of early summer. Some need to be very heavily weighted to get them down in strong seasonal flows. Upstream and "high-stick" nymphing along banks is commonly used by walking fishermen. Wading can be dangerous at times, and many fish will line the banks anyway. Consequently, you should not wade deeply, if at all.

Much river fishing is done from drift boats in the early summer period, with anglers casting along the banks. A serious downstream-angled reach cast is a must. This prolongs drifts of a dry fly and gives nymphs time

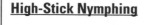

High-Stick Nymphing

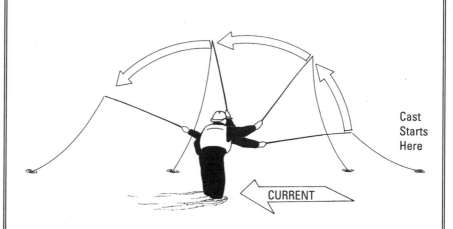

Cast
Starts
Here

CURRENT

High-stick nymphing features relatively short upstream casts of bottom-bouncing nymphs. As the current brings your fly downstream and alongside your position, you raise the rod tip to take up the slack. As the fly goes on by, lower the rod tip and point it downstream, following the line's and nymph's progress. Any unnatural movement of the strike indicator should be interpreted as a take by a fish. Employ a quick, short hook set, one that doesn't jerk the fly up out of the water, for there will be many false slams as the fly ticks along the bottom. Twitching the rod tip is the way to set the hook, for it will allow the nymph to continue on its path if no fish was encountered.

The usual option to high-stick nymphing is to cast farther upstream and strip line in as the fly drifts back toward you. The rod tip is held low and pointing upstream, so that you are ready to strike and pull any slack from the water.

to sink and tumble along. A cast straight in to the banks on a tight line will almost instantly be skidded away from the target bank water and drag back out toward midstream. This is due to the difference in speed between the slower and eddying bank flows and pushy midriver currents. Such casts will catch some fish, especially if a very heavily weighted Woolly Bugger is used, but not nearly as many as a well-controlled reach cast will.

The Drift Boat Reach Cast

When one is fishing from a drift boat, it's usually best to cast downstream at close to a 45-degree angle and use an exaggerated reach cast.

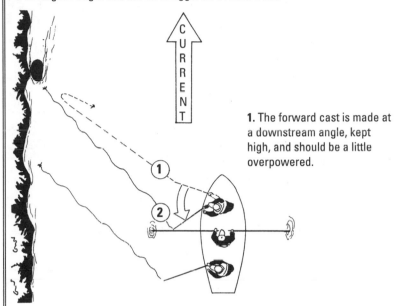

1. The forward cast is made at a downstream angle, kept high, and should be a little overpowered.

2. While the line is still straightening in the air, reach with your rod back upstream as far as you comfortably can. Then let the rod tip and line drop to the water. A quick mend at this point, and the allowance of some additional slack, can make for extralong drifts of your dry fly. It also allows nymphs to sink deeper. Additional mends may still be necessary, for the current out by the boat is usually faster than that by the bank and can belly your line downstream.

This technique puts your fly out in front of your leader and allows the best and longest presentations when fishing from a boat.

A few days after the first salmon fly nymphs emerge, adult mating swarms and egglayers are seen. Some almost scary mating swarms are seen at times, usually in the evening, moving upstream on salmon fly–rich rivers like the Yellowstone. Most other times you just see numerous egglayers flying this way and that, looking a bit like helicopters, carrying a black mass of eggs at the tip of the abdomen. They hit the water to drop the eggs, flop around, and take off again. Some get stuck on the water, making easy targets for fish brave enough to tackle the beasts. This is when the dry-fly fishing comes on. It can be exciting, mediocre, or a complete bust, varying from year to year, place to place, and hour to hour. Trout can also favor sunken adults or continue to take nymphs in preference. Timing is everything, because the hatch is short on a given piece of river, lasting perhaps a week. It starts at lower elevations when the water first hits that magic fifty-plus-degree mark and progresses upstream a few miles a day to higher elevations. Therefore, one has to chase the hatch and pin down its exact location. This is usually done by phone work and by watching which way the gravel- and dust-spitting Suburbans and drift boats are racing. A carnival atmosphere can ensue.

It is often said that trout become glutted on this hatch and soon quit feeding. This could well be so. They can continue taking salmon fly nymphs and adults a week after the main hatch is over, though, once they've had a day or two off to digest the initial feast.

There are times when the salmon fly hatch will fail to produce and caddis will provide the action, so have a variety of patterns on hand. The golden stonefly hatch can follow hot on the heels of the salmon flies in some places, possibly overlapping hatches. Elsewhere there will be a distinct break between the two of two to three weeks.

Salmon Fly

MATCHING FLY PATTERN SIZE:
       NYMPH—#2–8
       ADULT—#2–6

COLOR: NYMPH—BLACK OR DARK BROWN
       ADULT—GRAYISH BODY AND WINGS WITH SALMON ORANGE COLLAR AND
       HIGHLIGHTS ON THORAX AND ABDOMEN

Habitat: Swift mountain rivers and streams

Salmon fly fishing can be unpredictable. Too high a water flow often negates the importance of this hatch. In lower-water years, though, the action can be hot. The golden stonefly hatch that follows the salmon fly hatch is often a better fishing bet.

CHAPTER TWO

Golden Stoneflies (*Hesperoperla pacifica, Calineuria californica, Claasenia sabulosa*)

Golden stones are slightly smaller than salmon flies, about 1.5 inches long as adults. As the name suggests, they're lighter in color, too, a mottled tannish brown as nymphs and golden brown as adults.

Golden stones follow salmon flies in a predictable seasonal sequence. They are often the better hatch of the two for several reasons: They last longer, hatching for several weeks rather than several days; they tend to hatch in lowering and clearing river levels, too. There are other hatches around now, and trout are getting in a better surface-feeding groove (though nymphs will still be most productive overall). This makes golden stones one of the better hatches of the year in appropriate locations—medium to swift mountain rivers.

Golden stones begin hatching as early as May in some coastal and low-elevation drainages. They show up in June or early July in many mountain locales and can be found as late as August or even September at the highest elevations. The nymphs emerge in the same way as salmon fly nymphs do: crawling out, mostly at night. One difference is that freshly emerged adults can take a while to fully dry their wings. These nonflying adults can be seen in numbers scampering around bankside rocks and will be hiding underneath them. Birds, raccoons, and even bears can be seen haunting river corridors, picking them off. Gulls, which have an amazing instinct or accumulated knowledge, fly into Montana's Smith River Canyon just for the golden stonefly hatch. It's truly a hatch of plenty.

Golden stoneflies can be a destination hatch. They highlight the beginning of a productive freestone period that is worth targeting. Other hatches you might see at this time include green and brown drake mayflies; several species of what I refer to as fast-water mayflies (mostly olive-gray to pale yellow *Heptagenia* and *Epeorus* species); pale morning duns; smaller brown and olive stoneflies; and numerous caddis. As waters clear, this can be a banner fishing time. This could occur in late June but frequently doesn't come just right until early July in the Rockies. Hatches are numerous, occur at most times of day, and water temperatures are ideal for the trout's metabolism. Fish seem gung ho, taking a wide variety of flies with abandon at times, many in the #6–14 size range. Big fish often target big flies now, because the big naturals are there. Overcast days can prompt even better hatches and feeding.

This sometimes dreamlike fishing is in complete contrast to that found on spring creeks and tailwaters, where the bigger stoneflies and such are not found. There, it's prolific hatches of smaller fare that provides the day-in, day-out action; the use of bigger dry flies is often experimental in nature. Casting to rising fish or the systematic use of smaller #14–22 nymphs, sowbugs, and San Juan Worms brings more consistent results. These slower, richer flows will show continued midge and *Baetis* activity, along with pale morning duns and caddis from June on. Dry flies will be in the #14–22 range, but the sight fishing can be excellent if water levels don't jump up.

The exact timing of golden stone hatches will vary from water to water, state to state, and from coastal elevations to high mountain ranges. As with the salmon fly hatch, one could follow the golden stone hatch around the West and come up with some great fishing experiences. Successes are likely to be more routine than with salmon flies because of the lowering water levels. Other hatches would only add to the likelihood of good (or great) fishing.

Golden stonefly nymphs are attractively patterned beasts. The longer duration of the hatch (compared to salmon flies) often meets with lowering and clearing water. This and other booming hatches can make the clearing period an exceptional freestone fishing event.

Golden Stoneflies

MATCHING FLY PATTERN SIZE:

    NYMPH—#4–8

    ADULT—#4–6

COLOR:

    NYMPH—MOTTLED TAN AND BROWN

    ADULT—DULL GOLDEN BROWN

Habitat: Swift mountain rivers

Golden Stone Patterns

NYMPH:

    GOLDEN STONE #4–8

    GEORGE'S STONE #4–8

    MONTANA NYMPH (BROWN AND YELLOW) #4–8

ADULT:

    FLUTTERING STONE #4–6

    STIMULATOR #4–8

    MADAME X #4–8

One can also encounter smaller species of brown and olive stoneflies in late June. They can be overshadowed in importance by the larger salmon flies or golden stones, but you don't want to get in the habit of taking that for granted. If success doesn't come down one avenue, be sure to observe and try another.

Randall Kaufman's Stimulator has proven to be a better than average golden stonefly pattern. In various sizes and colors it can imitate different stonefly species, large caddis flies, and terrestrials, too. Golden-stone-colored Stimulators often pass for hoppers later in the season, making it a good multipurpose fly. Its buoyancy makes it a favored strike indicator pattern as well.

May and June Mayflies

The early-summer period starts off with a continuation of the spring *Baetis* and march browns discussed in Chapter 1. These can continue as late as June in higher elevations but can be overshadowed by larger stoneflies and rising water toward the end of their seasonal emergence.

There is another *Baetis*-like mayfly I see on Montana's Smith River, called by some the iron blue quill. It's a dark gray #16 mayfly that hatches in quieter water nearer the banks as a rule. Though possibly insignificant in many places, this *Paraleptophlebia* species can get fish attuned to it when it's found in abundance. A slate gray Parachute or Thorax pattern should catch such fish, as well as *Baetis* feeders.

The following May and June mayfly species are common across the West. In high flows they can be overpowered by murky water and the temporary presence of large stoneflies, at least when it comes to surface action. There are times, though, when fishing medium-size nymphs will outproduce larger salmon fly imitations. Fishing them in tandem covers both situations. It's a productive way to go if you don't mind the occasional tangles associated with wielding such rigs. It's not unusual to find fish taking the large mayflies of early summer in rising flows, either. Both fish and fly can end up in slower edge waters and tailouts, where flies are still obvious to trout. You might be dredging with golden stone nymphs, but keep your eyes open for other flies and risers.

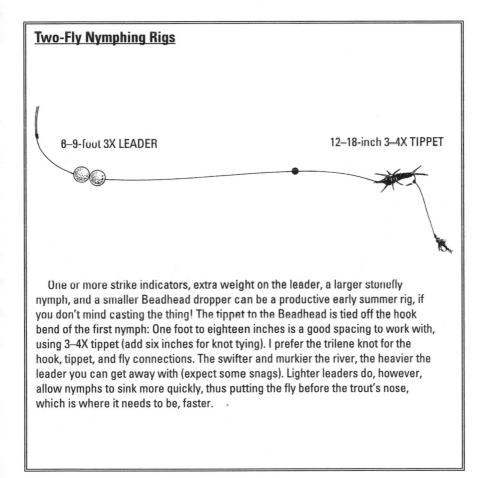

Two-Fly Nymphing Rigs

6–9-foot 3X LEADER

12–18-inch 3–4X TIPPET

One or more strike indicators, extra weight on the leader, a larger stonefly nymph, and a smaller Beadhead dropper can be a productive early summer rig, if you don't mind casting the thing! The tippet to the Beadhead is tied off the hook bend of the first nymph: One foot to eighteen inches is a good spacing to work with, using 3–4X tippet (add six inches for knot tying). I prefer the trilene knot for the hook, tippet, and fly connections. The swifter and murkier the river, the heavier the leader you can get away with (expect some snags). Lighter leaders do, however, allow nymphs to sink more quickly, thus putting the fly before the trout's nose, which is where it needs to be, faster. •

Green Drakes
(*Drunella grandis, D. doddsi, D. coloradensis*)

The legend of western green drakes often outweighs their fishing potential. The most famous green drake hatch that comes to mind is that of the Henrys Fork (late June), a clear tailwater fishery that doesn't suffer from high-water runoff. Many other green drake rivers are in or are coming out of the high-water period, making the short-lived green drake hatch an iffy proposition. One reads repeated discussions of this hatch not living up to its imagined potential.

The draw is that *Drunella* is about the biggest mayfly in the West, a full #8–12 in size. There are times and places when the hatch does produce good fishing, but you have to hunt the hot spots down and be right on top of them, because the windows of opportunity close quickly.

Western green drake duns feature stocky olive-green bodies with yellowish highlights. Some have hints of reddish brown. They have dark gray, heavily veined wings and three tails. The duns hatch from late

Giant green drake mayflies are similar to salmon flies in the hit-or-miss fishing experiences they create. These mayflies are so big, though, that anglers can't help but be attracted to the hatch!

morning to midafternoon, making life easy for those in pursuit of them. The dark olive to reddish brown nymphs are also stocky, with three tails and prominent gripping legs. They are poor swimmers and tumble along feebly until regaining a grip on the bottom if swept free. In slow water they wiggle slowly up and down with a swimming motion not conducive to long-distance or speedy results. (See color plate no. 6.)

During the green drake's two- to three-week emergence, there are usually some peak days in the middle with lots of duns. The perimeter days can have poorer showings, though toward the end the trout can be on the few that remain. It can take the trout a day or two to get used to the big duns when they first pop, for they are so much bigger than any other mayfly the trout have seen to date. Once they do catch on, though, the pleasures of fishing giant mayfly patterns can ensue. Green drake patterns can continue to work for a while, even after the hatch has met its seasonal demise. In a profuse flat-water hatch, trout can be picky, too. Having a couple of dun options and an emerger pattern would be advisable.

Though green drakes start hatching in June in many locales, there are places where they don't show until July. Other closely related species hatch sparsely in August and September at the higher elevations of Yellowstone Park.

Green drake spinners are of little concern. They hit the water at night and occasionally are seen near dawn on heavily overcast or foggy days. Few anglers ever fish over a green drake spinner fall.

Western Green Drake Mayflies

MATCHING FLY PATTERN SIZE: #8–12

COLOR: NYMPH—SHADES OF OLIVES AND BROWNS TO BLACK, USUALLY MOTTLED OR STRIPED, THREE TAILS

DUN—DARK GRAY, HEAVILY VEINED WINGS, OLIVE TO GREEN BODY WITH YELLOWISH HIGHLIGHTS, STOCKY BUILD, THREE TAILS

SPINNER—CLEAR WINGS, WELL VEINED; OLIVE-GREEN STOCKY BODY WITH YELLOWISH HIGHLIGHTS; THREE TAILS

NOTE: Spinner fall is rarely encountered

Habitat: Varying river types, from slow and weed-laced to medium-swift

Flav
(*Drunella flavilinea*)

The green drake has a smaller, #14–16, cousin known as the flav. This is an evening hatch that begins as early as May in California, shows in late June up around the Henrys Fork, and puts in July and August appearances in other locales. Its colors are similar to the green drake's, and it's often called the small western green drake. (See color plate no. 7.)

As is often the case, the smaller versions hatch more profusely and for longer periods of time than the largest models do. More consistent and predictable fishing is the result. On sunny hot days the hatch begins toward sunset. On overcast and rainy days flavs can hatch better and earlier, often showing sometime between 4:00 and 7:00 P.M. Such days will give the best fishing.

Flav spinners fall in the evening. They feature dark olive to olive-brown bodies, clear wings, and three tails. They can often be overshadowed by numerous emerging caddis, but it is possible to find trout keyed on them. The nymphs are stocky little brownish guys with the same crawler features as the bigger green drakes. Though trout may not focus on these, they will add to the early-summer nymph load and could be worthy of imitating in nonhatch periods.

Flavs are a major hatch in the Greater Yellowstone area and elsewhere. Like green drakes, they may not be found on all rivers, but where they are found they can be an important late-afternoon to evening hatch.

Flav Mayflies

MATCHING FLY PATTERN SIZE: #14–16

COLOR: NYMPH—BROWN, AMBER-AND-BROWN-SPECKLED LEGS, THREE TAILS

DUN—MEDIUM GRAY, HEAVILY VEINED WINGS, OLIVE-GREEN STOCKY BODY
WITH YELLOWISH HIGHLIGHTS, THREE TAILS

SPINNER—CLEAR VEINED WINGS, DARK OLIVE TO OLIVE-BROWN BODY,
THREE TAILS

Habitat: Various river types, from slow and weedy to medium-fast

Flav Fly Patterns

NYMPH:

BEADHEAD PHEASANT TAIL #14–16

HARE'S EAR, DARK #14–16

EMERGER:

OLIVE FLOATING NYMPH #14–16

OLIVE CDC TRANSITIONAL DUN #14–16

ADULT:

OLIVE PARACHUTE #14–16

OLIVE SPARKLE DUN #14–16

SPINNER:

OLIVE-BROWN SPINNER #14–16

Brown Drakes (*Ephemera simulans*)

The brown drake is another large, #8–12 mayfly, with populations around the country. It's an evening hatch but can be pushed up into late afternoon on overcast rainy days. Usually from 6:00 P.M. until dark is when they pop. It's possible to find green and brown drakes overlapping every once in a while, adding to the big-fish potential. These flies are large enough to turn on big fish during the hatch's two- to three-week duration. (See color plate no. 8.)

Brown drakes have brown bodies with lighter tannish brown undersides. Their light gray wings are heavily mottled with dark brown speckles and splotches. They have three tails. The large size, mottled brown wings, and evening appearances make them easy to recognize. This hatch begins in late June in most places and runs into early July.

The yellowish brown nymphs make tunnels in semisilted streambeds and aren't available to trout except at emergence. This limits them to that one habitat. You must find it in order to cash in on this big-fly hatch. Slower and lower reaches of river where silt loads can settle out, and upper meadow reaches, which give the same effect, are where this hatch is found.

When the nymphs emerge they swim quickly to the surface with a pronounced up-and-down wiggling motion. Wiggle Nymphs have been created to capture this movement and increase catch rates. Many attempts to tie effective imitations over the years indicate one thing—that the fish can be picky and hard to catch when they are focused on emerging nymphs. On some days the duns fly off almost immediately after hatching, giving trout little time to eat them. On cooler, moister days, they ride the currents longer, making better targets of themselves. I've seen brown drakes hatch from silty inside bends of Montana's Smith River while most of the fish were living on the rockier outside bends. In this particular pool and case, the hatch was totally ignored. Even on the same river, in the same mile, there might just be a few pools and runs where the brown drake habitat and good fish populations coincide. They're certainly worth hunting down. Trout gulping #8–12 mayfly duns are a real treat. And remember that these drakes might not show until the light has gone off the water and twilight reigns. You might be sharing the fishing with nighthawks and bats.

Spinner falls occur afternoons and evenings, but in a less predictable way. The big spinners have mottled brown wings, too, and are

Brown drake spinners are big enough to get a trout's attention, but sometimes they seem to be ignored. Every river has its own puzzles.

easy to identify. As with most spinners, they have otherwise clear wings, and longer tails and forelegs than the duns do. Body colors become glossier, too.

Brown drake spinners can be numerous enough to bring up big fish. I've also seen them totally ignored by the fish, something I can't quite figure out.

During these evening hatches, it's not unusual for caddis to emerge as well. Trout could even be focused on caddis in rockier parts of the river and on brown drakes in siltier zones. (Other hatches and spinner falls are likely, too, at this time of year.) Such niche-hatch experiences are common with aquatic insects. There are altitude niches (low and high), bottom-structure niches (silt, gravel, cobble, rock), temperature niches, and oxygen-requirement niches (fast cold water versus slower warmer water), among others. Some nymphs migrate to slower-water zones before hatching, too. This keeps life interesting for those wandering the river. As you become more experienced and keyed to this, you begin to anticipate both localized hatch activity and the trout's responding behavior. Consequently, you will tend to catch more fish.

Brown Drake Mayflies

MATCHING FLY PATTERN SIZE: #8–12

COLOR: NYMPH—YELLOWISH BROWN WITH FEATHERY GILLS AND THREE LONG
HAIR-FRINGED TAILS

DUN—MOTTLED BROWN ON LIGHT GRAY WINGS, BROWN BODY, LIGHTER
UNDERSIDES, THREE TAILS

SPINNER—MOTTLED BROWN ON CLEAR WINGS, BROWN BODY, LIGHTER
UNDERSIDES, THREE TAILS

Habitat: Semisilty to silty-bottomed rivers, usually in slower water

Brown Drake Fly Patterns

NYMPH:

BROWN DRAKE WIGGLE NYMPH #8–12
BROWN WOOLLY BUGGER #10–14
MARABOU-TAILED HARE'S EAR #8–12

EMERGER:

BROWN DRAKE PARACHUTE #8–12 (CAN HAVE MARABOU OR Z-LON TAIL)

ADULT:

BROWN PARADRAKE #8–12
BROWN DRAKE PARACHUTE #8–12

SPINNER:

RUSTY SPECKLE-WING SPINNER #10–12
BROWN DRAKE PARACHUTE #8–12 (I BELIEVE THAT ONE OF THE PARACHUTE
TYING STYLE'S GREATEST ATTRIBUTES IS THAT IT CAN LOOK LIKE DIFFERENT
STAGES OF A MAYFLY'S LIFE CYCLE TO MOST TROUT—EMERGER, DUN, OR
SPINNER.)

Pale Morning Duns
(*Ephemerella infrequens* and *E. inermis*)

These smaller mayflies are summer's most important and wide-spread mayfly species. They offer everything a fly fisher could desire and then some. Trout feed heavily on the nymphs, emergers, cripples, duns, and spinners, becoming very selective at times. This is one hatch that the studious angler will want to cover all bases on. It begins as early as May in warmer climates (and the hot-spring-fed water of Yellowstone Park) but more commonly shows in June. In some rivers it may not show until July. PMDs, as these mayflies are commonly known, continue through July into August, and even into September. (See color plate no. 9.)

This is a much smaller mayfly than the green and brown drakes, and different but similar PMD species range from #14–22 in size. Most are #16–20. The larger species show earliest in the PMD season. The smaller ones continue into midsummer. The majority of mid- to late-summer mayflies are much smaller than the early-summer models, and are lighter-colored as well. PMDs are a transitional group, beginning at the tail end of the high-water season but continuing into midsummer.

Pale morning duns get their name from the coloration of the dun. The basic color scheme features a very pale greenish yellow body and light gray wings. There is a vein of yellow running up the leading edge of the larger pair of wings. Body-color variations include hues of orange, brown, and even pink. This is sometimes thought to be a reason why trout can be so picky when feeding on PMDs.

The duns routinely float a long time on the surface after hatching before taking to the air. Many don't fully escape their nymphal shucks and die on the water that way. These are known to anglers as cripples. PMDs have a higher than average rate of cripples as mayflies go. The long-drift-ing duns and cripples give trout ample opportunity to feed on them in a steady, deliberate manner. Fish take up feeding positions where they can dine at leisure on this plentiful hatch. They have the time to inspect and refuse your presentation as well.

PMDs start the season as a late-morning emergence, showing up around 10:00 to 11:00 A.M. Hatches can continue into early and midafter-noon, especially on overcast rainy days. Hatches can last one or more hours, and in some cases four to five. As the hatch moves into the heat of summer, a split hatch can occur. On the Missouri we see a sputtering late-morning hatch (mixed with Tricos, PMD spinners, and caddis) followed by a more profuse early-evening one, from about 5:00 to 8:00 P.M. Fish are decidedly easier to fool at the beginning of the PMD's seasonal emergence than they are in the middle and end of it.

PMD nymphs vary in color, too, including many shades of tan, brown, reddish brown, olive, to almost black. Some are mottled. PMD nymphs are numerous in many habitats, showing up routinely in stomach samples. They are slowish swimmers, so trout have no problem finding and eating them. (See color plate no. 10.)

When the nymphs emerge to hatch, they are particularly vulnerable. They can make repeated undulating trips to the surface before successfully breaking through it. They often pause and drift helplessly just under the surface, summoning the energy for the last nymphal hurrah. Many sophisticated larger trout focus on these subsurface emergers, so have a few such pattern options in your fly box. In fact, because trout can be so annoyingly picky at times when feeding on PMD emergers, I suggest you buy every option in sight!

What I often see is that early on in the PMD season, trout aren't too hard to fool on dun patterns. Some big browns are surface-feeding with abandon in the midday hours. Caddis are booming at midday, too. If water levels are ideal (lower than their usual seasonal highs) these can be some of the best fishing days of the year. As the PMD season progresses, water levels drop and fishing pressure increases, trout target subsurface nymphs and emergers, often ignoring duns almost completely. These fish can be very hard to fool. One strategy I use as a guide is to move downstream a bit from the actual emergence sites (in gravel and weed-bed riffles and runs) to slower water zones where only duns and cripples ride the surface. Trout here can be a little easier to fool, and the PMDs are often mixed with caddis and midges. Some trout are definitely easier to fool than others.

You can tell that the emerging stage of a PMD is difficult to imitate by the number of names and patterns applied to it: cripples, transitional duns, floating nymphs, stillborns, emergers. There seems to be either a particular motion or moment of vulnerability that trout focus on during the PMD emergence. In any case, they often take a dragging pattern as you walk away after diligently making perfect casts of all kinds by the dozen. If you know a PMD hatch is in full swing, bring a complement of patterns if you have success in mind.

Despite its common name, the pale morning dun can often have a split or evening emergence. Note the duns, hatching mayflies, catching the evening light here.

Female PMD spinners are pale to yellowish olive. Males are a rusty brown. The spinner falls can become fishable events by themselves or when mixed with already-present Trico spinners, caddis flies, and the like. Keep a few imitations on hand that can also pass for the spinners of several other mayfly species around the West.

PMD spinners can be very important, too. These can hit the water mornings or evenings. The females are pale olive to yellow with clear wings. Males are rusty brown to almost pink. Varying colors between the sexes is common in mayfly spinners.

I see days on rich, slow-paced tailwater rivers when PMD spinners are littered in with morning Tricos, continuing in fair numbers through the afternoon and into the evening. Trout can focus on them exclusively during a concentrated morning or evening spinner fall or take them along with a variety of other surface fare. Keep some #14–22 PMD spinner patterns on hand, which can pass for those of some other species as well.

Pale Morning Dun Mayflies

MATCHING FLY PATTERN SIZE: #14–22, MOSTLY #16–20

COLOR: NYMPH—VARIOUS SHADES OF OLIVE AND BROWN, SOME MOTTLED; THREE TAILS

DUN—PALE GRAY WINGS WITH YELLOW VEIN UP LEADING EDGE; PALE OLIVE BODY, CAN HAVE OVERTONES OF PALE YELLOWS, BROWNS, ORANGES, OR PINKS; THREE TAILS

SPINNER—CLEAR WINGS; FEMALE HAS PALE OLIVE TO YELLOWISH BODY; MALE HAS RUSTY BROWN TO ALMOST PINK BODY; THREE TAILS

Habitat: Most river types, particularly dense and long-term hatches in spring rivers and tailwaters

PMD Fly Patterns

NYMPH:

BEADHEAD PHEASANT TAIL #14–18
OLIVE PMD NYMPH #16–20

EMERGER:

QUIGLEY PMD EMERGER #16–20
CDC TRANSITIONAL DUN #16–22

ADULT:

PMD SPARKLE DUN #16–22
PMD THORAX #16–22

SPINNER:

PALE OLIVE-YELLOW SPINNER #14–22
RUSTY SPINNER #16–22

The Fast-Water Clinger Mayfly Family (Heptageniidae)

Several genera and species of this common swift-water mayfly family are widespread across the West. Genus members include *Epeorus, Heptagenia, Rhithrogena, Cinygmula,* and *Cinygma*. Different species go by some of the following common names (among others): pale evening dun, little yellow mayfly, ginger quill, pink Albert, and western light cahill. These names indicate the pale yellow to cream to almost pink color tones displayed by this family of mayflies. Some begin hatching as early as April and May in coastal drainages. In the Rockies, June and July hatches are most common, with some continuing into August and even September.

The duns are characterized by their #12–16 size; cream, ginger, yellow, pinkish, and pale gray coloration; flattened heads; and two sturdy tails. You could initially mistake one for a PMD, but comparing the two tails of the swift-water types to the three wispy tails of a PMD should clear the confusion up. These are slightly larger as well.

Several species of fast-water mayfly duns might be encountered along mountain rivers. Many are light-colored and are in the #14–16 size range. Some are quick to take flight, giving trout fewer opportunities to sip them in. Splashy rises sometimes result.

Many of these duns hatch from morning to afternoon. Some push into evening. The nymphs of some species migrate to quieter waters near the stream's edge, or at least to the sides of heavier currents before hatching. They can be profuse enough at times to get fish rising if rivers aren't too high in this May-through-June period. The end of June is likely to provide more consistent action as waters drop and clear. Prime opportunities in the Rockies will continue to improve through July. Other mayfly, caddis, and stonefly species are likely to be seen as well.

These swift-water duns don't usually float on the currents as long as a PMD will, except on cooler, damper days. Even then, PMDs will drift longer. Quick swirling and splashy takes might be seen, for early-summer trout have to hurry a bit to capitalize on some fast-water species.

One notable feature of some of these mayflies is the subsurface escape from their nymphal shucks. Many rise to the surface from the bottom as winged adults with their wings folded and trailing over their backs.

Some fast-water mayfly species shed their nymphal shucks before reaching the surface. Traditional wet flies and soft hackles are used to imitate these duns. Because the duns can take off quickly, trout might focus on the subsurface stage.

CHAPTER TWO

This swift-water Epeorus *mayfly nymph has a wide stance, prominent legs and gills, and two sturdy tails. This is a common genus of mayflies that are found in clean mountain rivers. The standard Hare's Ear is a good imitation of them.*

These are some of the only mayflies that emerge this way. Consequently, traditional wet flies and soft hackles often prove to be better producers than dry flies. When waters are still a bit high and murky, wet flies are likely to be superior producers. Beadhead versions and extra weight on the leader might be needed to get the flies down a bit in high flows. At times you might be able to target swirling fish with them by using the traditional down-and-across wet-fly swing.

The nymphs of this clinger group of mayflies are well imitated by the classic Hare's Ear and its Beadhead offspring. They are wide and flat, with prominent gripping legs and gills. Colors vary from pale grays and tans to amber and darker shades of brown. Some are beautifully mottled. They're poor swimmers, but because of their tenacious grip they don't get washed off stones too often. Imitations should be well weighted and bounced along the bottom. Because some of these (and also some other) mayfly nymphs migrate to shallow edge waters before emerging, one could make a case for retrieving your bottom-bouncing nymph slowly back upstream and along the banks before recasting.

The Down-and-Across Wet-Fly Swing

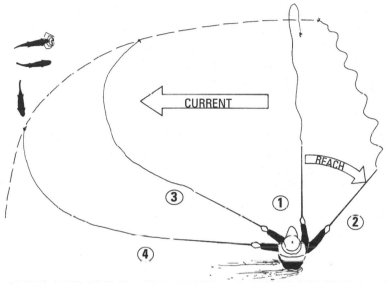

1. Start by casting straight across, or just a little down and across stream, but well above where your known or imagined quarry is finning.

2. Make an exaggerated reach cast. This will allow your wet fly to sink a bit while drifting drag free. Trout are used to seeing emergers come up from the bottom in front of them.

3. As your fly starts to drag, lift and swing it across the current, leading it shoreward with your rod tip. Be ready for strikes, and don't use too light a tippet for this presentation. Takes are typically bold and can pop light leaders. 4X is a good starting point. It helps to hold your rod tip high or way off to the bank side. This creates just enough sagging slack to soften the impact of the trout's strike while still allowing a solid hook-up.

4. It doesn't hurt to lead the fly into quieter water near the bank and even to strip it back up the edge water a little, especially if you are imitating insects with bank-migrational tendencies. Some fish may follow the fly before taking.

Fast-water mayfly spinners are often of limited importance, but fish will get on them when they occur in quantity. Evenings can be best when there are multiple insect species present. Edge waters and tailout flats are the best locations for finding spinner-sipping freestone trout. Typical colors include tans, pale yellows and olives, and pale pink to reddish browns. A good all around size is #14, though #12–16 spinners can be found.

Spring creeks and tailwater rivers won't feature too many of these hatches—some waters are just too slow. In these places it's the PMD group (similar coloration but smaller size) that dominates. When on freestone rivers and streams, though, expect to see some of these midday to evening emergences. Populations can vary from sparse to good, with fishing opportunities to follow suit. Remember that wet flies can at times provide the better action. When mixed with other hatches, though, attractor patterns that feature some of the natural's characteristics can work consistently enough. Yellow-bodied Humpies, Grizzly Wulffs, and Parachute Light Cahills are good examples. Dangle a Hare's Ear wet fly or soft hackle below for added results. You could be in for some fun fishing as the freestone summer waxes.

Swift-Water Mayflies

MATCHING FLY PATTERN SIZE: #12–16

COLOR: NYMPH—PALE GRAYS, TANS, AMBER, AND BROWNS, SOME WELL MOTTLED; TWO OR THREE TAILS

DUN—PALE GRAY TO YELLOWISH WINGS, SOME LIGHTLY MOTTLED; BODY COLORS INCLUDE CREAMS, YELLOWS, GINGER, PALE OLIVES AND GRAYS, AND EVEN PINK; MOST HAVE TWO TAILS

SPINNER—CLEAR WINGS; BODIES OF PALE OLIVES, YELLOWS, TAN, PINKS, AND REDDISH BROWN; MOST HAVE TWO TAILS

Habitat: Medium to swift mountain rivers that are clean and cool

---

Swift-Water Mayfly Fly Patterns

NYMPH:

BEADHEAD HARE'S EAR (LIGHT AND DARK) #10–16

PRINCE NYMPH #10–16 (BEADHEAD VERSIONS, TOO)

EMERGER:

HARE'S EAR WET FLY #12–16

HARE'S EAR, AND PARTRIDGE AND YELLOW SOFT HACKLES #10–16

ADULT:

LIGHT CAHILL #12–16

QUILL GORDON #12–16

PARACHUTE LIGHT CAHILL #12–16

GRIZZLY WULFF #12–16

PALE EVENING DUN #12–16

SPARKLE DUNS #14–16 (VARIOUS COLORS TO MATCH)

Other mayflies could be seen in the early-summer, May through June period, some of which can be locally important. Likely colors include slate gray– and olive-bodied flies with gray wings (similar to *Baetis* and flavs). Most are #14–16. The quieter edge waters are where some of these secondary species are likely to be concentrated and the fish most likely to rise.

Early-Summer Caddisflies

Many species of caddis begin profuse and prolonged emergences in the May and June period. As waters drop and clear in late June, the caddis really come out in force. Because caddis species dominate many rivers, you'll want to have a variety of caddisfly imitations.

Many species can be imitated with similar flies. Some variations in size and color are needed, but general-imitation styles can remain constant. For instance, a couple of larva imitations (cased and caddis worm in green and tan), a couple of emerger designs (Sparkle Pupae and soft hackles), and

Caddisflies are big players on the river scene. Have caddis larva, emerging pupa, and adult patterns on hand to increase your success rate. Diving egg-laying caddis imitations provide an additional twist.

a couple of dry-fly types (high-floating hairwing and a more realistic low-floating feather wing) will cover most situations.

The most common larva, pupa, and adult body colors are green, olive, yellowish brown, and tannish brown. Common wing colors are dark grays, mottled browns, tans, and black. Sizes range from giant #6–8 to tiny #24 microcaddis. Most are #14–20.

Following are the major early-summer species. Note that the grannom caddis we discussed in Chapter 1 can continue into May, June, and even July on some rivers. In other rivers it will be over in May. Related *Brachycentrus* species will emerge later in summer and in early fall.

Spotted Sedge (*Hydropsyche occidentalis*)

This is the dominant caddisfly on most rivers. (Several *Hydropsyche* species hatch over the course of summer. This is the earliest species. All look about the same.) It is matched by #14–16 fly patterns. Wings are mottled tan and brown. Bodies are tan to yellowish brown or green when the caddis first hatch. They all turn light brown after a couple of days. (See color plate no. 11.) (Caddis live much longer than mayflies as adults, up to a month. Mayflies die in one to three days.)

Adult egg-laying flights can occur morning or evening and can be scattered throughout the day. This stage presents the best dry-fly possibilities. Like many caddis, some females dive or crawl to the bottom of the river to paste their eggs on the streambed. When they do so, the hairy nature of their wings traps tiny air bubbles. You have to see this in action to understand how shiny it makes them look. Trout get to see hundreds of shimmering adult caddisflies swimming to and crawling on the bottom, then releasing and drifting back up to the surface. This is a major event that the majority of anglers totally overlook. Most anglers just see caddis bouncing on and riding the currents and figure it ends there. It's quite possible that most caddis species lay eggs in this way. Consequently, diving caddis patterns can be very productive.

Many caddisfly species swim to the river bottom to lay eggs. Air bubbles stick to their hairy wings when they are submerged. These swimming adults are highly visible to fish. Diving caddis patterns like this one imitate what's perhaps the most overlooked stage of a river's major hatches.

Spotted sedges are particularly vulnerable when they emerge, more than many other caddis species are. It has been noted by several writers that this is the prime spotted sedge fishing opportunity. (Remember that we're talking about the single most numerous insect trout eat in many rivers.) The emergers have a yellowish abdomen and brown thorax and wing area. What makes them so attractive to trout is the longer than average time these pupae drift just under the surface before breaking through and quickly flying off. Trout can pick them off at leisure because there are so many of them. This occurs late afternoons into evening and darkness. You may see plenty of swirls and porpoising trout, mistaking them for surface feeders, when the majority are likely to be taking pupae just under the surface. This action causes a boil on the surface that's easy to mistake for an actual rise. You might see dorsal fins and tails in the air at times, too.

Egg-laying flights can precede emergence in the evening. Another event confuses some anglers: Hordes of swarming male caddisflies form mating flights over the river. These can be so dense as to gag anglers when they go by. They whirl about in a dizzying manner with no seeming goal. These are not hatching caddis or egglayers, though. Trout can't reach them unless they jump up in the air. These mating swarms just continue upstream untouched, though they do encourage some anglers to switch to a caddis pattern.

Indeed, caddis hatches can be notable for the lack of adults, even though rising, swirling, and even jumping fish are seen in force. Most adults leave the water so quickly after escaping the pupal shuck that there can be little visual evidence the hatch is coming off. You might see a few caddis and many floating empty shucks, but it's easy for some of them to go unnoticed.

Spotted sedges are the river's most common species, emerging pupae are the most concentrated and important life stage, and caddis in general are the river's most numerous insect type (besides midges). I think I'll tie a few bonus brown-yellow caddis emergers before next June rolls around! I like to hang one off a caddis dry as a dropper, too. And the drys can be good searching patterns when the world seems to be made of caddis. Rough and tumble Elkhair Caddis do fine for general work, but keep some more realistic flat-water models on hand for pickier rising fish.

The larva of the spotted sedge is less important than its numbers would suggest. The larvae dwell in little homes made of silk they spin from streambed sand and debris. Trout don't get much of a chance to feed on

Caddis Emerging and Egg Laying

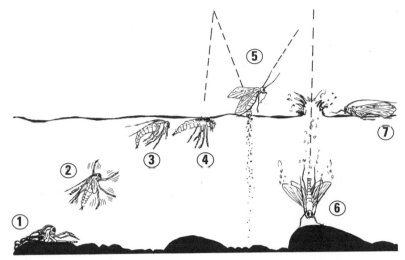

1. Caddis larvae change to pupae by sealing their cases, or constructing cocoonlike enclosures of spun silk and river debris. After a period of time the pupa emerges for its trip to the surface and transformation into a land-based fly. Upon breaking free of its shelter the pupa will often drift along the bottom for a while before journeying upward. Trout can focus on this.

2. The pupa then swims for the surface using vigorous leg motion and specialized sculling feet on its middle and forelegs.

3–4. Some species of caddis, the spotted sedge being one, then drift for a period just under the surface, readying themselves for the next effort—that of escaping the pupal shuck while breaking through the surface film. This subsurface stage can attract the attention of most trout. After that, most individuals fly off very quickly, giving fish little opportunity to grab them. Some species run across the surface instead, heading straight for the banks. Splashy rises and boils are often seen during caddis emergence, with the odd fish shooting completely out of the water.

5. Many caddisfly species lay eggs by bouncing off the surface and dropping egg clusters.

6. Others hit the surface hard to break through it, then swim to the bottom, grab hold, and paste their eggs there. Some crawl down items protruding from the river or along the banks. Because a coat of air bubbles sticks to their hairy wings, this is a very obvious maneuver for trout to see and capitalize on. (The Latin word *Trichoptera* means "hairy wing.") After laying her eggs, the spent female makes for the surface.

7. Some exhausted and dying egglayers then drift serenely along on the river's surface. Trout generally get to eat more adult caddis at this point than when the flies first hatched.

The high-floating Elkhair Caddis catches a lot of fish, but not all of them! Sometimes a more realistic flat-water caddis is needed to fool smooth-water trout, especially where fishing pressure is high. Carry some of both. Caddisflies in sizes #14–22 are common on most rivers. Have a few of the smaller versions on hand for stubborn fish.

these homebound larvae except when they come out to graze on the spider-like webs the larvae build on the streambed to filter out food particles. Even then they don't drift free as often as they might because they are secured with a safety rope of silk, just as a spider uses to lower itself. These tan to olive-brown larvae do occasionally find their way into trout mouths, but not with the regularity of the free-crawling green caddis or some cased species.

Spotted Sedge

Matching Fly Pattern Size: #14–18
Color: Larva—uncased, olive-brown
Pupa—brown thorax, yellowish brown abdomen
Adult—mottled tan and brown wings, tan to yellowish brown body

Habitat: Most rivers

Spotted Sedge Fly Patterns

LARVA:

OLIVE BROWN CADDIS WORM #12–16

PUPA:

BROWN AND DIRTY YELLOW SPARKLE PUPA #14–16
PARTRIDGE AND YELLOW SOFT HACKLE #14–16

ADULT:

X CADDIS (BROWN AND TAN-YELLOW) #14–16
TAN PARACHUTE CADDIS #14–16
ELKHAIR CADDIS #14–16

DIVING CADDIS (EGGLAYER):

BEADHEAD DIVING CADDIS #14–16
HARE'S EAR WET FLY #14–16

Little Tan Shorthorn Sedge (*Glossosoma* species)

This is a small but prominent caddis, though its hatches can be sporadic. Different species range from #16–24 in size. Adult colors range from tan-gray to almost black wings, and pale green to tan bodies. The "short horn" refers to the short antennae, as compared to most other caddis species.

It can be hard to see smaller caddisflies hatch. Trout rising to unidentified or unseen flies combined with numbers of small caddis bustling about streamside grasses and willows can clue you in. Small caddis become most important in slower waters that are low and clear. They can be numerous enough at times to overshadow larger insects that might be present in lower numbers. This scenario is only likely to be important in May and June in springfed or dam-controlled rivers, where having small versions of flies is always a good idea. Because this is a high-water period in general, larger flies are getting the trout's attention on most freestoners.

The larvae of this genus have one unusual trait that makes them

Caddisflies usually stay in the shade during the daytime. Float fishing and casting under willows is a standard fishing tactic. When shadows start to fall, the action picks up. A caddis dry with an emerging-pupa dropper can be a hot combination.

available to trout. They build what's known as a saddle case, which they outgrow at intervals. When they leave the old cases to build new ones, many of them wash free in the currents. This is a somewhat synchronized age-class occurrence, adding to the general nymph load of the prolific May through July period. Some of these caddis larvae are pinkish tan in color, differing from most other nymphs and larvae. A #14–18 pink caddis larva would make a good dropper off, say, a larger #10–14 Beadhead Hare's Ear, especially when waters have cleared and dropped a bit. This larva's niche is swift shallow water where algae coats the rocks (which is what the larvae graze on). Little algae-free trails can be seen on such rocks as evidence of this activity.

Little Tan Shorthorn Sedge Fly Patterns

LARVA:

Pale Pink Caddis Worm with Black Beadhead #14–18

PUPA:

Tan (thorax) and Pale Green Sparkle Pupa #16–20
Hare's Ear Soft Hackle #16–20
Tiny Gray Sparkle Pupa #18–22

ADULT:

Tan and Pale Green X Caddis #16–20
Elkhair Caddis (tan or pale green body) #16–20
Parachute Caddis (tan or pale green body) #16–20

DIVING CADDIS (EGGLAYER):

Beadhead Diving Caddis (pale green) #16–18
Gray Diving Caddis #18–22

Longhorn Sedge (*Ocetis* species)

This easy-to-recognize caddisfly is numerous and widespread. Its antennae are more than twice as long as its wings (hence the name) and its wings are longer than its body. It's a light ginger (not mottled) in color (both body and wings), though some males have distinct blue-green bodies. Hatches of this #12–16 caddis begin in June. They are dense and protracted enough to cause selective feeding by trout at times. This hatch can continue all through the summer. (See color plate no. 12.)

Late afternoon through evening is when both emergence and egglaying take place. The egglayers often ride the currents serenely for long periods of time, providing the best dry-fly opportunities. Realistic quill-wing-type drys and spent caddis imitations can be necessary to fool pickier fish. This is one caddisfly species where the adult and spent forms equal or outweigh the emergers in angling importance.

Longhorn sedge larvae are of the cased variety, preferring slower water areas to crawl about and feed in. Trout like cased caddis. They make good indicator searching patterns and also work well when cast to visible nymphing fish.

Little Sister Sedge (*Cheumatopsyche campyla*)

This smaller cousin of the spotted sedge is also very widespread. It's one of the most important caddisfly species across the West. With its

Longhorn Sedge

MATCHING FLY PATTERN SIZE: #12–16

COLOR: LARVA—LIGHT TO DARK CASE, WITH BLACK HEAD

PUPA—GINGER TO BROWN

ADULT—GINGER TO BROWN WINGS, YELLOWISH TO GINGER BODY, ANTENNAE
MORE THAN TWICE AS LONG AS WINGS

Habitat: Slower sections of rivers

Longhorn Sedge Fly Patterns

LARVA:

CASED CADDIS #12–16

PUPA:

GINGER SPARKLE PUPA #12–16

HARE'S EAR SOFT HACKLE #12–16

ADULT:

TAN PARACHUTE CADDIS #12–16

TAN GODDARD CADDIS #12–16

SPENT CADDIS:

LIGHT QUILL-WING CADDIS #12–16

ZING WING CADDIS #12–16

tan to gray brown mottled wings and green to olive body, it looks very
similar to the spotted sedge, too. These are one step down in size, from
#16–20. A fly selection of tan- to brown-winged caddis with olive-green
bodies from sizes #12–20 will cover many of the West's prime caddis
hatches. With some fast-water imitations (buoyant Elkhair Caddis types)
and flat-water models (truer profile low-riding quill-wing versions), an
angler can fool many rising trout.

Emerging caddis pupae are a favorite food of trout. Some caddis pupae, such as those of the little sister sedge, are important to imitate. The adults of this species will ride the surface a while before taking off. It's the kind of caddis both trout and anglers like!

This hatch is most important during emergence. Egglaying apparently goes on after dark. Little sister sedges can emerge at various times during the day as long as light levels are low. This includes mornings, evenings, and overcast afternoons. As is typical of most aquatic insects, hatches occur at midday in the cooler spring and early-summer period and push more toward evening in the heat of summer. They avoid the midday heat of mid- to late summer, unless a cooling thunderstorm or rain is threatening. Hatches with long seasonal durations tend to start the year off with slightly larger and darker individuals that become smaller and lighter colored in midsummer. This helps them ward off dehydration.

The little sister sedge is an early-emerging caddis, but it continues well into summer. Hatches start as early as April in coastal California. By May they are spreading widely across the West. In higher elevations of the northern Rockies, including much of Montana, they begin in June and can be quite important from then on. They can be mixed with salmon flies and at times provide better fishing.

Little sister sedges float on the surface quite a bit longer after hatching than do most caddisflies. This makes both emerging-pupa and dry-fly patterns excellent options. Hatches are easier to detect, too, with both caddis adults and rising fish easily seen (with many other caddis species this is not the case). An emerging-caddis-adult pattern like Craig Mathews's X Caddis or a CDC variation are good fish-catching choices, too.

The larvae of the little sister sedge are olive-brown caddis worms that, like their big cousin the spotted sedge, don't find their way into trout mouths as often as their numbers might suggest. Undoubtedly many do, though, and increase the early-summer nymph load, in which numbers, species, and sizes are approaching seasonal highs.

Little Sister Sedge

MATCHING FLY PATTERN SIZE: #16–20
COLOR: LARVA—OLIVE-BROWN WITH BLACK HEAD
PUPA—BROWN THORAX, OLIVE-GREEN ABDOMEN
ADULT—GRAY AND BROWN TO TAN AND BROWN MOTTLED WINGS, GREEN TO
OLIVE BODY

Habitat: Most rivers

Little Sister Sedge Fly Patterns

LARVA:

BLACK BEADHEAD OLIVE CADDIS WORM #14–18

PUPA:

BROWN AND GREEN SPARKLE PUPA #16–20
PARTRIDGE AND PEACOCK SOFT HACKLE #16–20

ADULT:

BROWN AND OLIVE X CADDIS #16–20
QUILL-WING CADDIS #16–20
ELKHAIR CADDIS #16–20 (CAN BE TIED WITHOUT HACKLE IN SMALLER SIZES
FOR FLAT-WATER USE)

Little Western Weedy Water Sedge
(*Amiocentrus asphilis*)

This is a #16–20 caddisfly of weed bed–laced rivers, as its long name suggests. Spring creeks and tailwaters are where it is seen in abundance, all across the West. Hatches begin as early as April in coastal regions, showing up in the Rockies in late June. This caddis has brown wings and a green-olive body. As is true of many spring creek–type hatches, smaller flies and picky fish can be the norm. Down-and-across slack-line casts and light tippets are often required. It's usually best to locate a rising or bulging fish (one taking emerging pupae just under the surface and creating a swirl) before making a cast.

Fish can focus on the evening emergers of the little western weedy water sedge and will at times prefer them to the adults. Subsurface pupal patterns should be on hand for pursuing sophisticated trout that live where this hatch occurs.

This is another cased larva, something trout seem fond of eating. The cases are constructed of finer materials than the small pebbles, sticks, and what have you used by other caddisfly species.

Small caddis-pupa patterns can be important tools for flat-water success.

Different Materials Used in Caddis Cases

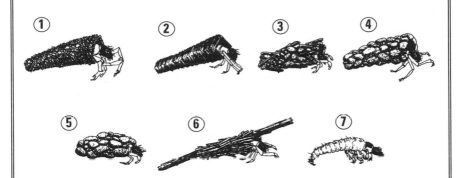

1. Fine grains of sand (including little plain brown sedge)
2. Four-sided cases of shredded plant material (including grannom species)
3. Rough cases of sticks, leaves, and pebbles (including snow sedge)
4. Larger cases of small pebbles (including October caddis)
5. Rounded cases of pebbles and sand, "saddle" type (including little tan shorthorn sedge)
6. Roughly built cases of twigs, with a longer stick(s) added (including black caddis species)
7. Free-roaming uncased caddis (including spotted sedge and especially green sedge). These worms are mostly shades of green, olive, brown, and tan.

Little Western Weedy Water Sedge

MATCHING FLY PATTERN SIZE: #16–20

COLOR: LARVA—DARK BROWN ELONGATED CASED CADDIS, BLACK HEAD
PUPA—BROWN THORAX, GREEN ABDOMEN
ADULT—BROWN TO BLACK WINGS, GREEN TO OLIVE BODY

Habitat: Spring-rich rivers with weed beds, generally mellower flows

Speckled Peter (*Helicopsyche borealis*)

This is a very small, #18–22, caddisfly that is most important on slower, richer tailwater and spring creek river types, though it can be found elsewhere. Many beginning anglers think of caddisflies as primarily #14–16 insects. Many species, however, go from #18–24. Most of the very small ones won't be important until mid- to late summer, but the speckled Peter is a widespread May through June hatch on the right water types (such as the Firehole and Henrys Fork).

The small adults feature light brown wings with a strong speckling of darker brown. Some approach a darker gray. Their bodies are a yellowish amber. Evening is the time for both emergers and egglaying. Egglayers seem to be the most important of the two to anglers. These caddisflies use the banks as staging areas, crawling or flopping into the water from streamside vegetation. The egg-laying females ride the currents serenely close to the shores. Some lay their eggs under water and even out of the water on overhanging vegetation. Consequently, one expects to see bank feeders with this hatch sipping insects in calmer edge waters. Such trout could be taking speckled Peter egglayers, spent caddis, midges, PMD spinners, and a variety of small foodstuff on the rich rivers these caddis dwell in. Go prepared if you're looking for large steady-rising trout! A seine net and stomach pump are handy tools in identifying the sometimes hard-to-fathom hatches of small flies.

The larva of the speckled Peter builds a curious snail-shaped case from tiny pebbles and sand grains. These seem to be unimportant to anglers.

Speckled Peter Caddis

MATCHING FLY PATTERN SIZE: #18–22

COLOR: LARVA—ROUNDED SNAILLIKE CASES, LIGHT TO DARK BROWN

PUPA—BROWN THORAX, YELLOW-AMBER ABDOMEN

ADULT—BROWN-SPECKLED WINGS, SOME ARE DARKER GRAY; YELLOWISH AMBER BODY

Habitat: Best on slower rich rivers

Speckled Peter Fly Patterns

LARVA:

NONE

PUPA:

BROWN AND YELLOW SPARKLE PUPA #18–22

PARTRIDGE AND YELLOW SOFT HACKLE #18–22

ADULT:

X CADDIS #18–22

QUILL-WING CADDIS #18–22

CDC CADDIS #18–22

Great Gray Spotted Sedge (*Arctopsyche grandis*)

At the other end of the early-summer size spectrum for caddis is the great gray spotted sedge. This is a giant, #8–10, fly common to higher altitudes and swift-flowing rivers. While its population doesn't compare to those of the smaller species, there are certainly enough of these big fellows around to get some trout's attention. The adults have gray-mottled wings and greenish brown bodies. Their size alone should make them unmistakable at this time of year.

Because this fly is largely nocturnal, its emergence and egg-laying activities are rarely encountered. The size and seasonal abundance of such a big fly seems to form a mental imprint in the minds of fish, which will smash them at times. They also hatch just after the tail end of the salmon fly hatch in some rivers. Other, medium-size stoneflies preceded those. Consequently, the trout have already gained some big fly experience by the time the great gray spotted sedges appear. Hatches of this fly can be heaviest around the salmon fly's upstream range in mountain rivers. A large caddis dry pattern with a nymph dropper would be an excellent searching combination as waters drop and clear. A fly like a #8 olive Stimulator could pass both for this large caddis and subsequent hatches of stoneflies that follow in the salmon fly's wake.

The larva of the great gray spotted sedge is important, too. It's a free-living caddis worm that roams about the streambed. Because of its size and availability to trout, imitations can produce well. Being a fast-water insect helps, too, for the fish don't have much time to decide what to eat as nymphs gush by. One could fish a big stonefly nymph with this larva pattern as a dropper and cover two large food-item bases at once.

This hatch begins as early as May, shows through June in some locales, but doesn't make an appearance until July in higher-altitude drainages. The salmon fly, great gray spotted sedge, golden stonefly progression can keep fish on the hunt for large surface morsels for over two months.

The females of this species dive under water to lay eggs, pasting them on the streambed. Even though this occurs at night, seeing these huge adult caddis swimming underwater can only heighten the trout's interest.

Great Gray Spotted Sedge

MATCHING FLY PATTERN SIZE: #8–10

COLOR: LARVA—OLIVE TO OLIVE BROWN, BLACK HEAD AND THORAX, UNCASED
WORM TYPE

PUPA—GRAY THORAX, GREEN ABDOMEN

ADULT—DARK GRAY WINGS WITH LIGHT MOTTLING, GREENISH BROWN BODY

Habitat: Middle to upper reaches of mountain trout rivers

Great Gray Spotted Sedge Fly Patterns

LARVA:

DOUBLE BLACK BEADHEAD OLIVE CADDIS LARVA #6–10

PUPA:

GRAY AND GREEN SPARKLE PUPA #6–10

GRAY AND GREEN SOFT HACKLE #6–10

ADULT:

DARK ELKHAIR CADDIS (OLIVE BODY) #6–10

OLIVE STIMULATOR #6–10

EGGLAYER:

GRAY AND GREEN BEADHEAD DIVING CADDIS #6–10

Traveler Sedge (*Banksiola crotchi*)

This is a big caddis found on lakes. Several larger caddis species are lake and slow-water dwellers. This one shows up two to three weeks after the ice goes off. This could be anywhere from April through July depending on elevation.

These tannish brown caddisflies are a full size #6–10. The common

Lakes that grow large trout also grow some extra-large caddis, including the traveler sedge.

name comes from their habit of running across the lake's surface after hatching (often over weed beds). This activity can bring smashing takes by big lake-bred trout when populations peak. Lake fly fishers will want to keep a handful of large caddis dry flies on hand—they can come into play throughout the summer. A few large caddis emergers in the tan to brown to reddish brown color range could be important at times, though the highly visible running action of the adults draws most trout's attention.

The larvae are of the cased variety, on a giant scale. The cases are cylindrical and built of shredded leaf or bark material. Trout like them too, especially in mid-April through June, when they are most numerous in weed beds. These larvae will also abandon their cases if disturbed. A #6–10 pale yellow caddis worm will imitate such behavior and should be crawled along the bottom a little quicker than other case imitations.

Other caddisflies play roles in lake fishing, too. The lake devotee will want to study them closely. Such information is becoming more readily available with each passing year.

Traveler Sedge

MATCHING FLY PATTERN SIZE: #6–10

COLOR: LARVA—BROWN CASED CADDIS, BLACK HEAD

PUPA—BROWN THORAX, TANNISH YELLOW ABDOMEN

ADULT—TANNISH BROWN WINGS AND BODY

Habitat: Lakes

Traveler Sedge Fly Patterns

LARVA:

CASED CADDIS #4–8

PALE YELLOW CADDIS WORM #6–10

PUPA:

BROWN AND YELLOW SPARKLE PUPA #6–10

PARTRIDGE AND YELLOW SOFT HACKLE #6–10

ADULT:

BROWN AND YELLOW DANCING CADDIS #6–10

TAN ELKHAIR CADDIS #6–10

TAN GODDARD CADDIS #6–10

Little Plain Brown Sedge
(*Lepidostoma pluviale* and *L. veleda*)

Here's another common caddisfly genus, with over a dozen species crawling around the Northwest. It's found in most streams and rivers and has a long seasonal duration. No doubt you've seen both the larvae and adults on-stream, even if you didn't know what they were. The plain brown sedge ranks among the most common and fishable caddisfly hatches to be found (along with the grannom, spotted sedge, and little sister sedge).

The larvae are of the cased variety, technically known as tube case makers. The several prominent species build varying types of cases. Most common are four-sided cases built of shredded leaf material and similar to those of the grannom caddis. Some are tubular and built of sand grains. A few species build "log cabin" homes of tiny sticks.

These cased caddis prefer eddies, pools, quiet backwaters, and slower areas near shore in which to dwell. They eat leaves and pine needles, so slower water is their choice for crawling, dining, and, later, pupating. This is yet another caddisfly family to add to the river's cased-caddis load. Always a favorite with trout, cased caddis deserve a little space in your fly box in the "searching pattern" department.

Plain brown sedges are evening emergers. As with most aquatic insects, a heavily overcast afternoon can push hatch and egg-laying times forward. These caddis tend to ride the currents longer than most when freshly hatched, giving trout and anglers more opportunities during this stage. In profuse hatches, trout are still likely to focus on the brownish emergers, though. These should be fished dead drift just under the surface and run repeatedly over swirling trout.

Females lay eggs in various ways both on and under the water. After egglaying, many adults of both sexes will be seen drifting helplessly along on the surface with their wings in the resting or spent positions. A caddis dry with a pupa dropper is always a good evening bet, because both stages are present then.

This caddis is classically imitated by Al Troth's olive-bodied

---

Little Plain Brown Sedge

MATCHING FLY PATTERN SIZE: #16–20

COLOR: LARVA—MEDIUM TO DARK BROWN CASED CADDIS, BLACK HEAD
PUPA—BROWN WING AND THORAX, OLIVE TO BROWN ABDOMEN
ADULT—LIGHT BROWN WINGS WITH NO MOTTLING, MALES HAVE A DARK GRAY
EDGE ALONG THE LOWER FRONT WING, OLIVE TO BROWN BODY

Habitat: Slower water zones of streams and rivers

Little Plain Brown Sedge Fly Patterns

LARVA:

> BEADHEAD PHEASANT TAIL CASED CADDIS #12–16
> BRASSIE #14–18

PUPA:

> BROWN AND OLIVE SPARKLE PUPA #16–20
> PARTRIDGE AND PEACOCK SOFT HACKLE #16–20

ADULT:

> ELKHAIR CADDIS (OLIVE AND TAN, BROWN BODIES) #14–20
> PARACHUTE CADDIS #14–20
> FLAT WATER CADDIS #16–20
> CDC CADDIS #16–20

EGGLAYER:

> BROWN AND OLIVE BEADHEAD DIVING CADDIS #16–20

NOTE: Caddis pupae are most important to trout when they first break free and drift along the bottom (before swimming upward), and when they are just under the surface, where they often pause and struggle to break through the surface barrier. (The slower the water and the more debris there is on it, the harder it is for aquatic insects to break through.) The midwater zone between the two is of secondary importance. Some caddis pupa designs, including Gary LaFontaine's, are largely meant to be dead drifted. Weighted ones are bounced along the bottom. Unweighted ones are fished just under or in the surface film. Regardless, trout take them on the old wet-fly swing, too. Soft hackles can be fished either way and can even be treated with floatant and fished in the film (barely floating, half-in half-out of the water). These can be hard to see on the water but imitate a caddis struggling to escape its pupal shuck quite well. The natural motion of the soft hackles heightens this effect.

Elkhair Caddis. In flat late-summer water, though, more realistic quill-wing models can routinely be necessary, along with subsurface pupae. Cast, inhale the evening river scents, and enjoy.

There are many more caddis species than the average angler is likely to comprehend. Fortunately, many are similar in shape, action, and coloration. Some of the caddisflies listed in this chapter will continue to hatch in July, August, and even September. Other species of the same genus have seasonal niches. For instance, one species can hatch in May through July, whereas a closely related species may hatch from August to October.

Because caddisflies are the most numerous aquatic insect in terms of population and variety of species in most rivers, a little extra study of them can only help your fishing success. They don't drift as nicely on the surface as mayflies do. Nor are they as large and dramatic as the biggest stoneflies. They are, however, the workhorse trout-stream insect that can form the bulk of a trout's diet at different times of year.

There are times in the May and June period when little is hatching. Late May through early June shows sparse surface action on some tailwater rivers in my area. At this time, fishing well-weighted San Juan Worms, sowbugs, Beadhead Pheasant Tails, and the like gives the steadiest results. On freestone rivers, deep stonefly nymphs with medium-size nymph droppers can work best. Woolly Buggers, streamers, and crayfish patterns are good bets, too, but might have to be fished slowly for the best results. By late June, though, both hatches and rising fish action can pick up dramatically if water levels aren't too high.

As the early-summer period ends, July brings the promise of ideal water levels and a continuing boom in hatch and trout activity. This is prime time on most mountain and tailwater rivers across the Rocky Mountain West, as the next chapter will illustrate.

Early-Summer Hatch Chart—May and June

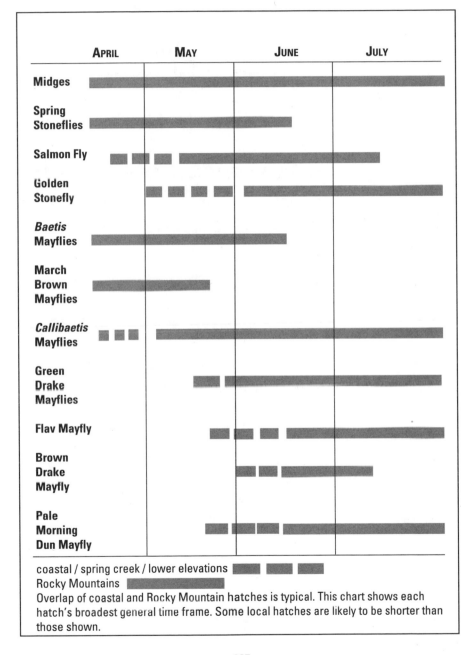

	April	May	June	July

Midges

Spring Stoneflies

Salmon Fly

Golden Stonefly

Baetis **Mayflies**

March Brown Mayflies

Callibaetis **Mayflies**

Green Drake Mayflies

Flav Mayfly

Brown Drake Mayfly

Pale Morning Dun Mayfly

coastal / spring creek / lower elevations
Rocky Mountains
Overlap of coastal and Rocky Mountain hatches is typical. This chart shows each hatch's broadest general time frame. Some local hatches are likely to be shorter than those shown.

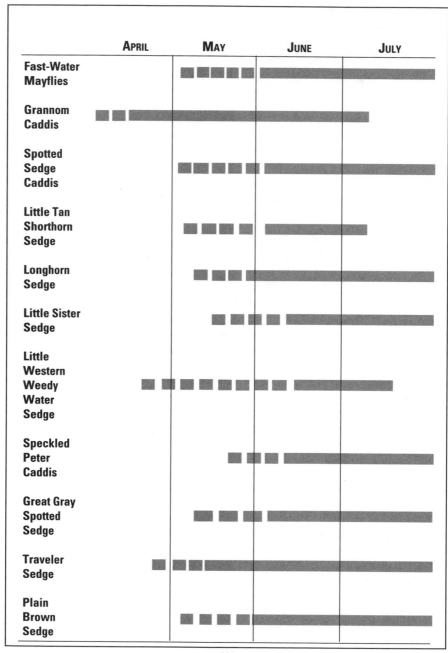

	APRIL	MAY	JUNE	JULY
Fast-Water Mayflies				
Grannom Caddis				
Spotted Sedge Caddis				
Little Tan Shorthorn Sedge				
Longhorn Sedge				
Little Sister Sedge				
Little Western Weedy Water Sedge				
Speckled Peter Caddis				
Great Gray Spotted Sedge				
Traveler Sedge				
Plain Brown Sedge				

3

HIGH SUMMER
July through Mid-September

Long days, the air and browning grasses alive with buzzing, clicking, and silent insects, low clear water and quizzical trout—hot summer days have an intoxicating effect, especially at midday. Huge blue-gray thunderheads roll east, lashing sun browned landscapes. On the river hatches come and go, bringing fish and anglers to life mornings and evenings. Twilight's pastels find swallows, nighthawks, and bats wheeling above, mixing with the up-and-down flights of mayfly spinners and the circular whirling orbits of caddisflies.

High summer doesn't start like this, though. It's often a continuation of June conditions. In years of high snowpack rivers are still settling, but they are also clearing. Cool mountain rainstorms can chill one to the bone. It's still very green out, and salmon flies and golden stones linger at high altitudes. With its diversity and clearing of the waters, this can be a banner time of year for anglers.

There is no better time to hit many freestone rivers than when they first drop and clear for the summer. Hatch diversity and densities are never higher. Larger insect types are still found, mixed with numerous medium and small ones. The trout have a free-for-all period of daylong hatch activity and ideal water conditions. Both dry-fly and nymph possibilities are maximized. This is the time of year when river trout can put on some weight.

Hitting a dropping freestone river just right can bring joyful days of pounding out bushy attractor patterns and watching trout greedily pounce on them. Because stoneflies, mayflies, and caddisflies are well represented at this time in the Rockies, a variety of fly shapes and patterns work well. Downwing attractors like Stimulators and Trudes; upwing flies, including Parachute Hare's Ears, Humpies, and Wulffs; straight-forward ties like Elkhair Caddis, Light Cahills, and Green Drakes can all find favor. Smaller Muddlers and Buggers can at times work wonders. It's not that all fish are temporarily dumb, but fish can feed indiscriminately when rivers suddenly clear and bustle with aquatic insect activity. There are certain times and certain emergences when they'll be picky. As high summer progresses this can soon become the rule rather than the exception.

As early summer turns late and August shimmers into September, the heat will cause many changes. Hatches will move toward mornings and evenings, avoiding the baking brilliance of midday. Warming water can cause trout to become lethargic, having shortened daytime feeding sessions. The insects become smaller and generally lighter in color, a natural mechanism that staves off dehydration, for many aquatic insects can't eat or drink as winged adults. It becomes a time for smaller and more realistic fly patterns. Trout grow wary, too, having seen a parade of hopeful humans slapping lines at the front door. Fraud and deceit are in the summer air!

So high summer can start as a time of easy successes and advance into a period of challenges. Fortunately, the angler will have honed casting skills in the high-water period and will be ready for the light tackle and precision casting demands of the low. Fishing adventures as varied as fast-water salmon flies, low-water Tricos, challenging PMD and caddis emerger fishing, and hopper action can all be found at this time. In many cases anglers can travel and seek the kind of fishing they want (instead of just heading for the latest hot "destination" river). A leisurely vacation tossing attractor patterns or sight-fishing to large and particular rising trout—it's all there for the choosing.

EFFECTS OF HIGH-SUMMER WEATHER

In early July, mountain mornings can still be cold. Rain and cool thunderstorms are common. Hatches still show in the midday period. A threatening storm, dropping barometer, and heavily overcast afternoon can certainly trigger some good hatches and rising fish. I see evening insects like brown drake mayflies and caddis coming off the water early in such instances. Most of the fish in the river seem to get in on the action. Trout and bugs still favor humid low-light conditions when they can get them, but sunny days have moderate hatches, too.

As we move into mid-July, the heat begins to kick in. One hatch in particular changes the trout's sun-related behavior enormously. This is the tiny #20–24 Trico mayfly (*Tricorythodes minutus*). This morning hatch is profuse. The duns quickly molt into spinners. Soon, cloudlike mating swarms line up over banks in a swirling up-and-down mass. It's not long, between 8:00 and 10:00 A.M., before tens of thousands of these little spinners hit the water. Bright sunlit days concentrate the hatches in these hours. Cool cloudy days can delay them a bit and sometimes spread out the duration. On slower-paced rivers, Trico spinners are still trickling downstream and circulating in eddies hours after the actual spinner fall is over. Trout rise and gulp, keeping an eye out for predators while they're in their shallow feeding lies.

All these thousands of tiny spentwings get most of the river's trout rising, despite the bright sunlight. The same fish that seemed to avoid bright light in spring now rise with abandon. Another late-morning hatch, the PMDs, further enhances this behavior. From this point on in the season, trout are more willing to rise to a variety of hatches and terrestrials in the sunlit hours, up until extreme heat starts affecting their metabolism and comfort. Nonetheless, afternoon thunderstorms and heavily overcast days will still trigger those bonus hatches and gluttonous feeding sessions anglers hope for.

Some larger browns, the same ones that took streamers at midday in early spring and rose to stoneflies and the first PMDs in early summer, now feed less on the surface in the bright daylight hours. You catch a few on hoppers and wet flies, but on the whole the low-light periods of early morning and evening will show the most active large summer trout.

There is also a dawn and dusk phenomenon known as "behavioral drift." Many nymphs basically let go of the bottom and drift downstream at these times, not necessarily very far, but in mass and into trout's mouths. The purpose of this is thought to insure the spread of insect populations downstream and perhaps to help thin out overcrowded areas. You'll notice on-stream that most adult mating and egg-laying flights move upstream. This further evens things out. The dawn and dusk behavioral drift, which can be quite pronounced, plays into the feeding habits of larger browns. I know Montana anglers who have caught 27–30-inch brown trout on dry flies at dusk—not many, mind you, just a rare few. Large wet flies and nymphs are likely to be more consistent producers, though.

The extreme heat of late summer combined with dropping river levels and slowing hatch activity spells a fishing lull come late August and early September. This is true of many rivers across the West. There are some high-volume rivers like the upper Yellowstone that take long enough to come down and are cool and swift enough to maintain good fishing through high summer. Some smaller ones really suffer, though, and the extraction of irrigation water only makes them worse. Trout become very lethargic and seek out springs, deep holes, swift runs, shade, and any combination of these that adds to their comfort and oxygen requirements (warm slow water holds less usable oxygen than cold rushing water does). The fishing potential can be quite grim, except perhaps in the morning and evening. It isn't a time period I'd base a trip on, unless I had some good options figured out. For instance, some rivers will have good hopper fishing at this time. Large-volume rivers can be more dependable than small-volume ones. Each year will be a little different. Nymphing the swift-water runs and dropoffs can give the steadiest results. Remember that most of late summer's insects are medium to small, including nymphs. A few exceptions would be the giant #6 cased caddis larvae of the soon to hatch October caddis, along with the ever-present crayfish and sculpin. There are also many cooler spring-fed lakes where hopper action can add to the damselfly, *Callibaetis* mayfly, scud scenario. The wind blasts many western lakes routinely, scattering hoppers widely, and 3–10-pound trout can smash them, towing float tubes over weedy dropoffs and shallows.

After a long, hot late summer, the first cold snap of fall can really invigorate fish. I remember one hot August on the Missouri. The fishing was slowing down as it usually does at that time. We had a freak snow-storm about August 22, not just up in the mountains, but down at river level, at 3,600 feet. The fish went wild. Hatches boomed and we saw no more rising fish that year than we did on this cold, snowy August day, and the day that followed. The first cool snap and snowstorms can really mark a turning point in the fishing, generally in mid-September. From then on, through October and most of November, is prime time on most waters.

Although threatening thunderstorms and light rain and snow often provide sensational fishing, the wind-blasting, hail-pounding, rain-drench-ing types seem to spook fish a little. The fishing often dies off during and just after a lashing storm, the kind that visits us frequently in the Rocky Mountains from June through July. Once one of these storms goes by, the fishing can turn back on again, especially if cool, dark, humid, and tran-quil conditions follow and continue into evening. Glorious sunsets often follow, with brilliant beams of light slicing between, over, and around the billowing thunderheads. Evening caddis and midge action can come on strong.

HIGH-SUMMER RIVER CONDITIONS

Summer is a time of change. Trout have endured winter's numbing chill, ice-covered waters, and the possibilities of bottom-ripping anchor ice and ice-jam floods. They eased into early spring's quiet moments of warming temperatures, increasing hatch activity, low clear waters, and in some cases, the rigors of spawning. They weathered the runoff and onslaught of rushing murky water. Now waters drop and clear rapidly. A procession of attainable hatches begin. Trout claim summer homes and favorite feeding positions, often in close proximity to one another. Many predators gain an advantage, too. Birds, people, and other mammals pursue them relentlessly, in a shrinking environment of summer-low rivers and streams.

Water temperatures begin the summer as ideal. Trout and flies flourish. (I wonder if the seasonal progression of dozens of species of insect isn't intellectually stimulating to the fish?) As green July bakes into a browning August, water temperatures again affect trout, especially in some smaller waters. Rivers go from a salmon fly 55 degrees to a PMD 60, and on up to a Trico 65. In many cases 70 degrees or more can be reached, which becomes life-threatening to trout at times. Trout then seek out springfed and deeper holes. Shade and swift running water give additional comfort and oxygen. Some fish may even head up cooler tributaries. They have temperature-related feeding periods and general slowdowns in metabolism. This is reflected in fishing results come late August and early September, when heat and low water can be at their worst. The drought years of the 1980s heightened this effect dramatically. Dry streambeds and fish kills weren't uncommon in and around Yellowstone Park during the year of the fire.

Although early July in the Rockies can still feature high but receding waters, mid-July generally marks the beginning of the low-water season. When freestone rivers first drop and clear for the summer is a prime time for fishing. It can be *the* prime time and worth targeting for a vacationing angler. The exact timing will vary a bit from year to year, depending on mountain snowpack and early-summer rain. Mid-July is a pretty good bet, though.

Hatches are diverse and numerous, with both daytime and evening emergences. Trout probably see more food items go by in this first clearing period than at any other time of year. Water temperatures and conditions are ideal. The trout have an upbeat, get-in-the-chow-line approach to life. Float fishing can produce splendid results. Wading can be a little limited at first but soon allows increasing coverage as waters continue to level out. Spectacular fishing is had from time to time.

By late July rivers have usually settled into their summer banks. Hatches are still numerous morning, afternoon, and evening. Trout are settled in for the summer and tend to stay in the same eddies, pools, and runs. Many can be concentrated in ideal locations. The water is not yet so warm as to make fish lethargic. July is certainly a top fly-fishing month.

Early August begins to bake. Green hillsides become brown. This can trigger good hopper fishing on many rivers as midday hatches dwindle. Hopper fishing might not pick up on other rivers until the end of the month. A daily fishing routine at this time can feature productive nymph and streamer fishing from dawn to midmorning. (Tailwaters and spring creeks can show more dawn-rising fish feeding on midges, spent caddis, and then Trico duns and spinners.) A Trico spinner fall usually gets freestone trout up on the surface from mid- to late morning. Some caddis may be popping, too. Deep-fished medium-size nymphs produce well through to the evening, perhaps with some good hoppers and attractor patterns thrown in (or used as strike indicators). A hopper with a beetle or ant dropper can be another good combination. Caddis emergences and egg-laying flights occur as shadows fall, possibly mixed with some fast-water mayfly or PMD spinners. (On many tailwaters and spring creeks PMDs will still constitute some of the best hatches of the day.) Nymphs and streamers can draw a few bigger fish as darkness approaches. The use of an oversized dry fly can bring some bold twilight takes at times. Sometimes it's fun not to match the hatch, just to see what you can get the fish to do. Big freestone trout will always be interested in large food items, especially as darkness comes on and many large food forms become active.

Late August to mid-September sees river levels bottoming out for the year, and water temperatures peak. Trout can get lethargic, and catch rates drop. Hoppers, cicadas, and the like can keep some midday fish greedy. On some rivers I fish this is the best hopper time, though other fishing techniques sour a bit overall with the heat. Hatches, too, are fewer now.

As mid-September approaches we look for fishing to improve with cooling weather. Another boost to many smaller rivers now is the end of the irrigation season. River flows increase slightly and cool. Fall weather and a slight increase in precipitation helps, too. Rivers are rejuvenated after the late heat, and some of the year's best dry-fly fishing is soon to come.

I guide on two rivers with distinctly different natures. They will give a good cross section of the trout's and fisherman's world in high summer. One, the Missouri, is a lower-altitude large tailwater (dam-controlled) river. Think of it as most of Yellowstone Park's rich spring water all channeled into one sprawling flow. Fish and insect populations both are high.

The other river is the Smith, a higher-altitude Montana river that's small, basically shallow, and enriched by many springs. It entails a sixty-mile, five-day float trip dropping about a thousand feet in elevation and progressing through a wide variety of trout and insect habitats. It runs through a magnificent canyon and could be seen as the perfect trout stream.

Summer affects these rivers in different ways. Runoff on the Missouri can last into early or mid-July because its upstream tributaries (the Madison, Gallatin, Jefferson, Big Hole, and Beaverhead) drain such a vast mountainous region. Though high at runoff, the water is usually clear, coming out from a series of silt-settling dams that have been in place for many years. As summer goes on, water temperatures change slowly. They're not big dams, though, so waters aren't superchilled, as they are in the Colorado or Bighorn. We're soon wading in shorts and sandals. Hatches proliferate in late June, July, continue into early August, and thin out a bit by late August and early September. This is when river levels are lowest and water temperatures highest. Here, the upper sixties is about as warm as the Missouri will get. The shallow edge waters where a lot of trout like to feed often feels like tepid bathwater by late afternoon. Strangely enough, the trout will still hang in there, so habituated are they to feeding stations that accommodate the easy capture of small-fly species that dominate here.

The combination of peak water temperatures and lowered hatch intensity in the late August to early September period generally brings a slowdown in overall fishing results at this time. Hopper fishing can turn on, though, and be quite good. There are still morning hatches, midday "leftovers," and evening emergences to fish as well. The trout don't show any marked on-and-off feeding behavior due to daily water-temperature fluctuations because these are minimized by the dam. Feeding activity is largely hatch-triggered, and much of the caddis and midge hatches and egg-laying flights now push into dusk. Dawn, too, brings midges and caddis, then Trico duns, and rising fish. The Trico spinner fall still brings up daytime risers, but not with the intensity of late July. And this *is* a river known for rising fish, due to its superabundance of surface fare.

The Smith, on the other hand, is a small freestone river starting in a 5,000-foot-high valley, and it has many springs. It suffers the usual ravages of winter and spring ice jams, high runoff waters, and occasional floods. By late July it can be so low that you can hardly get a boat down it some years. This only gets worse in August and early September. In the Yellowstone fire year, parts of it almost dried up. Even the springs dried up in many places. Fortunately, there were springs enough to save some if not all the fish. It has rebounded well, though a major population shift has occurred. It used to be about 60 percent rainbows before the drought. It's about 80 percent brown trout now, which is the larger species by far here.

Hatches on the Smith progress from the large salmon flies of late May to the golden stones and brown drakes of late June on to the smaller

The prime dry-fly season on the Missouri is from mid-July into November.

117

CHAPTER THREE

PMDs, pink Alberts, caddisflies, little yellow and green stoneflies, and Tricos of July. Tricos, a smattering of swift-water mayflies, terrestrials, and caddis carry on through August and into September. Cicadas and spruce moths can enhance the fishing when they are present in numbers. In the worst drought years, when the water dropped and heated extremely fast, there were salmon flies and Tricos in the air at the same time, something that would normally never happen.

On the Smith, the daily response of fish to water temperature is quite different than it is on the Missouri. Because the Smith is mostly shallow (alternating with deep holes), it heats up quickly once the sun begins beating on it. I took daily temperature readings for years and found that the river temperature in midsummer would change on average 10 degrees a day, and at times 15 degrees, from about 60 degrees Fahrenheit at dawn to 70 degrees in late afternoon. This is a big change for a trout river, and the fish behave accordingly. (If it weren't for the numerous springs, they'd have a harder time surviving.) What you see here is well defined on-off feeding behavior that is both temperature and hatch triggered. In early morning, when the river is at its coolest, the fishing is fairly good, especially with streamers and nymphs. Nothing much is hatching yet. Because this is a swift river overall, midging trout aren't seen with any regularity, not compared to a slow-paced and midge-rich tailwater like the Missouri, anyway.

Just after the morning sun hits the river and first begins warming it, the trout turn on. Some spotty hatches including Trico duns and caddis are seen, but the trout most days will take about anything that's reasonable and cast well—wet or dry. The bigger fish like bigger-to-medium-size flies like Stimulators, Humpies, and Woolly Buggers, because larger naturals have been present. Midmorning usually provides some good and consistent dry-fly and nymph fishing. Sometimes it's great. This is due to the varied food base this river has, and to the ideal water temperature that is attained for only a brief period of time. As noon approaches and bakes into early afternoon, things slow down. The river begins superheating, and hatches fizzle. If it's a good hopper or cicada year, some trout will still recklessly attack the surface, as will the odd bank hugger and foam-eddy cruiser. Many trout now concentrate in spring holes and swift-water dropoffs. Deep, systematic "put it in their faces" nymphing with medium-size nymphs will still catch some midday fish. As the cliffs (this is a

Freestone-river trout can exhibit more of an on-off feeding behavior when temperature swings are dramatic. Niche hatches are common, too, as these undammed rivers drop in elevation and run through a variety of microenvironments.

canyon river) begin blocking the late afternoon and then evening sun and temperatures cool, hatches begin to pop again and the fish reactivate. By dusk they usually turn on well enough, and hatches, spinner falls, and egg-laying flights of various species might be seen. (A freestone river like this one—dropping a thousand feet, starting in high meadows, traversing pine forest and canyon, and winding down to coulee-type prairie country—goes through many aquatic ecosystems and thus shows a tremendous variety of niche hatches.) This off-and-on feeding behavior is very noticeable. Once summer chills into fall, the fish hit through midday with more regularity. Mornings can be slower then, for the water cools rapidly overnight. The rest of the day, water temperatures are ideal and hatches few. This translates into "grabby" trout at times, a freestone pleasure. Many rivers would fit into one or the other of these summer patterns, but every river is a bit different, as are its fish.

Midsummer fish react to both temperature and hatch changes. During long midday nonhatch periods they nibble at such things as cased caddis, snails (snails can be very important to trout diets in both summer and winter), terrestrial insects, and whatever food inadvertently drifts in front of their faces. They often appear quite listless in the water without the active finning and weaving body motions that belie a fish on the hunt. Many of the late-summer foodstuffs are small—leftover Trico spinners, ants, spent caddis, beetles, and the like. A few are big, like hoppers, crickets, cicadas, and spruce moths. These can solicit bolder rises in the midday sun, when streambed gravel glows its brightest. On the Missouri, damselflies add an unusual river twist. These are as numerous as nymphs and adults where slow rivers grow rich weed beds. Otherwise the damsel is primarily a lake fly important to anglers in still-water environments. Crawfish, sculpin, and minnows still find their way into summer-trout stomachs. The big-fish hunter should never totally ignore these.

Another effect the low clear water of summer has on fish is in their enhanced ability to see and perceive anglers. They are constantly pursued by mink, otters, herons, kingfishers, ospreys, eagles, and the like, as well as by numbers of anglers. Many casual anglers don't give wild trout their due. They walk right up in plain sight and wade into a pool, apparently thinking trout can't see or hear them. Many potential catches are scared off this way. I routinely see the faintest of wakes pushed forward by a careful wader's feet put down trout, and sometimes at amazing distances. One should get in the habit of staying back from the bank a bit and looking for rising and nonrising trout before immediately wading in. Your eyes should be your main ally in locating summer trout.

Trout can hold in amazingly shallow edge waters, eddies, streambed depressions, and flats. Stalking them by sight can be quite exciting and educational, and should be a major summer tactic. Stalk first; blind-cast later if you want to increase your awareness of trout behavior. It takes practice to spot trout under water, but in midsummer it can be well worth the effort. You'll probably locate more incidental risers, too. Fishing blind can be a great distraction from trout hunting, though it certainly hones casting skills.

The low clear water, wary trout, and smaller prominent insects of summer can require long light leaders and small flies. You may be inclined to stick to hoppers and other flies that are easily seen on the water. Try using them as strike indicators, too, and hang smaller drys and

Plate no. 1.
Several stonefly species can be found hatching on most spring days. These March nymphs came form Montana's Bitterroot river.

Plate no. 2.
Baetis *mayflies are the season's first and last mayfly hatch. They begin protracted afternoon emergences in March or April all across the country. The dense hatches, which are often mixed with countless midges, can bring up steady-rising fish if the rivers remain low and clear.*

Plate no. 3.
Western march brown mayflies produce prominent spring hatches across the West. Noticeably bigger than Baetis. *they capture the eye of many a trout too.*

Plate no. 4.
The entire riparian world seems to liven up when salmon flies hatch. Every bird, fish, and mammal wants a piece of the action, including human anglers. Though the hatch is short-lived and waters are often high, this seldom seems to thwart the spirit of traveling fly fishers.

Plate no. 5.
Imitating salmon fly nymphs is often the most productive technique to use, especially if you hit the upsteam wave of the hatch just right. Even when the hatch is over, large stonefly nymphs can continue to be big-fish producers.

Plate no. 6.
Green drake nymphs are stocky representatives of the mayfly family.

Plate no. 7.
The flav, or small western green drake, is a major evening hatch wherever it is found. Its hatches last longer and generally occur in better fishing conditions than do those of its larger sister species, the green drake.

Plate no. 8.
The brown drake is a big #8–12, evening-hatching mayfly. The nymphs are of the silt-burrowing variety, which limits them to silty habitats.

Plate no. 9.
Pale morning duns are among summer's dominant mayflies. Their hatches are found most everywhere and last for many weeks. Trout can become ultrapicky at times when feeding on the different stages.

Plate no. 10.
PMD nymphs come in a variety of colors and hues, from olive to reddish brown. They are not fast swimmers, but trout seem to home in on moments of vulnerability in their trips to the surface just before emerging. Very picky fish are the rule when trout target PDM emergers. Have several pattern choices on hand.

Plate no. 11.
The spotted sedge is perhaps the most common caddis-fly across the West. Trout can really focus on these emergers in the evenings. If fish ignore your dry fly, think sub-surface.

Plate no. 12.
Longhorn sedges feature uniformly tan wings and antennae that are twice as long as the wings. The long antennae and the habit of the egglayers of riding the surface serenely for a long time makes these flies easily recognizable on-stream.

Plate no. 14.
It's the dense Trico spinner fall that's the real highlight of the Trico hatch. The concentrated mating flights and immediate spinner fall means thousands of tiny flies are on the surface, enticing many a rising trout.

Plate no. 13.
Little olive, brown, yellow, and green stoneflies can be numerous on early- to midsummer rivers. Even if trout don't focus on them exclusively, they increase the stream's insect load and help keep fish interested.

Plate no. 15.
What appears to be smoke or fog over the river here is actually a mating flight of Trico spinners. Mid-July to mid-September is the typical time to find this small-fly action.

Plate no. 16.
Callibaetis *duns feature intricate wing patterning and a mottled body. This fly is from the year's first brood in May. Later-summer specimens will have lighter wing coloration and less-noticeable patterning.*

Plate no. 17.
Callibaetis *and* Siphlonurus *nymphs are active swimmers. They have large large gills and three feathery tails that aid in propulsion. Imitating one in nonhatch periods is always a viable option for fishing lakes and slow-paced rivers.*

Plate no. 18.
Late-morning Callibaetis *spinner falls bring up trout in lakes and slow, weedy rivers. Note the mottled front edge of this female's front wings. A speckled body and two sturdy tails aid in identification, too. The typical size is #16.*

Plate no. 19.
The giant gray drake produces a hatch that may have to be looked for. The spinner fall is the most important stage, occurring in late morning. Note the bold color patterning on the body, and clear but heavilly veined wings. At #10-12, it's hard to confuse with anything else!

Plate no. 20.
Cased caddis are plentiful in most streams and rivers. Imitating them between hatches is always a reasonable tactic. Bounce one along the bottom under an indicator, or cast it to visible fish.

Plate no. 21.
Damselfly adults can bring lake fish charging to the surface. This is great dry-fly fun when you can get it. Slow-paced rivers with weed beds can afford the same kind of action. Windy periods on midsummer days blow damsels in and get trout looking. This offers an alternative to hopper fishing.

Plate no. 22.
Damselfly nymphs are numerous in weedy lakes and rivers alike. They often have concentrated emergences, that bring them swimming slowly to shore. Damsel nymph patterns are always good lake options.

Plate no. 25.
The nymph of autumn's mahogany dun is easily identifiable by its tusks and forked, stringy gills.

Plate no. 24.
Mahogany duns are among the few mayflies that can crawl out of the river to hatch. Wind can blow them back in, though. Expect to find modest populations along quiet edge waters of medium-swift rivers.

Plate no. 23.
The tiny blue-winged olive, or Pseudo, is a major slick-water hatch. Though a tiny #24, it can bring up picky and steady-rising fish, especially in late summer. It precedes the last fall hatch of Baetis mayflies.

Plate no. 26.
Spotted Sedges continue hatching into late autumn. They're often mixed with fall Baetis, *midges, October caddis, or* Ephoron.

Plate no. 27.
October caddis are big flies and are widespread across the West. They bring up many a large fish and make great strike-indicator patterns, too.

Plate no. 29.
Midges can face a struggle in getting out of their shucks. This makes an obvious target for surface-feeding trout.

Plate no. 28.
October caddis pupae are big, lumbering orangish nymphs. They're much bigger than most other insect forms eaten by autumn trout.

Fishing to Bank Feeders

Low-water bank feeders can call for a lot of finesse on the part of an angler. In some cases, wading quietly out to a midstream position can afford the best angle of approach. Go slowly, quietly, and avoid crunching gravel underfoot or pushing out noticeable wakes.

1. Some trout, especially in big tailwater rivers and flats, will fin along nondescript slick-water banks. Rising and holding are easy here. It's easy to spook some of these fish by casting up and over them—their view of the world is just too good. Down-and-across slack-line reach casts from midstream can be a better option if you can attain that position without scaring the fish. Trout holding in bank-formed ripple lines will be your best bets for up-and-over presentations.

2. Trout in eddies can be facing downstream, and circling currents can make drag-free presentations difficult. Consider all your options and move into the best casting position before making the first presentation. Every situation can be unique. Flat-water fish may not take more than a couple of casts before spooking, so make every one count.

3. Some trout, because of their holding positions, are difficult or impossible to approach from any angle other than upstream. The down-and-across reach cast is a versatile tool in these situations.

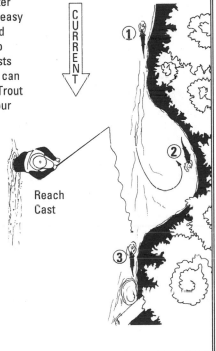

CURRENT

Reach Cast

nymphs off the bend of the hook as droppers. Eighteen inches or so of 5X tippet between the two flies should do the job in most cases. When casting to a fish that's already proven to be particular, remember to cover him with the smaller offering, not the bigger one you can see.

Down-and-across slack-line reach-cast presentations can be a must. Some summer fish just won't tolerate being cast over, unless the cast is flawless. There are many cases where it's better to wade out to midstream (slowly, so as not to create wakes or crunching footsteps that trout easily perceive) and cast back toward the banks, should trout be located there. This can require extreme patience and stealth when dueling with flat-water fish. Every overhead movement of leader and line, every bit of spray sprinkled from a false cast, each surface-creasing, shadow-casting tippet becomes obvious to such trout. Show them the fly before the leader when conditions suggest it.

THE TROUT, THE RIVER, AND FEEDING BEHAVIOR

Trout begin the high-summer period settling in as high water recedes. They are active feeders because water temperatures are ideal and hatches plentiful. When the river was higher in June and larger stoneflies began migrating bankward, many trout lined up along the shores—by no means all of them, but still a fair percentage. They found refuge from bar-reling currents and a good source of food. The conditions carry over into early July for as long as the water levels stay medium-high to average. Golden stones and other species still show bankward emergences, and such trout lies are ideal.

Now, though, the bottom structure of the river becomes more apparent to anglers. With declining volume and clearing water in the river, fish settle into a variety of holding positions where their needs are met: protection from strong currents, channeled food, and a safe retreat. Some lies can be used the rest of summer and fall. Other, shallower holds will continue to change as summer water drops farther still. Dropoffs, inside bends, eddies, bellies of pools, edges of main currents, undercut banks, and streambed depressions are among the prime holding lies. Edge waters and tailouts will remain among the favored rising positions during heavy mayfly hatches and spinner falls. Blind-fishing dry flies and nymphs through good-looking pockets, rather than targeting rising fish, can be very productive at times, and a lot of fun.

As July turns into August and early September, waters drop farther still. Although the main stonefly hatches end, smaller species do con-tinue. Terrestrial insects—hoppers, cicadas, beetles, ants, moths—tumble out of streamside grasses and spin down trout feed lanes. Where depth is sufficient (and this could be about four inches of water but also could be four feet), trout may continue to haunt the banks. An undercut bank or overhanging foliage, anything that adds cover or shade, is a further induce-ment. In many other cases bank lies get too shallow, too slow, and too warm for trout. This is especially true on freestone rivers, where tempera-ture fluctuations are greater than on most tailwaters. Tailwater fish often continue to hang in shallow, coverless edge waters, since they're such effi-cient feeding locations. They must be on guard against winged predators, but it's obviously a worthwhile trade-off.

When freestoners get really warm, trout start looking for refuge from the heat. Faster, deeper, shaded, or spring-fed locations are top choices. The added oxygen and rushing water of riffle dropoffs, the heads of pools, and swift runs become favorite late-summer haunts. Some trout will move from shallow banks to the edges of the main current and longi-tudinal dropoff zones. Shaded banks and deep pools draw fish, sometimes in schools. Springs are of great value. I've seen dozens of fish pile into spring holes during droughts. Weed beds in an otherwise rocky-bottomed freestone river is one sign of spring seepage. Wading in shorts and wading shoes allows you to feel temperature changes in the water. Locating major spring seepage areas in your home water over the years will add to your fish-catching potential both in summer and from late fall to spring.

Late-summer fish can grow lethargic. It can be necessary to get nymphs right in their faces to draw a take. There are few larger naturals around now. Medium to small nymphs can be more productive overall, fished with added weight to the leader and a strike indicator or buoyant dry fly above. The systematic working of dropoffs, broken runs, and deep or shaded banks should fool a few summer fish at midday. Morning and evening hatch activity can slow, too, though some rising fish are still likely to be found. There are still fish that will smash or inhale a hopper under the summer sun, so using one for a strike indicator can cover two bases at once.

As the lazy summer hardens into a more invigorating fall, most trout continue holding out in their late-summer haunts. In many cases they've been concentrated there. Productive daytime fishing begins to pick up as waters become more comfortable to trout, increasing their metabo-lism for a fall feeding fling. Browns begin moving up- or downstream to the tailouts of their births. This scatters some big specimens around, adding to the hopes of fall anglers. Pools above and below major spawning areas, and pools off the mouths of spawning tributaries (especially if they are running low), can get stacked with big browns. Many are reluctant to hit anything, but just enough do to boost flagging egos from time to time.

Naturally, the food of the high-summer season affects the way trout feed. In early July, many aquatic insect species are present. Quite a few are medium to large in size. Ideal water temperatures and swift-flowing water can prompt trout to eat heartily. They're used to seeing plentiful nymphs tumble by and can be happy nymphing the day away, saving rising activity for the densest of hatches or larger insects. Every trout is different, though. One can nymph, whereas the next one, perhaps in some protected bankside eddy, scans the surface. Because of the heady variety of early- to mid-July insects, trout can feed indiscriminately at times. This is usually a prime attractor-pattern period on freestone rivers. Swift but clearing waters plus abundant daylong hatches often result in "grabby" trout. Have fun while it lasts!

As waters drop, clear, and warm from the end of July to early September, the number of insect species hatching declines a bit. There is a major shift from medium and large insects to medium and small ones, too. Most hatches avoid the heat of midday now and push into morning or evening. Waters slow, giving trout more time to inspect your offering in shallow, languid flows. Fishing pressure takes a toll. Trout become "educated" and leader-shy. Lighter and longer leaders often become necessary, along with smaller, truer-to-form fly patterns. The #20–24 Tricos become the main morning hatch and spinner fall. These can be mixed with #16–22 PMDs, #14–16 swift-water mayflies, #16–22 caddis, and a smattering of terrestrials. Hoppers, craneflies, crickets, cicadas, and damselflies in #6–10 carry on the big-ticket-item interest to fish. Trout like hoppers sunk deeply in swift water even better at times.

On some rivers golden stones and gray drakes (*Siphlonurus occidentalis*) can be found. The big flies are less consistent producers than the smaller ones as a rule, especially when steadily rising summer fish are encountered. Big flies can, however, provide just enough action to keep some anglers happy.

Another trend that develops as waters drop and clear, or at least one that becomes more painfully obvious at times when the quarry can be seen, is the trout's growing preference for certain emergers. Pale morning dun and caddis emergers are prime examples. Trout often ignore adults on the surface because it's easier for them to see and obtain nymphs and

By late summer rising trout become educated. More realistic fly patterns; light, long leaders; and down-and-across presentations can be the order of the day now.

emergers just under it. Mid- to late summer is when such challenges become the greatest, especially with larger flat-water fish. Whereas you might have slaughtered (figuratively speaking) freestone trout in early July on #12 Humpies, you now might have to work and pray for every flat-water victory, particularly on tailwaters and spring creeks. Your leader now looks like a clothesline throwing immense shadows across midday streambeds and trout. Many surface-feeding fish are eating tiny little dead things, like Tricos and microcaddis spentwings, or puny kicking terrestrials that aren't easily imitated. You cause wakes like miniature ocean waves lapping up and over gravel bars. Another deliberate Trico sipper retires from active duty!

This is when the skilled light-tackle artist shines. Others may wish to seek swifter water and more gullible fish. Thank God there are rivers and lakes where summer trout slam hoppers and damsels, where Wulffs and Buggers still bring mixed results, where Beadhead Prince Nymphs dance through broken runs and get sound takes, and where trout don't laugh at 4X and 5X tippet!

As late summer gets its first front or wayward snowstorm, waters cool. Trout seem to grow less picky as fall advances, feeding more heartily through the shrinking daylight hours. Maybe it's the lower sun angle causing less leader shadow or the fact that there are fewer fall hatches left to choose from. In any case, I always look forward to autumn as a respite from the tough challenge late summer always offers.

HIGH-SUMMER HATCHES AND FLY PATTERNS

Early July sees a continuation of many hatches that started in late June, plus new ones of great significance. Salmon flies are still out in the highest elevations. Golden stones are quite widespread for a while longer. Smaller brown, olive, yellow, green, and yellow and red stoneflies become prominent as water levels continue to drop.

Mayflies include the possibility of the big green and brown drakes, though these are usually done by mid-July. Flavs carry over until early August on some waters. Pale morning duns are long-lasting hatches and of particular importance on tailwaters and spring creeks. These, too, can show until mid-August and even September. Several of the fast-water species, including pale evening duns (*Heptagenia* species), and pink ladies, or pink Alberts, which had just started in June, carry on strongly into July, August, and September, though hatches can be sporadic.

Many caddis have more drawn-out hatches than do some mayflies. Several of those discussed in Chapter 2 also hatch in July and even later. The spotted sedge, longhorn sedge, and little sister sedge are most conspicuous and can hatch until August. Some spotted sedges (especially *H. cockerelli*) will continue through September, even running into mid-October.

The little western weedy water sedge and speckled Peter can hatch well into July. The giant species, including the great gray spotted sedge (to mid- and late July) and the lake-dwelling traveler sedge (July into August) continue, too.

July in the Rockies shows the greatest diversity and number of hatches. On many freestone rivers the trout's willingness to pounce on attractor drys and generalized nymphs can eliminate the need to recognize and copy each aquatic insect. There are certainly times, though, when that knowledge and preparedness will increase catch rates. As summer waxes and water levels drop, matching the hatch will become more and more important on most waters.

In general, the importance of stonefly species will wane as waters drop and summer progresses. Mayfly species will lessen a bit and become smaller in size. The ones encountered can require a close match. They can be so profuse in summer-clear waters that a trout can observe and choose the fly that suits its tastes, and not just the surface-sailing insects, but the emergers as well.

Caddis go on strongly through the summer. Emerging pupae and egglayers can dominate the trout's attention at times. Smaller flat water models can be necessary to fool choosier trout. Bushier elkhair types continue to produce on swift broken runs, but downsizing may even be necessary here, too. Some caddis naturals are as small as #24 in mid- to late summer, which catches more than a few anglers off guard.

Let's look at this dry-fly time of plenty more closely. It's bound to get a bit confusing, but prolonged exposure and fishing experience (plus some reading and rereading) will help piece together the puzzle in a personally profitable, home river sort of way.

High summer is dry-fly time. Success comes here in a PMD hatch.

HIGH-SUMMER STONEFLIES

Golden Stones (*Calineuria californica, Claasenia sabulosa, Hesperoperla pacifica*)

We discussed golden stones in Chapter 2, but they can continue to be such a major player on many waters that they deserve to be highlighted again. The tan- to brown-mottled nymphs and tannish brown adults, both imitated on #4–8 flies, are very important to fish and anglers along the swift rivers where they dwell in force.

The nymphs take two to three years to mature. They are active predators, which makes them frequently available to trout. When they begin their prehatching bankward migration (from May to August, depending on altitude, location, and species), many more find their way into contented trout stomachs. Golden stone nymphs make excellent year-round nymph searching patterns, though it can be better to downsize them a bit from late summer through winter, going from #4–6 in higher flows to #8 and even #10 when waters are at their lowest. Long-shank 2–3X hooks are usually used, with curved models offering a more realistic look.

Golden stone drys continue to catch fish even after the main hatch is over, for the adults seem to linger around much longer than do the bigger salmon flies. Stimulators are excellent patterns, Fluttering Stones and Trudes produce well, too, coaxing some big fish to the surface. Golden stone patterns can even pass for hoppers. Patterns like the Madame X and Stimulator can go either way and continue to deceive fish. They also make good high-summer strike indicators, with dangling smaller summer nymphs below for midday trout that are reluctant to rise. See page 63 for golden stone patterns.

Little Olive and Green Stoneflies (*Alloperla* species)

The biggest trend you'll notice with high summer's stoneflies (and other aquatic insects as well) is their rapidly declining size when compared to most high-water species. Their colors lighten and brighten, too. The warmth-absorbing blacks and dark browns of spring evolve into neutral browns and grays during high water. This could add a degree of camouflage, too, because their high-water size is so big as to attract many

This big brown was released after taking a golden stonefly nymph. Note that the water is high, up in the grass, but it's clear. The clearing period can be a banner time to catch fish.

CHAPTER THREE

predators. Midsummer stoneflies quickly become smaller and lighter in color as water levels bottom out. Light colors reflect excess heat and possibly attract mates in an insect-filled summer world. Most stonefly hatches are finished by August, though in some high places they linger into September. (See color plate no. 13.)

The little green stones of the *Alloperla* genus are numerous and widespread. It's hard to figure how important they are to fishing, though. I see plenty of them scattered about, flying randomly overhead, and marching this way and that over streamside rocks and bushes. I can't say that I've ever been in a serious hatch or egg-laying event while fishing and guiding, with trout targeting them exclusively.

On Montana's Smith River, where I've spent many years guiding, there are many of these species. Often, there will be several emergences and egg-laying flights going on simultaneously, including stoneflies, mayflies, and caddisflies. This can put trout in a grabby mood. A variety of patterns will work, including the downwing variety that best imitates little olive and green stoneflies: #12–16 olive Stimulators, chartreuse Royal Trudes, and the like catch lots of fish, but so do upwing Wulffs, Parachutes, and Humpies.

In any case, the smaller stonefly silhouette is no stranger to the trout. Such #12–16 downwing patterns should be on hand once rivers are easing through summer banks. The adults can be very plentiful, and the brilliant lime green stoneflies are particularly notable. These are beautiful little scampering creatures, whether the trout are selectively feeding on them or not.

The nymphs of these little stoneflies are equally numerous but stay well protected under rocks much of the time. Like all stoneflies, they have bankward migrations and emerge by crawling up on the banks and out of the water. This afternoon and evening behavior is easy to miss because of the insects' smaller size and less concentrated emergence. It's not the event experience associated with the larger salmon flies and golden stones. I suppose it could be, perhaps being one of those fly fishing opportunities as yet unpublicized, and thus unfished. The analytically minded, armed with a stomach pump, might identify such occurrences on home water over the years. Daily fishing activity combined with a close eye on streamside rocks for shucks could unmask localized opportunities.

The nymphs of little olive and green stoneflies are mostly shades of brown, though there are some green ones. Crossover generic patterns like Zug Bugs and dark Hare's Ears can catch plenty of fish. More realistic ties are not usually commercially available, though one would be simple enough to tie in #12–16. For instance, a slimmed-down Montana Nymph tied in brown would be a good workable option. Tick this along the bottom, just downstream of rapids, riffles, and dropoffs. Let it slowly swing into edge waters, then slowly strip-crawl it back up along the bank a bit before recasting. Trout might take it anywhere along its flight path.

Little Olive and Green Stoneflies

Matching Fly Pattern Size: #12–16

Color: Nymph—mostly browns, some green
Adult—pale to medium olive to bright lime green

Habitat: Medium to swift mountain rivers and streams

Little Olive and Green Stonefly Fly Patterns

NYMPH:

Dark Hare's Ear (Beadhead, too) #12–16
Montana Nymph, brown #12–16 (Beadheads, too, copper or black for a more realistic look; silver, gold, or brass for added flash)

ADULT:

Chartreuse Royal Trude #12–16
Elkhair Caddis, green body #12–16

Little Yellow Stoneflies, Yellow Sallies (*Isoperla* and *Isogenus* species)

These bright, active little stoneflies really liven up lazy summer riverside settings. They fly and scamper about so freely that you can't help but like them. Their yellow color (which in some species features a bright red portion on the abdomen) epitomizes summer's aquatic-insect shift to lighter coloration.

Here is a populous, widespread fly of debatable fishing stature. In some quarters and years it's reputed to be an important hatch and egg-laying event to both fish and anglers. Elsewhere, it's been duly noted that the fish seem to completely ignore them. My experiences on the Smith River, where they are very numerous and often mixed with little green stoneflies and other hatches, is that the trout couldn't care less. I can't recall ever seeing the fish focus on them, though they add to the river's surface load and no doubt help keep the fish looking up. Generic downwing and upwing attractor patterns seem to work just as well as do any closer attempts at imitating them. In other places and states that I don't get to fish, the trout–yellow Sally relationship could certainly be different. The yellow Sally is reported to be an important and fishable hatch on such rivers as the Bighorn (at least in some years) and North Fork of the Platte. Fish over them, pump a few stomachs, and see for yourself!

Yellow Sally nymphs are predatory and active. This makes them more available to fish. (Predatory nymphs eat other nymphs. It's pretty dramatic down there!) They, too, migrate bankward for nightly emergences. Nymph colors vary from bright yellows, some with orange and red abdomens, to tans and browns. Some have distinct longitudinal tan or brown stripes and mottling. Both nymphs and adults vary from #10–16, depending on species. They become most populous after rivers have first dropped and cleared and are usually mixed with various other stonefly, mayfly, and caddis hatches.

High-Summer Mayflies

The mayflies of midsummer show the same trend as the stoneflies do. Species in general become smaller and, with the exception of short-lived Tricos, become lighter in color. Hatches also tend to have longer seasonal durations and can be more profuse.

Little Yellow Stoneflies, Yellow Sallies

MATCHING FLY PATTERN SIZE: #10–16

COLOR: NYMPH—YELLOWS, SOME WITH ORANGE OR RED ABDOMENS, ALSO TANS
AND BROWNS, SOME WITH LONGITUDINAL STRIPES AND MOTTLING

ADULT—PALE YELLOWS AND TANS TO BRIGHT YELLOW, SOME WITH RED PORTIONS
ON THE ABDOMEN

Habitat: Medium to swift mountain rivers and streams

Yellow Sally Fly Patterns

NYMPH:

LIGHT HARE'S EAR #10–16
MONTANA NYMPH, TAN OR PALE YELLOW #10–16
BITCH CREEK NYMPH, BROWN AND YELLOW #10–16

Few if any commercial imitations are likely to be found. Ties should be kept fairly thin. Simple stonefly nymphs are easy to tie with just a few inexpensive ingredients like chenille for bodies; goose biots, hackle fibers, or rubber strips for tails and (if desired) antennae; and hen hackle or partridge soft hackle for legs.

ADULT:

YELLOW SALLY #10–16
STIMULATOR, YELLOW OR TAN #10–16
PARACHUTE CADDIS (TAN WING, YELLOW BODY) #10–16
HUMPY, YELLOW BODY #10–16

Patterns like the Stimulator, Humpy, and Parachute Caddis can pass for several insect types and are quite productive. They just look good to a lot of fish. Keeping them small in late summer can fool additional and jaded trout.

Although the big green and brown drakes of early summer do continue into early and mid-July in some locales, they finish up quickly after that. As midsummer settles in, many of the somewhat confusing niche hatches of late June and early July thin out. Things settle into a high-summer routine that's a little easier to figure out. You can set your watch by some summer hatches and plan your hours on the river accordingly. Midday lulls in hatch activity now become the general rule, because aquatic insects tend to shun brilliant sunshine. Morning and evening hatches are common, with most midday hatches popping only on rainy days and heavily overcast, humid weather. This isn't to say that fish don't find things to eat at midday—they do, including leftover morning-hatch and spentwing casualties, wayward terrestrials, snails, damselflies, and the like.

Of the mayflies that carry over from the early-summer period, PMDs, flavs, and fast-water mayflies are the most important. PMDs are particularly widespread, with profuse daily hatches, especially on tailwaters and spring creeks. PMDs epitomize summer dry-fly fishing to many anglers, particularly those of a technical bent.

Flavs continue into early August in some locations as a major evening hatch. As with many mayflies, overcast and rainy conditions can prompt the best hatches, with emergence times usually pushing forward into late afternoon and early evening rather than twilight.

Several swift-water species, including pink ladies, also known as pink Alberts (*Epeorus albertae*); pale evening duns (*Heptagenia solitaria*); ginger quills (*Heptagenia simplicioides*); and western light cahills (*Cinygma dimicki*) carry on into high summer. These can be locally important but are less profuse and spottier than PMDs (which they are at times mistaken for). Most of these are #14 and light tan, cream, or pale grayish olive in color. Some have hues of pink and ginger. They can provide good fishing when found in numbers, usually on swifter rivers and streams, and often to the bank side of heavier flows. Refer to Chapter 2 to refresh your memory on these carryover hatches.

The following are the high-summer mayfly hatches of note, those that capture both the trout's and anglers' attention across the West.

Tricos (*Tricorythodes minutus*)

These tiny morning mayflies begin their profuse hatches and spinner falls come early to mid-July, carrying on strongly until mid-September,

A school of trout gulps away at a dense morning spinner fall of Tricos. This hatch lasts a full two months on many waters across the country.

and in some cases October. They provide two full months of predictable rising-fish activity on most easy-paced rivers and on many lakes as well.

This is a major morning event with an almost cultlike following, so dense are the spinner falls and numbers of trout they can bring to the surface. Trout will actually feed in schools, overcoming most territorial instinct, because the food is so plentiful. Most rise and gulp steadily, even rhythmically, ingesting as many of the #18–24 spentwings as they can while the morning glut lasts.

Trico duns hatch in two stages. Males hatch the evening before the next morning's spinner fall, just at dark, but don't molt into spinners until sunrise. Female duns begin hatching shortly after sunrise, continuing until 8:00 A.M. or so (later on cool overcast days). On slow, rich rivers, morning midge hatches and spent caddisflies add to the surface load, making it possible to find rising fish from dawn on.

Although the Trico duns become more and more numerous, this isn't the stage that attracts most of the trout's attention. The female duns

135

Trico duns get some early-morning trout up and rising, especially when mixed with midges, caddisflies, and other surface fare.

rapidly molt into spinners, some taking off with their shed skins still trailing behind them. They quickly join the hordes of males that now form swarms over the riverbanks. This is one of the fastest molts of any mayfly.

Clouds of spinners swirl parallel with the stream edge up and down the valley. So dense and shimmering are they that they appear as fog or smoke from a distance, despite the individual fly's small size. They'll line up over roads, too, mistaking those shining ribbons of asphalt for rivers. It's not long before egglaying takes place. Tens of thousands of these little olive and black clear-winged spinners soon coat the surface. The hours between 8:00 and 10:00 A.M. see phenomenal spinner falls and, usually, gluttonous rising fish. Cool weather pushes the spinner fall back an hour or two, even into afternoon. On slow rivers, leftover spinners keep trout rising much longer, especially in big eddies and sluggish inside-bend flats. Trout might still be taking Trico spinners mixed with other fare into early evening. (See color plate no. 14.)

Trout have to eat many a #20-ish spentwing to become full. Protracted rising sessions ensue. Picky, spooky fish feed visibly in morning-lit pools and runs. This midmorning feast carries on from mid-July to mid-September on many rivers. On some, this time period can be pushed up or back a bit. This gives two full months of challenging sight fishing.

Because the spinners are so small, trout, especially large ones, feed in locations where they don't have to fight much current. Surprisingly shallow edge waters, inside-bend and tailout flats, and big eddies and eddy lines are prime lies. This is certainly a hatch and spinner fall where you want to walk and look for rising fish before even thinking about casting. When you find rising trout, consider the best angle of approach. When fish are feeding heartily, this can be quite close.

On flat water, down-and-across reach casts are usually best and are sometimes a necessity. Educated trout may only take presentations that show them the fly before the leader (see the illustration on page 20). In many places, wading quietly out to midstream and casting back toward the bank can provide the best results when combined with down-and-across presentations. This spooks fewer bank fish than does repeatedly casting up and over their backs. Backcountry fish and trout pushed up into ripple lines can take upstream presentations more freely.

Because the naturals can be so numerous during Trico spinner falls, it can take many perfect casts to fool a particular fish. Trout set up a rising rhythm. Your fly must go over them just as they tilt back up for another bite. (My book *Small Fly Adventures in the West* from Pruett Publishing Company gives greater detail on the technical aspects of fishing these challenging small-fly hatches.)

What this requires is a series of casts, because fish don't usually go out of their way to get your fly. You must intercept them in their feeding rhythms at times. It may take five, ten, twenty, or even more casts to fool a fish. Quick repetition and perfect reach casts are your secret weapons. Once you experience these spinner falls, all this will become brilliantly clear. (See color plate no. 15.)

There are Trico-feeding fish that will occasionally take larger flies, though, especially where fishing pressure is light. Small, #16–20, Royal Wulffs can work well. Perhaps the fish view the two clumps of peacock herl as Trico bodies. Parachute Adamses in that size can work, too, because Parachutes seems to pass for emergers, duns, and spinners in the minds of many trout. Spent caddisflies and aquatic moths can be mixed in with Trico spinners. Flat-water caddis can produce well at times. PMD duns and spinners might be mixed in, too. Each trout has its own preferences. Some will pick out a larger food item that twirls by while others get into a rut on Trico spinners alone.

One trick I often resort to as a guide is to use the two-fly rig. I use one of the just-mentioned larger flies as a strike indicator and hang a #20 or so Trico spinner a foot below it. A fair percentage of trout end up taking the larger offering after a series of casts. Some will have none of it, disdaining anything attached to a leader. I'll also substitute a small nymph or tiny soft hackle emerger for the Trico spinner, still using the larger dry for an indicator. Trout that become reluctant to rise due to fishing pressure usually begin feeding again first beneath the surface. The tiny wet fly hides leaders better and fools additional fish.

If you like casting to steadily rising trout that are easily visible in bright morning sunlight, you'll want to hunt down this challenging spinner fall. It shouldn't be too hard to find, for most rivers across the country have Tricos, especially in their more placid stretches.

Trico Fly Patterns

NYMPH:

UNIMPORTANT, NONE

DUN:

OLIVE SPARKLE DUN #18–24
PARACHUTE TRICO #18–24
CDC TRICO #18–24

SPINNER:

ALL THE ABOVE, PLUS POLY WING TRICO SPINNER #18–24 (OTHER WING MATERIALS, INCLUDING CDC, SPARKLE FIBERS, AND TURKEY FLATS, CAN BE SUBSTITUTED. BOTH SPARKLE DUNS AND PARACHUTES GIVE A SPINNER SILHOUETTE WHEN VIEWED FROM BELOW AND CAN PASS FOR BOTH DUNS AND SPINNERS.)

Callibaetis Mayflies (*Callibaetis americanus*)

This is *the* mayfly of importance to most lake anglers (even though Tricos are found on many lakes, too). Also known as speckled duns and spinners, they can be found in slow reaches of rich rivers that support weed-bed growth. In either case, weed beds, often near shorelines, are the preferred habitat. (See color plate no. 16.)

Trout will feed on all stages of this mayfly, and because *Callibaetis* species have two to three generations a season, there is ample opportunity to do so in the weedy lakes and slow rivers where the insects are found. The year's first emergence is seen in April toward the coast, and in May in the higher elevations of the Rockies. Succeeding generations can overlap, peaking July through September.

The nymphs are active swimmers, with feathery tails and noticeable gills. These propel them in half-foot bursts that are easily imitated by the strip-pause-strip retrieve of a fly line. They're streamlined, a mottled light to medium gray to tannish brown. Shades of pale olive are seen, too. They're imitated on #14–18 2X long hooks, which should be weighted. It can be important to get nymphs down to the trout's cruising and feeding levels. Lines of various sink rates could be needed for serious lake work, though much *Callibaetis* activity is centered around weed-bed areas nearer a lake's shores. Nymphs can be of added importance when hatches begin, for many fish will favor ascending nymphs over duns, especially if those ever-present western winds are disturbing the water's surface. Because *Callibaetis* hatch from late morning to early afternoon, largely between 10:00 A.M. and 2:00 P.M., it's not unusual for the wind to be picking up at this time. Light wind can concentrate hatches along downwind banks, but heavier wind can put fish down. When this happens, letting your nymph sink, then steadily retrieving it toward the surface, can bring some solid takes. (See color plate no. 17.)

When conditions are calm and these late-morning duns are numerous, trout can switch from emerging nymphs to drys. Fish will cruise, picking off duns, sometimes in zigzag courses that make it hard for anglers to lead with flies. Sometimes you can see fish under water, which helps immensely. At other times you can tell which way a fish is heading because his nose, back, and wake will point the way. Some fish randomly switch direction, though, or sense an angler's presence by the wakes he creates. This leads more than a few trout to move out of casting range. At times it can be better just to leave your fly floating in an area that's part of a trout's feeding beat and wait for it to come back under it. Repeated casting scares off some of the more alert individuals.

Lake-bred trout that cruise and feed on *Callibaetis* and Trico mayflies are often referred to as gulpers, because an audible slurp is heard as the roof of the fish's mouth comes up and over the fly and plops back down into the water. Gulper fishing has become an institution in lakes around the West Yellowstone area and is also seen in slow-water sections of some rivers.

Callibaetis duns are distinctive-looking. Their speckled bodies (hence the name speckled duns) and mottled wings make them easy to recognize. Their two tails are another trademark feature.

As the summer season progresses, *Callibaetis* species usually decline in size. The first spring hatch brings #14 or even #12 flies. Summer and fall generations are more likely to be #16 or even #18. Spring insects are darker, with very contrasting dark splotches on a light gray wing background. Late summer *Callibaetis* have lighter gray-tan bodies, and the contrast in wing mottling becomes less noticeable because the overall tone is lighter. As with most mayflies, the underside of the body is lighter than the back and is the hue to imitate with an artificial.

Callibaetis spinners hit the water from late morning to midafternoon, often mixing with freshly hatched duns. Trout may or may not feed on the spinners, depending on how calm the water is and how numerous they are. Some writers have noted them to be unimportant; others find them to be an excellent fish-producing event. Apparently this varies.

"Gulper" fishing is an institution on some lakes, and on rivers, too. The trout's head comes out of the water a bit when engulfing the fly. The roof of its mouth comes down on the water and fly, producing a little popping sound, hence the name. If you look closely, you can see a fly about to go down this trout's throat.

The spinners' bodies are a pale speckled tannish gray. Female spinners have clear wings with brown mottling along the leading edges. The males' wings sometimes have no mottling at all. Males also have larger eyes. Both have two almost rigid tails. The "spread-eagle" form of these spinners make them easily recognizable along a lake's edge waters. Some are seen twitching or taking off from the water only to quickly land again, exhausted in their last struggle. (See color plate no. 18.)

On rich, slow, weed-laced rivers where *Callibaetis* are found, trout may or may not focus on them. It may only be in the biggest, slowest eddies where they might accumulate in enough numbers for cruising trout to target them. They can be overshadowed in importance by the much more prolific Trico spinner falls, which overlap with their own. Damselfly adults can add another twist and are likely to be found hovering and egglaying in the same weed-bed habitat, especially when weeds reach the surface. If the weather is calm and wind-free, trout may be found sipping *Callibaetis* and Tricos. As the wind picks up steady risers can go down, but the same winds blow damselflies in. Trout can slash at the surface or sip them in. Switching to a damselfly dry and fishing it along weed beds can be a lot like hopper fishing in such *Callibaetis* habitat. Going back to *Callibaetis* and damselfly nymphs is always a good wind option, too.

Callibaetis Mayflies

MATCHING FLY PATTERN SIZE: #14–18

COLOR: NYMPH—MOTTLED TANNISH BROWNS TO PALE OLIVE GRAYS, THREE FEATHERY TAILS, PROMINENT GILLS

DUN—LIGHT GRAY WINGS WITH DARKER PATTERNING, PALE TO MEDIUM GRAY OR TANNISH BROWN SPECKLED BODIES, TWO STURDY TAILS

SPINNER—CLEAR WINGS WITH BROWN TO DARK GRAY MOTTLING ALONG THE LEADING EDGE OF THE FEMALE'S WING, SIMILAR BODY COLOR TO DUN, TWO STURDY TAILS

Habitat: Weedy areas of lakes and slower rivers

Callibaetis Fly Patterns

NYMPH:

FLASHBACK Callibaetis Nymph #14–18
Marabou Tail Hare's Ear #14–18

(*Callibaetis* nymphs are usually tied on 2X long hooks and weighted. More options are likely to be seen near lake fisheries.)

DUN: ADAMS #12–18
PARACHUTE ADAMS #12–18
CALLIBAETIS THORAX #12–18
CALLIBAETIS SPARKLE DUN #14–18

Gray Drake (*Siphlonurus occidentalis*)

This is mid- to late summer's largest mayfly in the Rockies, though its lifestyle and habitat requirements make it of limited importance to anglers. Where found in abundance, its nymphs and spinners can offer some unusual sport. (West toward the Pacific gray drakes hatch earlier, from April to June or so.)

Like *Callibaetis*, gray drake nymphs are active swimmers preferring slower-water habitats. They're streamlined, have three feathery tails, and are grayish in tone. There's a darker band of color across the tails. In addition to weed beds, they can be found in river eddies and cut banks that have root or tree limb debris. They are also found in medium-paced open water. They are large enough to get the trout's interest, and are matched by patterns up to size #10 on 2X long hooks. Strip-retrieved nymphs in slow-water areas and the wet-fly swing provide nonhatch technique options where these flies dwell.

This is one of the few mayflies that emerges by swimming to the shore and crawling up streamside rushes and rocks to hatch. It hatches sporadically and, it is thought, at night. This activity obviously takes the duns out of the trout's realm, making them unimportant to anglers. It has been noted that wind can blow freshly emerged land-based duns back out onto the water, but even then their giant size and sporadic appearance don't always attract the attention of summer trout used to prolific hatches of smaller fare.

The spinner fall is the main attraction, because big gray drake spinners hit the water in a concentrated and well-defined manner. Late morning is the time to find these big spentwings on some waters, from about 10:00 A.M. to noon. It's not unusual to find Trico and *Callibaetis* spinners mixed in with them. Fish could be selective to one or all, as their preferences dictate. Gray drake spinners can fall afternoons and evenings, too, depending on weather conditions. Some writers have noted that using slightly smaller imitations fools more fish, because some trout are suspicious of #10 flies.

Besides their size, which separates them from the general summer mayfly crowd, gray drakes feature bold body patterning in the form of angled stripes. Both duns and spinners have thick tannish gray abdomens with reddish brown markings on each body segment. The dun's wings are pale gray and heavily veined, the spinner's are clear and also heavily veined. These big flies have two tails. There are other closely related species found toward the West Coast, with variations in color even from drainage to drainage. These range from yellowish olive to darker grays. The species are otherwise similar in lifestyle and size. (See color plate no.19.)

Many anglers will find this hatch to be unimportant. If hunting big-fly hatches is your thing, though, look for gray drakes in slower and meadow-type rivers and even lakes. This is the only extralarge mayfly found during much of the high summer, with peak emergences from July to mid-September.

Gray Drakes

MATCHING FLY PATTERN SIZE: #10–12 (MOST APPROACH #10, BUT SMALLER IMITATIONS CAN MORE EASILY PERSUADE SUSPICIOUS TROUT TO RISE.)

COLOR: NYMPH—LIGHT TO DARK GRAY WITH DARKER HIGHLIGHTS ON ABDOMEN, THREE TAILS WITH FEATHERY HAIRS AND PROMINENT GILLS

DUN—PALE GRAY HEAVILY VEINED WINGS, PALE TO MEDIUM GRAY BODY WITH BOLD BROWNISH STRIPES ON ABDOMEN, TWO TAILS

SPINNER—WINGS CLEAR BUT HEAVILY VEINED, BODY SIMILAR TO DUN, TWO STURDY TAILS

Habitat: Slower rivers and some lakes

Gray Drake Fly Patterns

NYMPH:

> DARK HARE'S EAR, MARABOU TAIL #10–14, 2X LONG HOOK
>
> BEADHEAD ZUG BUG #10–14

(Few if any commercial gray drake nymphs are likely to be found. Focus on the grayish color, streamlined shape, and wiggling swimming motion. Let the fly sink, and strip it slowly in half-foot bursts. Seek slow-water areas and weed or stick cover between hatches.)

DUN:

> GRAY PARADRAKE #10–12
>
> GRAY WULFF #10–12

(No use tying too many of these, you may seldom need them except as attractor patterns.)

SPINNER:

> GRAY DRAKE SPINNER #10–14
>
> PARACHUTE ADAMS #10–14

(Rib abdomen with heavy brown thread for a more realistic look.)

Small Western Red Quill (*Rhithrogena undulata*)

This smaller cousin of spring's western march brown (*Rhithrogena morrisoni*) is a high-summer mayfly that is common around the West from July into August, and in some places into September.

This mayfly is of the fast-water clinger group (Heptageniidae family), which includes a variety of genera and species. You can see wide, squat nymphs scuttling about on rocks picked out of fast water, and keeping a tenacious grip thereon. Small red quills have the ability to live in slower water, too. This increases their hatch status by making them more widespread than other fast-water mayflies. This mayfly has been rated by some fishing writers as the most important of all the swift-water species.

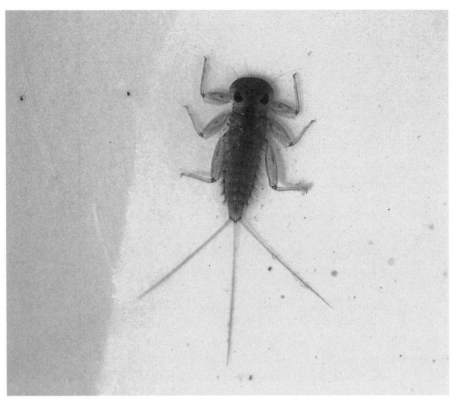

Rhithrogena *nymphs feature the wide stance of most fast-water mayflies. Reddish brown is the color of all the stages of this common insect.*

In some places the same fly is called the western black quill or the blue-winged red quill. This is why common name applications can be confusing, and why serious anglers tend to pursue the more dependable and exacting Latin terminology.

This #16 mayfly has a reddish brown body and brownish gray wings. The two tails are speckled brown. Like its relative the march brown, its wings are mottled, but in a subtler way. The nymph and spinner are reddish brown. All are matched on #16 hooks. Spinners have clear wings and paler or tannish undersides.

As is true of many fast-water species, the duns exit the nymphal shuck beneath the surface. The faster the water, the closer to the bottom they tend to emerge. Many nymphs will migrate to the sides of heavier flows before emerging. In mellower currents they usually emerge about six inches beneath the surface. On flats, they might even emerge on top.

As is true of many fast-water species, the duns tend to take off quickly, giving trout little time to sip them in. Quick splashy rises can be the result. Trout will often target the subsurface emergers. Traditional wet flies and soft hackles can be consistent producers during a hatch. A two-fly rig with a dry and wet fly is another choice.

Small western red quills are late-morning hatchers, showing around 10:00 to 11:00 A.M. Better hatches occur on overcast days, when they could last longer or continue later. As with some other swift-water mayflies, the spinner fall can end up being a better fishing event. Small red quills can have concentrated spinner falls that hit the water toward dusk. They're likely to be seen before that, performing their ritualistic mating dances overhead. Spinners hover about five to ten feet over the water, making three-foot rise-and-fall flights. These are usually over riffle areas. Trout can become very selective to evening spinners of this and other mayflies. The lower light level favors their vision, and the spent-wings can be concentrated enough to get trout to ignore other food items.

Red quill spinners are common sights on freestone evenings. Once the direct sunlight is out of the trout's eyes, these twilight feeders can become more selective.

Small Western Red Quill

MATCHING FLY PATTERN SIZE: #16

COLOR: NYMPH—REDDISH BROWN, THREE TAILS

DUN—MOTTLED BROWNISH GRAY WINGS, REDDISH BROWN BODY WITH LIGHTER UNDERSIDES, TWO TAILS

SPINNER—CLEAR WINGS, REDDISH BROWN BODY WITH LIGHTER UNDERSIDES, TWO TAILS

Habitat: Medium to swift rivers and streams

Small Western Red Quill Fly Patterns

NYMPH:

DARK HARE'S EAR #14–16 (REDDISH BROWN DUBBING COULD BE USED, PLUS A COPPER OR BLACK BEADHEAD, OR WEIGHT BUILT IN.)

RED SQUIRREL NYMPH #14–16

EMERGER:

RED QUILL SOFT HACKLE #14–16

MARCH BROWN WET FLY #14–16

BEADHEAD PARTRIDGE AND PHEASANT TAIL SOFT HACKLE #14–16

DUN:

RED QUILL #16

RUSTY SPARKLE DUN #16

PARACHUTE PHEASANT TAIL #14–16

RUSTY HAIRWING DUN #14–16

SPINNER:

RUSTY SPINNER #16

TAN SPINNER #16

Little Western Blue-Winged Olives
(*Attenella margarita* and *Serratella tibialis*,
formerly listed as *Ephemerella margarita* and *E. tibialis*)

These related species are fairly similar in size and color. One (*S. tibialis*) is slightly larger and darker than the other. (The season's mayflies tend to get a bit larger and darker as fall approaches.) Both are in the #16–18 range. Their olive to olive-brown bodies and medium to dark gray wings fit them into the somewhat overused "blue-winged olive" color pattern, though the larger model pushes a mahogany tone. These smaller cousins of the green drake, flav, and PMD are widespread across the West and important on slow- to medium-paced rich rivers. They hatch from midmorning into afternoon.

Trout can show a decided preference for the emerging nymphs of these species, taking them at or below the surface. Because slow clear waters are the places where these flies are important, sight-fishing to feeding trout is the name of the game. Ideally, you should get into a position

Serratella tibialis, the late-summer-to-fall-hatching cousin of the pale morning dun, features darker gray wings and an olive to olive-brown body. It's most important on flatter stretches of rich rivers.

where you can not only see a fish rise but see it under water as well. In this way you can present nymphs (if the trout won't take the duns) and watch them take, so as to time the hook set properly. By this time of year, late July through early October, trout have been fished to repeatedly in low clear water. Fishing pressure can make them a little surface-shy and opt for emerging nymphs, which, in this case, are easy for them to intercept. Pheasant Tails are a good imitation of the nymph's general brownish color. I have found trout eating the duns, though, on rivers as different as Montana's lower Bighorn and the upper Smith.

At first glance, these little blue-winged olives look like *Baetis* on the water. The more obvious hind wing and three tails of these species help separate them from the *Baetis*, which has a shrunken, almost nonexistent hind wing and two tails. Both mayfly groups can be on the water at once or can overlap, especially toward the tail end of high summer, and are often mixed with midges. Both can be imitated with similar flies.

This family (Ephemeridae) is also noted for its rather high percentage of duns that fail to completely emerge from their nymphal shucks. Cripples, therefore, can be important additions to a fly selection. Many *Baetis* duns have trouble getting away, too, and end up dying on the water sprawled like spinners but with the obvious opaque wings of a dun. Slow edge waters and eddies can harbor numbers of such cripples even after the main hatch wanes. Picky and inspiring flat-water fish can be found rising here, taking the odd midge and spent caddis as well. Ants and beetles can add to the mix. Think 6X!

The spinners of these little blue-winged olives tend to be overshadowed by those of other species and unimportant on their own. There is a chance you could find fish targeting them, though. Having a basic spent-wing collection is a good idea. Include tans, pale yellows, olives, reddish browns, and tiny blacks in sizes from #14–20. These will cover a high percentage of spinner situations, whether you know what the fly is or not.

As high summer cools into early fall, mayflies again show a color and size shift. Hatches will turn back toward afternoon, with early-morning and late-evening hatches disappearing. The blue-winged olive color pattern will go on as a dominant theme, and prolific *Baetis* hatches will be widespread. Some mahogany duns will be seen, too. The insects at this time will be darker and larger than those of high summer. The tiniest olives of August and September, down to #24, will fade. Large, #18–16,

Little Western Blue-Winged Olives

MATCHING FLY PATTERN SIZE: #16–18

COLOR: NYMPH—SHADES OF BROWN, SMALL AND STREAMLINED, THREE TAILS

DUN—MEDIUM TO DARK GRAY WINGS, OLIVE TO OLIVE-BROWN BODY, THREE TAILS

SPINNER—CLEAR WINGS, OLIVE BODY IN FEMALE, TRANSLUCENT ABDOMEN AND

BLACK THORAX IN MALE, THREE TAILS

Habitat: Slow- to medium-paced rivers, best on spring-rich waters

Little Western Blue-Winged Olive Fly Patterns

NYMPH:

PHEASANT TAIL, UNWEIGHTED #16–20
BEADHEAD PHEASANT TAIL #16–18
CDC OLIVE EMERGER #16–18

DUN:

OLIVE THORAX #16–18
OLIVE PARACHUTE #16–18
OLIVE SPARKLE DUN #16–18

Shades of medium olive to darker olive-brown can be encountered among the naturals. Their wings are medium to slate gray, a color than can be hard to spot on the water when incorporated in a fly pattern. Try black wings on some duns, because these show up well against gray glaring sky. Trout seem to like them just fine, for they present a bold wing silhouette. White wings show up better in darker areas. Gray wings may be desired by some fish and are most realistic but are best used where viewing conditions are ideal.

SPINNER:

OLIVE SPINNER #16–18

specimens will take their place. Some fall mayflies in the #12–14 size range are seen, too, though they're of less overall importance. We'll explore these in the next chapter.

HIGH SUMMER'S CADDISFLIES

To many anglers, this part of summer seems like caddis time. Evening caddisfly activity can be overwhelming and often seems difficult to fully capitalize on. Emerger-choosy trout have browbeat the most sophisticated angler more than he would care to admit. Spent caddis and early morning emergers and egglayers can be found at first light. Deep-fished pupal and cased-caddis patterns are very productive. Low-water freestone rivers show numbers of cased caddis wandering the sunlit stones. Sight fishing to spotted fish becomes a viable and interesting option. Buoyant caddis drys still make good searching patterns, though "downsizing" might be in order.

Microcaddis are widespread, too, some as small as #24, individuals that can crawl through the screens of riverside windows! Many anglers are unfamiliar with or unwilling to fish such small imitations. They can be locally important to flat-water summer trout, though, especially when mixed with midges and other small insects.

Because caddis species can have long hatch durations and closely related species and can live longer after hatching than mayflies do, emergences can go on for months on a given stretch of river. We'll reconsider some of the species discussed in Chapter 2, as well as note the most important caddis of high summer. Although caddis hatches and species are numerous, I'll do my best to simplify them. But even this streamlined approach will be a bit confusing. There's no doubt that reading, rereading, fishing, observing, and reading again will be necessary for most novice anglers to begin understanding the complex world of aquatic insects and trout. There's no need to be in a hurry. Have fun. Skilled casting and a fair variety of flies will catch enough fish to keep most people happy.

Most summer caddisflies are from #14–20 and down to #24 in size. They have tan-brown to gray wings and green-olive to tan-brown bodies. Don't neglect the smaller species, especially on slower, flatter rich rivers. Trout can be found dining on them from dawn to dusk in their larval, pupal, adult, and egg-laying forms. Here are a few brief points to remember:

This trout took an amber-glass-bead soft-hackle caddis emerger fished deep. Though this pattern worked well enough, glass beads break easily. Translucent plastic Larva Lace over tinsel gives a similar but more durable glistening effect.

- At dawn and dusk the behavioral drift of caddisfly larvae (free-living worms and cased larvae) is a natural phenomenon of interest to anglers.
- At dawn there will be some emergers and egglayers spent on the water.

- Daytime emergences and egglaying will be sporadic. Larva and pupa patterns fished deep are a good bet as searching flies.
- Fish caddis drys during the daytime under willows and in riffle lines as searching patterns with a dropper.
- There will be increased caddis activity from late afternoon on. Deep pupae work best first, then subsurface pupae, diving caddis, and adults. Overlapping species emergence and egglaying can be going on at the same time.

Summer Grannom (*Brachycentrus americanus*)

We discussed the spring caddisfly or Mother's Day hatch in Chapter 1. This high-summer grannom species is lighter in color, as most high-summer aquatic insects are. It has lighter gray-brown wings and an olive to green body. It is in the #14–16 size range and can emerge early in the morning during the heat of summer. Egg-laying flights occur when it's cool, in the mornings, evenings, and on storm-threatened afternoons, too.

Realistic caddisfly patterns can become necessary by mid- to late summer. Some caddis species float sedately on the surface after laying eggs, and trout sip them at leisure after inspecting them. Such educated fish may bypass oversized and overhackled fly patterns.

Egg-laying females either crawl or swim to the bottom to lay eggs or deposit them on the surface in the traditional manner. In any case, spent egglayers are of prime concern to anglers. Because many trout will have become educated by this time, realistic flat-water imitations could be necessary to fool picky rising fish. Pupal, emergent, adult, diving, and spent caddis patterns can all be of use, for this is a major hatch around the West.

The larvae are of the cased variety that make those four-sided little fragment-built homes commonly seen crawling over shallow rocks in western rivers. These make excellent nymph models. At times they can be fished to visibly nymphing trout in summer's low clear waters. A cased caddis fished deep under a strike indicator is never amiss at this time. (See color plate no. 20.)

Hatches of summer grannom begin in mid-July to August and continue to late August and September.

Summer Grannom Fly Patterns

LARVA:

Black Beadhead Cased Caddis #12–16

PUPA:

Brown and Olive or Gray and Green Sparkle Pupa #14–16
Peacock and Partridge Soft Hackle #14–16
Traditional Coachman Wet Fly #14–16 (also used as diving caddis
   and spent egglayer)

ADULT:

Olive-body Elkhair Caddis #14–16
Olive X Caddis #14–18
Olive Flat-Water Caddis #14–18
Olive CDC Caddis #14–18

EGGLAYERS:

Beadhead Grey and Olive Diving Caddis #14–16
Beadhead Coachman Wet Fly #14–16

Green Sedges (*Rhyacophila bifila* and *R. coloradensis*)

These are the adults of the green caddis worms mentioned in Chapters 1 and 2, free-living, bright green caddis larvae found in cobble and stone in swift shallow riffles. Imitations of green caddis worms are among the top searching nymph patterns to use in swift riffles, dropoffs, and broken pocket water. They should be bounced along the bottom, with weight added to the leader when needed. Some consider the larval stage of the green sedge to overshadow the importance of the adult. Trout see the larvae from spring through fall, making imitations good swift-water standbys when no hatches are in progress. Trout can congregate in swift-water areas during the heat of summer, especially in freestone rivers. These are just the places green sedge larvae occur in numbers. Dawn and dusk periods of behavioral drift are when they are most active and best imitated, but fish will take them at other times as well.

The pupae emerge in the afternoon to evening from riffles and swift-water areas, where their entire life cycle is focused. When emerging, they are fast swimmers and quick to take wing. Trout are even seen shooting up into the air as they chase them from the bottom to the surface. Though the naturals are numerous, hatches are often reported as sparse or sporadic. It can be difficult to see caddis emerge from choppy water. If you see swirls and boils and the odd airborne fish in or just downstream from riffle areas, suspect caddis emergers and tie on a subsurface pupa. These pupa imitations feature brownish wing-thorax areas and bright green to olive abdomens. Fish them in sizes #12–16. The adults have mottled gray and brown wings that

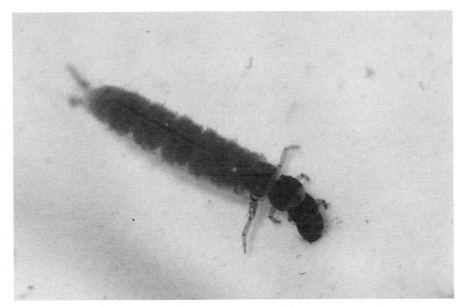

Free-roaming green sedge larvae are abundant in swift riffles and runs. Trout eat lots of them from spring through fall. Bright greens, olive, tan, and brown are colors found in this and other caddis species with worm-type (uncased) larvae. Bounce imitations along the bottom in swift water.

sport a few blackish spots and some whitish ones at the rear. Their bodies are green to olive. Adults can be seen in profusion along banks and riverside vegetation, but they're in the air more than on the water.

Egglaying takes place in riffled areas, too, in the late afternoon and evening. Many egglayers crawl or swim to the bottom, then drift back up to the surface. Some anglers see egglayers return to the surface and mistake them for emergers. The females float back up (coated in a layer of air bubbles, which stick to their hairy wings when they dive), climb up on the surface, and just lie there. Because freshly hatched adults take off quickly, an appearing caddis that floats along serenely should clue you in to egglaying activity. Diving caddis egglayers are undoubtedly the least-fished major insects in the West. A high percentage of caddis species lay their eggs this way.

Trout will feed on resting and spent egglayers in and just downstream of swift-water areas. Other egglayers can be bouncing around on the surface, too. Both subtle and splashy takes of the natural can be seen. Imitations can be fished on a dead drift or twitched. Larger trout are likely to lie off to the side of the current, in some willow-protected edge water, sipping the spent ones in at leisure.

There are two primary green sedge species, which look similar. The first, *R. bifila,* hatches from as early as May but more commonly in the Rockies from July through August. The second species, *R. coloradensis,* hatches from late August through October. Green sedges make good models for late-summer and fall caddis patterns around the West.

Green Sedge Fly Patterns

LARVA:

GREEN CADDIS WORM #12–16

DOUBLE BLACK BEAD GREEN CADDIS WORM #12–14 (CAN BE TIED ON CURVED LONG-SHANK HOOKS FOR A MORE REALISTIC LOOK)

PUPA:

BROWN AND GREEN SPARKLE PUPA (DEEP AND SURFACE) #12–16

PARTRIDGE AND GREEN SOFT HACKLE #12–16

COACHMAN WET FLY #12–16

(BEADHEAD VERSIONS OF SOFT HACKLES AND WET FLIES ARE GOOD, TOO.)

ADULT:

ELKHAIR CADDIS (GREEN BODY) #12–16 (DARK ELK-HAIR WINGS ARE MORE REALISTIC BUT MORE DIFFICULT TO SEE ON THE CHOPPY WATER THESE CADDIS HATCH FROM)

X CADDIS (GREEN OR OLIVE BODY) #14–16

PARACHUTE CADDIS (GREEN BODY) #12–16

EGGLAYER:

BEADHEAD BROWN AND GREEN DIVING CADDIS #12–16

BEADHEAD PARTRIDGE AND GREEN SOFT HACKLE #12–16

BEADHEAD COACHMAN WET FLY #12–16

Spotted Sedge (*Hydropsyche cockerelli*)

We discussed *H. occidentalis* in Chapter 2, but the summer and fall emergence of *H. cockerelli* is so important and widespread that it deserves another mention. This species can emerge in numbers from August into November. The #14–16 adult's wings are tan to mottled brown, and the body is tan to dirty yellow to green. It's regarded by many anglers as the most important of all caddis hatches.

The larvae are olive-brown worms that don't drift in the currents as often as their numbers would suggest. They use anchor lines of spun silk to keep themselves attached to the bottom. Some anglers, including Gary LaFontaine, have even imitated these silk anchor lines by whitening the last eighteen inches of tippet, reporting a greatly increased catch rate. Otherwise, larval imitations of the spotted sedge are of secondary importance.

It's the emerging pupae that trout target most. Spotted sedge pupae take an extra long time to fully emerge and break through the surface. They drift for long periods just under it, now struggling, now motionless, becoming easy targets of trout. Because their numbers are high and they're easily taken, fish consume them in a big way.

Egglayers dive to the bottom, after which they drift back up to the surface, then float downstream, spent. This can occur in the mornings or evenings. Diving caddis (or even caddis drys fished wet and stripped or twitched) and flat-water caddis are both important, too.

Hatches can occur at dawn during the heat of August but are usually encountered during evenings into darkness by anglers. As the emergence carries into autumn, hatches turn more toward midday. This is true of most aquatic insects.

Spotted Sedge

MATCHING FLY PATTERN SIZE: #14–16

COLOR: LARVA—OLIVE BROWN WORM TYPE

PUPA—BROWN WING-THORAX, DIRTY YELLOW ABDOMEN

ADULT—TAN TO BROWN MOTTLED WINGS; TAN, YELLOW-BROWN, AND GREEN BODIES

Habitat: Most rivers and streams

Spotted Sedge Fly Patterns

LARVA:

OLIVE BROWN CADDIS WORM #12–16

PUPA:

BROWN AND YELLOW SPARKLE PUPA (DEEP AND SURFACE) #14–16

PARTRIDGE AND YELLOW SOFT HACKLE #14–16

BEADHEAD AND UNWEIGHTED HARE'S EAR SOFT HACKLE #14–16

ADULT:

TAN ELKHAIR CADDIS #14–18

TAN PARACHUTE CADDIS #14–16

TAN X CADDIS #14–18

FLAT-WATER CADDIS (TAN TO DIRTY YELLOW BODY) #14–18

EGGLAYER:

BROWN AND YELLOW DIVING CADDIS #14–16

BEADHEAD PARTRIDGE AND YELLOW SOFT HACKLE #14–16

BEADHEAD HARE'S EAR WET FLY #14–16

Black Caddis (*Mystacides alafimbriata*)

As the name implies, this #16–18 summer caddis has black or very dark gray wings. Its body is amber and its antennae are very long. It has a low-flying wing profile and is most common in slower rivers and lakes.

Black caddisflies are active early in the morning, as they hover and swirl over banks. This activity has given them another common name—the black dancer. Some anglers report that they emerge at dawn by crawling out of the water along the banks. Others dispute this. In any case, they can be found floating along quiet edge waters before the day gets too hot. Trout like to sip them in. Realistic flat-water patterns can be necessary to negotiate with picky fish. Egg-laying flights are in the evening and can provide good fishing, too. The egglayers dive or crawl underwater to lay their eggs, with many returning to the surface spent. This, too, can be concentrated around the banks or objects that protrude from the river. Egglayers can be seen at other times and across midriver as well.

Gordon Rose, a well-known Bighorn River outfitter, enlightened me about that river's black caddis. He noted that emergence dates can vary by several weeks, due to the dam-regulated flows. These affect not only volume but temperature as well: Warmer releases mean earlier hatches. Normally the hatch shows around the twenty-fifth of August and runs through September. It begins around 10:30 A.M. and continues sporadically throughout the day. Trout will feed on the emergers and surface-riding black caddis, though not as well as they will on overcast days. Then, both hatch and fish activity is greater. The more important stage, Gordon related, is the evening egg-laying session. These black caddis are divers, preferring to crawl down objects to the bottom rather than to swim there, if such a protrusion is available. This could be a wading angler, an anchored boat, a streamside log, or an exposed boulder. It can also be the banks themselves. Gordon likes to use a diving caddis pattern in the evening with a green egg sac as an abdominal enhancement. Bighorn trout will feed on these #18–20 black caddis into darkness. Try them around and just downstream of any protrusions, because these not only give egg-laying caddis a ladder to the bottom of the river, they also provide eddies for trout to hold and dine from.

The larvae build curious cases from a variety of materials, often adding longer sticks. The end result is a case that's much longer than the larva, one that's presumably more difficult for predators to ingest. These seem to be of little importance to anglers.

Black Caddis

MATCHING FLY PATTERN SIZE: #16–20

COLOR: LARVA—ROUGH CASED CADDIS WITH LONGER STICK ATTACHED, BROWNS

PUPA—BLACK WING-THORAX WITH YELLOWISH ABDOMEN

ADULT—BLACK TO DARK GRAY WINGS, AMBER ABDOMEN, EXTRALONG ANTENNAE

Habitat: Slower rivers and lakes

Black Caddis Fly Patterns

LARVA:

NONE AVAILABLE, CONSIDERING THE CASE; COULD BE IMITATED, BUT NOT VERY IMPORTANT

PUPA:

BLACK AND AMBER SPARKLE PUPA #16–20

STARLING AND AMBER SOFT HACKLE #16–20

ADULT:

BLACK ELKHAIR CADDIS #16–20 (HACKLE CAN BE OMITTED FOR FLAT-WATER MODELS)

BLACK FLAT-WATER CADDIS #16–20 (THERE ARE FEW IF ANY STANDARDS FOR THIS; THEY'LL VARY BY FISHERY WHERE AND IF THEY'RE IMPORTANT.)

EGGLAYERS:

BLACK AND AMBER DIVING CADDIS #16–20

BLACK BEADHEAD SOFT HACKLE #16–20

Microcaddis (Family: Hydroptilidae.
Important genera: *Agraylea*, salt and pepper microcaddis;
Hydroptila, varicolored microcaddis; *Leucotrichia*,
Ring Horn microcaddis)

Most fly fishers call any small caddis "microcaddis," though the name really only applies to the Hydroptilidae caddis family. There are naturals in it that are surprisingly small, down to #28, though #18–22 is more common. As is true of many aquatic insects, population numbers can make up for small body size. Microcaddis tend to be most important on slow-water fisheries, including lakes, tailwaters, and spring creeks. The flows in those places are gentle enough to make it worthwhile for trout (including some big ones) to sip the insects in. Microcaddis do live in swifter rivers, too, such as Montana's Madison.

The larvae are for the most part unimportant to anglers. They have the distinction of roaming free for much of their larval life, building cases only in their final larval stage. They're dull shades of tan, gray, and olive with darker heads early on, much like midge larvae. Cases are built from a variety of materials, are quite small, and sometimes drift freely in the currents.

Emergers, egglayers, and spent microcaddis can be of importance to anglers and fish in high summer. Hatches begin in June and continue into September or October. These can occur at various hours of the day, and often endure for long periods of time. They're easily overlooked by anglers due to their small size. Riseforms similar to those provoked by midges are likely to be seen as the trout intercept emerging pupae just under the surface and spent adults just under or on it. Keeping a small seine net and stomach pump handy will greatly aid you in recognizing when these "little" opportunities are getting the trout's attention. Because the general trend of high-summer insects is to come down in size, consider this in your caddis fishing, too. You can even tie dry flies that will pass for midges or caddis. Tiny soft-hackle patterns have worked well for me, and I often fish them as droppers below a Parachute Adams on the fly-rich Missouri.

Microcaddis lay their eggs by diving or crawling to the bottom, then drifting back up to the surface, spent. Diving caddis patterns can be important, because the naturals are very obvious to fish. The hairy filaments of their wings usually catch tiny air bubbles. Their exaggerated

Caddisflies as small as #24 are common on mid- to late-summer rivers. Keep a few tiny caddis patterns on hand; they can also pass for midges.

swimming motion, added to their adult forms coated with shimmering air bubbles makes an easy target for trout. Other insects crawl down midriver on exposed boulders, or on bankside protrusions. Fish around and just downstream from these if numerous adult microcaddis are scuttling around on such objects (or on you). Tiny, simple diving caddis patterns, wet flies, and soft hackles could do business here.

Trout can be found taking the adult forms, too, in quiet edge waters, flats, eddies, and inside bends. This is especially true on tailwaters and spring-rich rivers of a slower nature. They could be getting some freshly emerged microcaddis, though it's more likely they'll be feasting on spent surface-riding ones, along with the other small fare summer offers.

Here are some major color trends for the various genera and numerous species of microcaddis:

Pupa:
- gray wing-thorax, bright green abdomen
- gray wing-thorax, yellow abdomen
- brown wing-thorax, orange abdomen
- brown wing-thorax, brown abdomen
- black wing-thorax, brown abdomen

The major color trends of the adults, egglayers, and spent caddis are:
- speckled gray and white wing, bright green body
- tan to gray to brown wing (some mottled), tan to yellow to orange to brown body, many shades
- dark brown to black wing (a few light spots), brown body

Microcaddis

MATCHING FLY PATTERN SIZE: #18–24
COLOR: AS LISTED ABOVE

Habitat: Especially important in slower rivers and lakes, but numerous in medium-swift rivers, too

Microcaddis Fly Patterns

LARVA:
NOT IMPORTANT, COULD EVEN USE MIDGE LARVA PATTERNS, PLUS BRASSIES, #18–24

PUPA:
TINY SOFT HACKLES, WET FLIES, AND SPARKLE PUPAE IN THE COLORS DISCUSSED ABOVE. THESE ARE NOT LIKELY TO BE FOUND IN MOST FLY SHOPS.

<u>Silver Stripe Sedge</u> (*Hesperophylax* species)

This is summer's giant caddis, a #8 insect with beautiful coloration. Its wings are a patterned ginger with a black and silverish white stripe running lengthwise through the center of the wing. A lighter patch of ginger is seen toward the rear of the wing. The body is bright olive to amber. Size, color, and season easily set these insects apart from the rest of summer's caddis clan. (They look similar to the giant orange sedge, also known as the October caddis, which becomes prominent from September through October. Those insects are of a darker hue, with a rusty orange body and patterned to dark grey wings.)

Silver stripe sedge hatch from early July through August. They emerge at night. Adults can be active in the cool of morning and lay eggs in late morning to afternoon. This is when fishing the dry form can be best. They're big enough and have an extended enough emergence that some trout get to know and relish them. They're never very numerous, but they're so big in a summer world of small aquatic insects that trout might take a slash at one any time of day. They also have a habit of running across the surface of the river, which brings out the aggressive nature of certain fish. Several of the largest caddis seem to share this post-hatching or egg-laying surface-trotting behavior.

Using a #8–10 Stimulator or Bucktail Caddis can bring up the odd thrashing fish. These make good strike indicators, too, trailing either a nymph, emerger, or smaller dry. You can continue using the big caddis dry as a searching pattern or strike indicator into autumn, because that season's October caddis (*Dicosmoecus* species) is similar in size to the silver stripe sedge.

The larvae are case makers, gluing small pebbles and debris together in constructing their mobile homes. The larvae can be quite large, as big as #2. They tend to group up on certain boulders, especially for pupation.

Because it emerges at night, the pupal stage of this caddisfly is of little consequence, except to those who prowl streams by moonlight. Skating and twitching caddis patterns across starlit rivers is known for getting some thrashing takes from above-average fish, though.

Females deposit eggs by diving to the river bottom from late morning through midafternoon. This easily conjures mental images of aggressive trout following suit! If a number of egg-laying females are seen at this time, a Beadhead Ginger Diving Caddis could bring some aggressive takes. It would be hard to ignore the dry-fly possibilities, though, especially because these big caddis often run across the surface toward the banks after laying their eggs. They can favor areas where trees and vegetation come down to the water's edge. They spend time hiding and mating in wooded habitat between emergence and their demise. They'll often be close to the banks during the egg-laying process, where bold trout pounce on them. There will never be a lot of them. Numbers are likely to be counted in the dozens, not in the hundreds or thousands, as with smaller caddis.

If midday hatches are sparse and you like to gaze around at the scenery, tie one of these big caddis dry flies on. Cast, look about, and don't be surprised if trout occasionally smash your fly just as it starts to drag! You could be imitating the surface-running action of the giant silver stripe sedge.

Silver Stripe Sedge

MATCHING FLY PATTERN SIZE: #8–10 (CASED LARVAE EVEN BIGGER)
COLOR: LARVA—CASED CADDIS, MEDIUM BROWNS, VERY LARGE
PUPA—(HATCHES AT NIGHT) GINGER
ADULT—PATTERNED GINGER WINGS WITH A BLACK AND SILVER HORIZONTAL
STRIPE DOWN CENTER WING, MEDIUM OLIVE TO AMBER BODY

Habitat: A variety of mountain river types

OTHER IMPORTANT SUMMER TROUT FOODS

In addition to the high-summer hatches, the following insects and fish can also be important to imitate at the right place and time.

Midges

We discussed midges in Chapter 1, but they should not be forgotten during the rest of the season. Whereas spring, fall, and winter midges are primarily dull shades of olive, gray, and black, summer midges show more variety. They come in those colors and in tans, reds, greens, and even chartreuse. Sizes vary more, too, down to those too small to imitate. Lake midges are bigger and bring trout to the surface morning and evening.

On humid days midges hatch better and can fill in the surface-feeding voids between hatches of larger mayflies and caddis, especially on slower-paced rivers. Trout can even prefer the smaller but more numerous midges over less populous hatches of larger insects, or they can take both. You'll want to keep some on hand as last resorts for overachieving selective trout.

Let me describe one summer midge from Montana's Missouri River. High summer sees many midge hatches here, from dawn 'til dusk. One is of particular interest due to its midday emergence and color. This is a bright lime green–colored midge, one that's not too small and catches the interest of trout. The color alone is striking—chartreuse all over. It's about #18–20, big enough to rub shoulders with the prominent Trico hatches here. It hatches from midmorning into early evening in moderate density. Stomach pumping shows the trout like it. No commercial patterns are available.

The emerging pupae struggle a bit at the surface, which is common with midges. This makes an easy-to-capture and enticing target for surface-gazing trout. The fish don't become selective to these midges in my experience. They just take them in stride, along with the more abundant Trico spinners, spent caddis, PMD spinners, and the like.

Anyone fishing rich tailwater rivers and spring creeks will want to include a variety of midge patterns. Lake anglers will want to have some, too. Swift freestone rivers have less consistent midge fishing, but even there they could be needed in eddies and tailout flats. Using smaller fly patterns often fools much-fished-over veteran trout.

Hoppers, Beetles, Crickets, Ants, and Cicadas

These land-based insects become important to trout in high summer. Because hatches of aquatic insects push toward morning and evening at this time of year to escape the dehydrating sun and midday heat, these crunchy bugs fill in the midday void. Heat activates them, increasing their appearance on the water. They helplessly trudge the surface film, get carried down bankside glides, and twirl tantalizingly in eddies. Trout love to sip them in.

By high summer, trout have chosen feeding positions in the river that become habitual haunts. Anglers should take time to scan river edges for quiet rings or visible subsurface fish. The low clear water allows stalking, but patience becomes a virtue. Walk slowly, look hard, and stop to stare into the water where the habitat looks promising. Anywhere a foam-specked food lane wanders near a protected bank hold deserves an extra look. Ideal positions are usually occupied. Large feeding trout like to sit just upstream of bank protrusions, too, not just downstream of them. The upstream side of turf clumps, rocks, and logs should be watched closely, then fished blind if no trout give themselves away. The downstream side should of course be investigated, too. Rocks, streambed depressions, and

Most anglers look forward to hopper season. After a summer of shrinking insects, fishing big dry flies to gung ho fish is an eagerly awaited event. This action never lasts as long as you'd like!

other holding water just off the banks will be important. Wherever the edge of the main channel flow is will be a holding zone for trout. Edge waters in some cases get overheated in high summer, and too shallow to be of comfort. They'll move out to a dropoff zone where currents push food their way. Rock and boulder cover along the edge of the main current and at the heads of pools offer fish more comfort and plenty of food.

Not all land-based insects fall in along the banks. Heat-inspired hoppers and cicadas are just as likely to crash-land midriver. Endless western winds help distribute them widely. Midriver trout can be every bit as happy to gulp down one of these satisfying morsels as would an undercut-bank hugger. And they're not as likely to be repeatedly cast to and made as nervous as their bankside brethren.

Such terrestrials can also sink as wave action rolls them under. Wet hoppers and ants can be every bit as productive as surface models. When the midday hatches are sparse, these bugs become a major tactic of choice. Late

July through mid-October is the time of terrestrial action. There's a lot more land than water in the Rockies, and these "hatches" never stop. When streamside grasses turn brown and hoppers march in search of better meals, some fat browns will be smiling!

Land-Based Insect Fly Patterns

HOPPER:

DAVE'S HOPPER #4–10	HENRYS FORK HOPPER #6–10
WHIT'S HOPPER #4–10	PARACHUTE HOPPER #6–10
MADAME X #4–10	

ANT:

CDC CINNAMON ANT #14–20	FLYING ANT #14–20
HI-VIS BLACK FOAM ANT #14–18	BLACK FUR ANT #14–20
PARACHUTE ANT #14–20	ELKHAIR CADDIS TYPE ANT #14–20

BEETLE:

HI-VIS FOAM BEETLE #14–18	BLACK DEERHAIR BEETLE #14–20
COCH-Y-BONDHU #14–20	PEACOCK TRUDE #16–20

OTHER:

BLACK CRICKET #6–12	CICADA #6–8
SPRUCE MOTH #12–14	INCHWORM #10–14
CHERNOBYL ANT #8–12	

Damselflies

These common aquatic insects are especially important to lake anglers. They also live in numbers in slow rivers with weed beds and big eddies. Both the swimming nymphs and adults are taken by trout.

Damselfly nymphs are pale tan to various shades of green. They're almost translucent and have prominent eyes, legs, and a fanlike tail sprouting off a long narrow body. They swim with an exaggerated side-to-side motion that doesn't allow them much headway. Slow-stripped retrieves of marabou-tailed flies are good imitations. (See color plate no. 22.)

After growing, damsel nymphs migrate to shores, where they climb up grasses and bankside vegetation to emerge, not unlike the stoneflies. They sometimes migrate in numbers and at the same time. This can get the attention of shore-patrolling trout. Look for freshly emerging nymphs and adults along bankside grasses, and the swirls of trout taking subsurface food. Sinking and slowly retrieving a damselfly nymph or damsel-scud combination should bring some results.

Damselfly adults hover over weed beds, lake edges, and still-water eddies. Trout will even jump and try to grab them out of the air. The adults come in shades of metallic blue and tan. These often get blown into the water on windy afternoons, as do hoppers. They are most active during the heat of midday. I've seen cases on the Missouri where damsels were much more numerous on the river than were hoppers. In such river environments few people imitate them, but trout eat them at will.

Adult damsels lay eggs by injecting them into aquatic plants just beneath the water's surface. The flies are often seen in tandem, laying eggs in weed beds. Damselfly patterns make good alternatives to hoppers in the right river habitats and are standard flies for many lakes. Trout can sip them in or smash them, providing some exciting high-summer midday action when other hatches are sparse. (See color plate no. 21.)

Damselfly Fly Patterns

NYMPH:

Olive Woolly Bugger #10–12
Beadhead Marabou Damsel #8–12 (shades of olive)
Marabou Damsel #10–12

ADULT:

Blue Damsel #10–14
Parachute Damsel #10–14

Forage Fish

Minnows, sculpins, and crayfish are big food items for river trout. Leeches add to the menu in lakes. All these are reasonable alternatives when little is showing, and at dusk, night, and dawn. Big-fish devotees will want to ply them with regularity.

As we approach mid-September a subtle change begins. There is less daylight. Nights cool. The first snowstorm and cooling trend is likely to hit. The Trico summer comes to an end. PMDs are gone, too. Hatches begin shifting from morning and evening back toward afternoon. The body colors of the naturals begin to darken, and many species become a bit bigger overall. Fish get reinvigorated when the extreme heat of August and early September ends and waters begin to cool. The beginning of an excellent fishing period begins—that of autumn and the next chapter's focus.

HIGH-SUMMER HATCH CHART–JULY THROUGH MID-SEPTEMBER

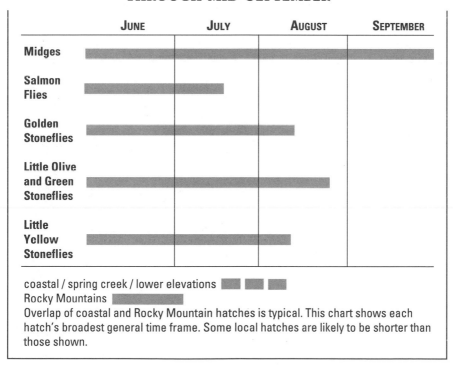

CHAPTER THREE

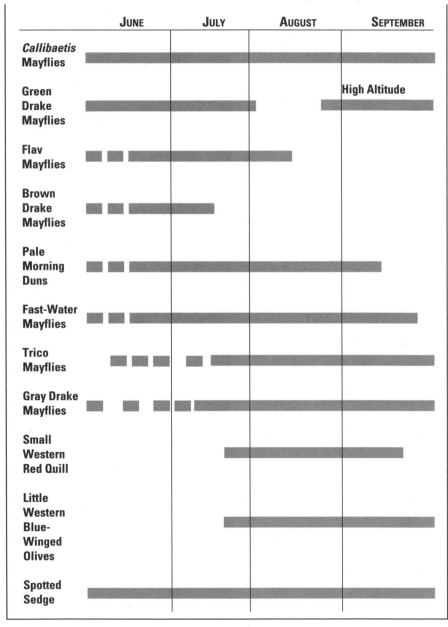

	JUNE	JULY	AUGUST	SEPTEMBER
Callibaetis Mayflies				
Green Drake Mayflies				High Altitude
Flav Mayflies				
Brown Drake Mayflies				
Pale Morning Duns				
Fast-Water Mayflies				
Trico Mayflies				
Gray Drake Mayflies				
Small Western Red Quill				
Little Western Blue-Winged Olives				
Spotted Sedge				

HIGH-SUMMER HATCH CHART–JULY THROUGH MID-SEPTEMBER (CONT'D)

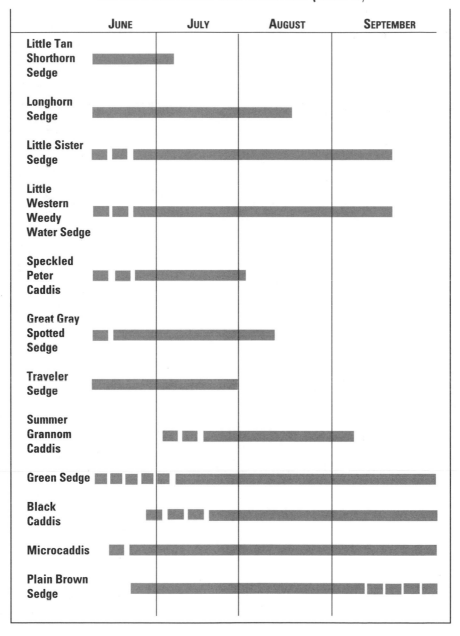

HIGH-SUMMER HATCH CHART–JULY
THROUGH MID-SEPTEMBER (CONT'D)

	JUNE	JULY	AUGUST	SEPTEMBER
Silver Stripe Sedge	▬ ▬ ▬ ▬▬▬	▬▬▬▬▬	▬▬▬▬▬	
Damselflies	▬▬▬▬▬	▬▬▬▬▬	▬▬▬▬▬	▬▬▬▬▬

4

AUTUMN
Mid-September through November

AUTUMN FISHING is certainly worth savoring. Water conditions and temperatures become ideal. Trout are reinvigorated. The scenery, texture, and scent of autumn overwhelms the senses. And the sport often lives up to expectation. Hatches continue. Trout tend to become less picky. They seem bolder and more ready to capitalize on the few hatches and feeding opportunities at hand, or should I say "at fin."

Then there are those prespawning browns—big ornery fellows that dwell in the imagination more than they spend time on hooks. Their image keeps one casting streamers and such, often beyond the bounds of reason. Trout could be rising to awesome afternoon *Baetis* hatches, but you'd hate to miss that one chance at a trophy by switching to a dry.

The good thing about autumn is the reduction of hatch species and flies needed for daily river work. Everything you need in most cases could fit into one or two fly boxes. Hatches become afternoon and evening events, with the addition of possible midge and rising-fish activity in the morning. I often find myself slinging streamers from dawn to midday, then breaking down and fishing the *Baetis* and midge hatches of midafternoon until dark. By then a few more slams of the streamer again feel compulsory. (There's little doubt that fishing a couple Beadhead Pheasant Tails under an indicator would provide the most consistent day-long action, but I'm prone to the more aggressive streamer style at times, regardless of results.)

There are other fall options and oddities, too, from hoppers to *Ephoron*, twilight's unusual white fly. Caddis still fly, ants still scurry, and the crayfish are never crunchier. One can fish autumn as the imagination dictates. It just seems as though the cottonwood limbs become bare and brooding all too soon. The promise of winter blows chill wind down your collar until the desire to be on-stream begins to wane. Football, the World Series, and the holidays begin chipping away at fishing time, along with the much shorter daylight hours. Premium late-fall fishing can be distilled into afternoon sessions with rising fish on drys and streamer fishing for big imagined browns. We always wait eagerly for autumn to arrive, but it always ends too soon.

EFFECTS OF AUTUMN WEATHER

Indian summer days, the fluttering gold of cottonwood leaves, frosty fog-strewn mornings, and glittering starlit nights—such dreamlike images are only part of autumn's world. Bone-chilling rain and snow-storms, high winds, and less than enthralling conditions make up the rest. Conditions in between the two usually provide the best fishing. A heavily overcast day, perhaps a little drizzle or light snowfall, and little or no wind generally prompts the best action. It's then that hatches boom and trout feed heartily. The difference between a glaring, sunny (and usually breezy) fall day and an overcast one can be remarkable in terms of steady-rising fish. *Baetis*, the dominant fall mayfly, avoids bright sunlight when possible but hatches in droves when a dank darkness pervades.

The fish respond better, too. After a summer of rising to Tricos, PMDs, and other sunlit fare, fall trout are much more willing to rise in sunlight than spring fish were. Some bugs will hatch in autumn's lower-angled sunlight, although not as many as on those darker days. Big browns seem to take streamers better on overcast days, too. At least I always expect them to.

Autumn weather should never be underestimated in the Rockies. Though it's not too common, it's not out of the question for a big cold

Overcast drizzly days often provide the best hatches and dry-fly action.

front to come sweeping down from the Arctic, plunging temperatures down into the subzero range. Temperature drops of more than 50 degrees in an hour are sometimes experienced. This can occur in late October and usually does at least once in November. On the whole, though, daytime temperatures will average from the seventies in late September to the sixties and fifties through October to the forties of November. It's not usually as cold here as people make it out to be. Highly variable, yes, but consistently cold weather doesn't usually start until December. Be sure to have a good stock of warm clothes, hats, and gloves on hand, though, plus some lip balm and skin cream. A flashlight isn't a bad idea, either, because darkness comes quickly, before some floaters get to the boat ramp.

On the whole, mid-September through November are excellent fishing months. Small rivers will cool faster than big ones, and their hatches can sputter out sooner. Tailwaters and spring creeks maintain their temperatures longer, providing better match-the-hatch fishing right into December (unless unseasonably cold weather dominates). When the wind drops and clouds build, it's time to be on-stream! Warm fronts are usually heralded by wind and sun. Optimal fishing conditions often fall between battling weather fronts.

AUTUMN RIVER CONDITIONS

Autumn sees a coming together of factors that generally lead to improved fishing after late summer's heat and low water. Rivers cool to temperatures that trout find comfortable. Irrigation ceases, which raises river levels just a bit, clearing some up as well (irrigation water in summer tends to warm and muddy its meager returns to the river). Autumn rivers flow clear, cool, and a little more full. Precipitation in the form of rain and snow can also increase a bit. There are fewer food sources for the fish, and they take flies aggressively at times. All these factors favor the trout and improved fishing.

Western rivers are dependably good at this time of year, more so than at any other time. Clear flows, perfect wading conditions, and ideal water temperatures for trout all come together now. The only exception is in extreme drought years, when water flows can be lower than average, though temperature and clarity will still be right. Summer droughts can cause some fish kill and make it difficult or impossible to float smaller rivers, even in fall. But such fall conditions make the wading potential better. Drought-shrunken large rivers concentrate trout, making the rivers easier to cover. The odds of having heavy rain or dam releases ruin your fishing are very low in autumn.

Summer water temperatures on many rivers push the 70-degree mark by late August. This sees a slowdown in the trout's metabolism and in fishing results. From mid-September on the waters cool, first into the lower sixties, then fifties, then forties. Trout are much more active in these temperature ranges, though drastic sudden changes in either direction can bring feeding to a temporary halt. Small shallow rivers heat and cool more quickly than big ones. I've seen the fish shut down hard after a big cold front settles on Montana's little Smith River while on the nearby Missouri trout feed on.

Change is the rule in autumn, though, and the trout will soon be back on the feed. Snow or rain fronts without drastic temperature changes and little wind prompt some of the best fall fishing experiences. The remaining hatches burst forth and fish respond. Even wind doesn't deter *Baetis* and midges from hatching. Fish will gladly rise in wind-free slicks along banks or wherever they happen to be. Wind is more likely to deter anglers than fish. The wind usually seems less of a hindrance once you're out there than it does when you're sitting in the car bemoaning the conditions. A fall day most always holds promise.

The Trout, the River, and Feeding Behavior

Autumn trout are still in their summer lies for the most part. Low clear water concentrates them in the ideal water types they prefer. Because the problem of extreme heat and lowered potential oxygen is over, and because river levels can come back up a bit when irrigation ceases, trout might also return to edge waters and tailout flats that become dangerously warm and shallow in high summer. There's less need for them to concentrate in riffle dropoffs and swift runs now, though some will always choose those spots.

An event that will draw more trout to quiet edge waters, eddies, and flats is autumn's *Baetis*, midge, and mahogany dun hatches. All these insects ride the currents a very long time after hatching and before flying away, especially on the cool overcast days they hatch best in. *Baetis* and midges can hatch in very dense numbers and are easy for fish to pick off at leisure. Mahogany duns are fewer but can be seen along quiet edge waters, which is where they migrate to hatch. Slower water and often shallow feeding stations are where trout can capitalize on these fall hatches the best.

As fall draws closer to winter and river temperatures drop into the thirties, some trout will opt for warmer water if it's available. This is especially true on smaller freestone rivers that chill more quickly with every cold front and may soon be locked in ice. Fish will gravitate to spring seepages, deeper pools, and in some places may even drop downstream until they enter larger rivers or lakes with warmer and more stable temperatures. Other trout seem to want to hold out in the area that's become their home over the course of the summer, areas that were chosen when spring runoff flushed clear and dropped and as the pecking order of size and aggression allowed.

Autumn Spawning

Both brown and brook trout are autumn-to-early-winter spawners. In fisheries that are dominated by either of these species the fishing will naturally show a marked change when it comes to where the big fish are located. They then become more concentrated and vulnerable to anglers. In some cases such spawning areas will be closed to fishing.

Whitefish spawn in late autumn to midwinter, too, and their freely scattered eggs become food for a variety of fishes. Egg patterns, pink scuds, and the like are always a good bet for trout in fall, winter, and spring. Where once they were oddities, they have now become standards.

Spawning movement of brown trout will see mature specimens, including some very large ones, move up or down rivers, streams, and creeks to the places of their birth. I've read reports of them moving as far as two hundred miles. They can be seen holding in deep pools in the sunlit daylight hours where rivers and streams give the benefit of an elevated view and clear water.

This isn't a salmon run, though. Individuals and small groups are all that will be seen in most places. The places where spawning tributaries come into rivers can find more browns stacked up, especially when the creek is too low to ascend. The fish might choose to wait for some added precipitation before making the final trip. Big spawners usually wait until nightfall to swim up small waters in order to hide their uneasy presence from predators.

Brown trout spawn as early as September and continue to do so through October and November. In some places spawning can run even later than that. Like most trout, they prefer tailouts and side channels where a certain velocity and depth of water are found to suit their needs. These areas provide clear gravel where sediment isn't likely to be deposited, and a medium-paced current to feed oxygen through the gravel and into the eggs. (Silt settles out of the river in pools and is generally clearer by the time it reaches the medium-swift tailout.)

One problem with the locations most trout choose to spawn in is that they are shallow enough—one and a half to three feet—that anglers often wade through the spawning beds, or redds, without knowing it. Tailouts and side channels are some of the very places anglers choose to walk down and wade-fish. This can destroy future generations of brown trout.

Big brown trout linger in the backs of the minds of most autumn anglers!

Take special care in spring and fall to avoid walking through possible nesting sites. Look for bowl- or oblong-shaped depressions with clear gravel showing through on an otherwise algae-coated bottom. Spawning fish can be seen on the beds at times, too. They should be left alone.

Brown trout differ a bit from most rainbows and cutthroats. They're not as fanatical about finding small tributaries to spawn in. Many will, but a good percentage will spawn in main-stem rivers as well. They seem to tolerate spawning on cobble bottoms as well as on finer gravel, too. On the whole they're just a more adaptable fish.

Brook trout have the distinction of being effective lake spawners, as well as of using rivers and streams. Their preferred spawning sites are where springs upwell from the bottom, supplying clean water and steady temperatures. They'll also use traditional spawning sites like tailouts and side channels in streams where spring upwellings aren't available. Their spawning activity can offer trophy potential in certain areas of some lakes, where bigger than average individuals are found. Most stream brook trout are much smaller, and may even be stunted by overpopulation.

One can expect to find larger brown and brook trout pools above and below the tailouts and side channels chosen for spawning when that time draws near. Such areas can be fished with big flashy streamers, which can bring strikes from aggressive males and females that become more territorial and defensive. A lot of weight can be needed to get the fly near the bottom. It may only be effective if it's right in a fish's face. Egg patterns also work well. I'm prone to using two big streamers of varying colors. I've seen examples of pooled-up big browns neglecting one color only to jump on another, even after repeated presentations. The two-streamer setup looks like one small fish chasing another, something that seems to bring out the aggressive tendencies in large fish. Egg-head variations seem to work especially well. Perhaps the trout think some small fish is making off with eggs from their redd.

What keeps fall fishing interesting is the fact that an extralarge brown trout could be intercepted most anywhere. Trout that have hidden through the summer in unfished places now cross paths with hopeful anglers. In most cases one can't see into the water well enough to stalk them. They're caught with deep-sinking, systematically cast rigs. Sight-fishing smaller tributaries with steep hillsides that provide good viewing does open up that prospect to trout-hunting anglers. Stealth is needed.

These fish are wary from their travels through unaccustomed watery arterials and may avoid the majority of presentations in sunlit hours. Some will take, though, and it's an exciting pastime. You'll get some good terrain-stomping exercise by the end of the day!

Autumn Hatches and Fly Patterns

Fall provides some enjoyable and productive fishing. Trout can be gung ho to feed because the hatches and food choices are fewer. Pattern selection can be less critical and the fish more opportunistic. This isn't to say they're dumb. They have been fished over all summer. But I do see a lowered level of selectivity, even among educated trout. Sometimes I think the lower angle of the sun in the sky might play a role. Leader shadows are reduced because more of the sun's rays bounce off the surface rather than penetrate it. Fish that were notoriously picky in high summer now take a well-cast Parachute Adams with regularity. Freestone trout grab nymphs from runs with vigor. A Prince Nymph, Hare's Ear, or Zug Bug can keep the rod flexed. Streamers and Buggers are a good choice anywhere, especially for big fish.

Some of high summer's hatches carry over into fall. Other, fresh hatches take place, too. Many anglers have traditionally overlooked autumn's outstanding dry-fly potential, which is among the best of the year.

On the whole, though, aquatic insects are finishing up their yearly scheduled emergences. Rivers will soon be traveled only by midges. Tiny and immature nymphs now populate the streambed, many of which stay hidden over the course of winter, showing little cold-water growth. Trout often respond to this shrinking food supply by aggressively feeding on what's left. This can play to the angler's advantage.

The remaining autumn hatches are made up of mayflies, caddisflies, and midges. Stonefly species have disappeared for the year. Terrestrials remain important through the first half of autumn, catching many fish from mid-September into mid-October. Hoppers, beetles, and ants continue as top midday offerings. Beyond mid-October the cooler daytime temperatures greatly reduce their presence on the water (though any sipping trout might take an ant pattern).

Though many anglers look at autumn in a streamer-fishing kind of way, it's also one of the best dry-fly times of year.

As a rule, autumn's aquatic insects run a bit larger and darker than those of high summer. Darker gray wings and olive to mahogany bodies set the mayfly trend. There is one notable exception, an almost pure white mayfly that we'll discuss later in this chapter. A few caddis species continue in the medium-to-small size range, plus one famous giant of a caddis—the October caddis or giant orange sedge.

Outside of midges, which can hatch at any hour when conditions are right, emergences all push into the late morning through afternoon. *Baetis* and midges can be found on the water until darkness in some places, for it now comes so soon. The *Baetis* will be thinned by then, however, but trout can still be looking. Dry-fly anglers can hit the river about lunchtime knowing that some rising-fish action is likely to be encountered the rest of the day. This is especially true on tailwaters, spring creeks, and rivers with easy-paced flows. And because sunset comes sooner now, one's concentration and dry-fly energies are concentrated into a shorter, four- to six-hour, time frame. It's easy to keep your fishing intensity up on a beautiful fall afternoon! Humid mornings can still provide excellent midge action, and there's always the promise of big fish on streamers, egg patterns, and nymphs. The fanatic will want to spend every scenic daylight hour on an autumn stream.

Autumn Mayflies

Mayfly species now drop off like, well, flies. Only a few hatches remain. Because there are so few, trout capitalize heavily on those that continue. There are some carryover hatches from high summer. Most others end their seasonal span around the mid-September period. Gone are the prolific Tricos and PMDs. (There are a few exceptions where Tricos linger into October.) Most of the fast-water species have fizzled, too. Those that carry over conveniently fit into either the blue-winged olive or mahogany dun autumn color patterns. These carryover mayflies include *Attenella margarita, Serratella tibialis* (which we looked at in Chapter 3), and some *Baetis* species that may only have showed during high summer's most inclement rainy weather. These are all in the #16–20 size range, with gray wings and olive to olive-brown bodies. The one great exception to this is the localized fly *Ephoron*, the white fly.

The White Fly (*Ephoron album*)

After a summer that features some tiny mayflies, down to #24, how does a profuse hatch of an all-white #14 mayfly sound? This hatch only occurs in the lower reaches of some large trout rivers where silt starts contending with gravel as bottom structure. The nymphs of this species burrow, digging tunnels in slow-water silty riverbeds. This eliminates their presence from popular stretches of most trout streams. One has to look this hatch up along the quiet cottonwood bottoms and lower reaches of such rivers as the North Platte, Yellowstone, and forks of the Snake. Fish populations are lower in such stretches, but fishing pressure is lower still. One can catch more fish in these locales at times, because the trout are more innocent of fly fishers and their ways.

The white fly hatch actually starts in late August in many western locales. It continues through all of September and ends in early to mid-October. The flies emerge only at twilight in a brief flurry that can show

Ephoron *mayflies, or white flies, only hatch from silt-bed areas in the lower reaches of large trout rivers. It's a twilight affair that can rouse every fish in the river.*

thousands of flies and numerous rising fish. Burrowing mayflies have some of the highest densities, which, coupled with their large size, provides a feeding bonanza to twilight trout.

Ephoron mayflies exhibit some unusual traits. The females never molt into spinners and mate quickly in the dun stage. They also have poorly developed legs. Males do molt and have developed forelegs that are needed for mating. The males hatch first, quickly molt, then mate with freshly hatched females even before they leave the water. All this takes place in a short twilight time. Some #12–14 flies, including White Wulffs, Cream Parachutes, and Sparkle Duns, make good dry-fly imitations.

The nymphs are swimming emergers, bursting free from their streambed tunnels and wiggling quickly to the surface. Jointed Wiggle Nymphs have been developed on eastern rivers to fish related hatches. Fish can be very picky when focusing on this nymph's up-and-down undulating swimming motion. Marabou is an obvious choice for tail material, and swiveling two-part flies have been tied to imitate the wiggle. The nymphs are #12–14, dirty-cream-colored creatures with tusks and prominent gills and tails. Because the white fly has gone largely unnoticed in the West, you'll have to tie your own nymphs, should the trout prove picky before getting on the duns. Late evening, *just* before the sun sets, is when nymph fishing should pick up. Let them sink, then short-strip them quickly to the surface on a floating line. You should be seeing some swirls made by subsurface fish as the hatch begins. It shouldn't be long before the duns and rising fish appear to clear up any misgivings.

It has been noted that all the fish in the river will get up on this hatch where it occurs. You'll have to stay out until dark to encounter it, though. Competition between your fly and the naturals for the fish's attention can be fierce.

The time period of the white fly hatch—from late August to mid-October—features daytime fishing that can include Tricos, caddisflies, and good hopper fishing. Toward the end of its seasonal emergence in October, afternoon *Baetis* and midges are likely to precede the white flies. Twilight *Ephoron* hatches can be the frosting on the cake once you've figured out where they are. Remember that they'll take you into darkness. Make sure the boat ramp or access point isn't too far away! Good night vision and a flashlight are advisable.

The White Fly

MATCHING FLY PATTERN SIZE: #12–14

COLOR: NYMPH—DIRTY CREAM, THREE TAILS (ONLY AVAILABLE TO TROUT WHEN
THEY HATCH)

DUN—WHITE WINGS AND BODY WITH HUES OF LIGHT GRAY OR DIRTY YELLOW;
FEMALE HAS THREE TAILS, MALES HAVE TWO

SPINNER—(MALE ONLY) CLEAR WINGS, WHITE BODY AS ABOVE, TWO TAILS

Both duns and spinners are on the water at the same time. One pattern, such as a Parachute, should pass for both.

Habitat: Lower reaches of large trout rivers where silt infringes on gravel streambeds. This is sometimes looked upon as marginal trout water, but the fish are there. Many will rise to hoppers in the daytime and to the white fly toward dark. This can also be good streamer water for larger fish.

White Fly Patterns

NYMPH:

EPHORON WIGGLE NYMPH #12–14

MARABOU-TAIL HARE'S EAR #12–14

DUN AND SPINNER:

WhiteWulff #12–14

CREAM/WHITE PARACHUTE #12–14

CREAM SPARKLE DUN #12–14

Faint hues of gray or yellow can be seen in the otherwise white naturals. Both duns and spinners are on the water at the same time, so the above patterns can pass for both.

Tiny Blue-Winged Olive
(was *Pseudocloeon edmundsi,* now *Baetis punctiventris*)

This is a smaller cousin of the #16–20 *Baetis* species seen on most waters. The tiny blue-winged olive ranges from #22–26, one of the smallest western mayflies to be encountered. They used to be listed as a *Pseudocloeon* species. The common name Pseudo was often heard among anglers in the know. Now that the Latin terminology is being revised, common names are making good reference points for people who just want to fish, not devote their time to language studies. We still call them Pseudos to differentiate them from the already abundant number of *Baetis* species. (See color plate no. 23.)

Despite all that, these tiny blue-winged olives are a pale green to almost lime green in body color, with light gray wings (no hind wing at all—something that used to separate them from *Baetis*), and two tails. The males have larger eyes and can run more toward pale brown or tan. The overall coloration is noticeably lighter and brighter than the other *Baetis* species.

These flies have two generations a season, as is the case with most *Baetis.* The first shows between May and July. The second hatches from September into October, when they are replaced on-stream by larger autumn *Baetis.* The first generation can be overshadowed by larger green drakes, PMDs, caddisflies, and the like on some rivers, along with runoff conditions. On controlled-flow rivers, though, the first generation can get the trout's attention, because it tends to include more flies than some of the larger insect species. (Small aquatic insects generally hatch in more profuse numbers.)

In my experience, it's the second generation that's of most importance to fly fishers. Where I fish, it kicks in just as the Trico hatch ends for the year, in mid-September. Pseudos become the dominant hatch for several weeks, mixed with midges and caddis. On sunny days the hatch starts in mid- to late afternoon and carries on into early evening. On rainy days, denser hatches start earlier in the afternoon, just after lunch, and continue longer, again into early evening. On those dark damp days, incredible numbers will pile up in feed lanes. As with other *Baetis* species, they appear to float forever on the currents, with few seeming to fly off. On some rivers both large and small trout feed steadily on these tiny duns. On other rivers, larger trout reportedly ignore them, even though they're superabundant. On the Missouri River, where I guide, most trout target them in low-water years. This is the main late-September hatch here, occurring with tremendous numbers. Fewer and smaller trout focus on them in high-water years. Apparently, the farther from the surface a good trout is holding, the less likely it is to rise to small flies if there is a sufficient quantity of other foodstuffs to keep him occupied.

Tiny blue-winged olives prefer slow flat water. Rich rivers with abundant weed beds have the best populations. There, large trout can feed efficiently, using slow-water feeding stations to harvest the small-fly bounty. Spring-fed rivers and tailwaters are the best water types for this mayfly, but I see them in quiet pools of autumn freestoners, too. Small schools of trout often form when feeding on this fly, using slow-water areas to gang up on abundant numbers.

The most important fishing factor is matching the size of this hatch. There are days when trout will gulp oversized imitations, but as a rule they'll ignore anything bigger than a #20 if they are focused on Pseudos. The naturals run #22–24, and this size must be used most days to insure some success during this prolific hatch. Trout will hit a variety of patterns if they are the right size. Because the naturals show variations in color, that aspect of imitation is decidedly of secondary concern. Bright to medium green bodies and pale dun wings and hackle are top color choices.

The tiny nymphs are of less concern, but small Pheasant Tail and pale olive nymphs are good imitations, in #20–24. The duns float so long on the surface that trout usually focus on that stage. If a bulging fish is encountered, one taking its meal just beneath the surface, such tiny nymphs will come in handy.

Tiny olive spinners can create fishable events. Whereas some other *Baetis* species prefer to crawl under water to lay eggs, Pseudos tend to lay them in traditional mayfly fashion—dropping their eggs on the surface and falling spent there. Spinner falls can occur mornings or evenings. I've been in a few good evening spinner falls in September. The female spinners have bright green bodies and clear wings. The males are browner, with larger eyes and clear wings, too. I've also seen many morning spinner falls in the season's first generation, but these were so diluted with Trico spinners as to be of little consequence on their own. They do help

Tiny Pseudo spinners can be on the water mornings or evenings. At times they can create a fishable event. In the mornings they can be mixed with Trico spinners.

keep morning fish looking up, though, adding to the trout's interest in abundant small flies.

Tiny Blue-Winged Olives

MATCHING FLY PATTERN SIZE: #22–26

COLOR: NYMPH—PALE BROWNS AND OLIVES TO BRIGHT GREEN, THREE TAILS

   DUN—PALE GRAY WINGS, MEDIUM TO BRIGHT GREEN BODIES IN FEMALES, PALE BROWN BODIES IN MALES, TWO TAILS

   SPINNER—WINGS CLEAR, BODY AS ABOVE BUT GLOSSIER (AS IS TRUE OF ALL MAYFLY SPINNERS), TWO TAILS

Habitat: Medium- to slow-water areas of rich rivers

<u>Mahogany Duns</u>
(*Paraleptophlebia bicornuta* and *P. debilis*)

This autumn mayfly exhibits the darkened coloration common to most early- and late-season aquatic insects. Its body is a rich brown or reddish brown. Its wings are medium gray. It has three prominent tails in both the dun and spinner stages, easily separating it from any fall *Baetis* species. Mahogany duns are #16, even pushing into the #14 range, which makes them easier yet to tell from the smaller, #18–20, *Baetis*. Related species hatch in spring and summer, but autumn's mahogany dun is generally the most important of the three. (See color plate no. 24.)

This is a sparse late-morning through afternoon hatch that exhibits some unusual mayfly characteristics. The nymphs begin life in swifter water, but as they mature they migrate to slower edge waters. Many crawl out of the water in stonefly and damselfly fashion onto rocks, grass, or sticks. Consequently, the duns don't always provide the dry-fly opportunities they might. Some do hatch in the river, though, and others stumble or get blown back onto the water after their emergences as duns. (See color plate no. 25.)

In any case, quiet edge-water zones and slicks are where these mahogany duns are likely to be seen, and where trout can sip their obvious, long-floating forms at leisure. Because of their fairly large size compared to Pseudos, *Baetis,* and midges, and because they drift for fair distances along slow edge waters, some fish will lean over a bit to procure them. On the whole, though, it's a sideline affair, not a blitz hatch. The numbers are sparse and the hatches sporadic. Have a few suitable fly patterns on hand when wandering beautiful autumn streams and rivers. Brown floating nymphs are also recommended for bulging or rising trout in quiet edge waters. Down-and-across presentations could be in order to show spooky flat-water trout the fly before the leader.

Mahogany dun spinner falls are sparse, too. The females have reddish brown bodies, clear wings, and three prominent tails. Male spinners are brownish with a very noticeable clear area in the middle of the abdomen. (This is seen in some male *Baetis* spinners, too.) A brown Parachute pattern could pass for both dun and spinner.

Mahogany Duns

MATCHING FLY PATTERN SIZE: #14–16

COLOR: NYMPH—BROWNS, SOME WITH TUSKS AND STRINGY TWO-PART GILLS, THREE TAILS

DUN—MEDIUM GRAY WINGS, BROWN TO REDDISH BROWN BODY, THREE TAILS

SPINNER—CLEAR WINGS THAT ARE WELL VEINED, REDDISH BROWN BODY (TRANSLUCENT WHITE MIDSECTION OF ABDOMEN IN MALES), THREE TAILS

Habitat: Small, medium, and large rivers, especially those with some swift water

Fall Olives (*Baetis* species)

The fall edition of the *Baetis* hatch is one of the year's best. Waters are dependably low and clear. Trout are still in a surface-rising groove after summer's insect extravaganza. Other hatches are fading fast, so trout look to these mayflies as the mainstay of their surface diet. If I had to rate my overall favorite hatch experience of the year, this would be it, at least on the Missouri River, where I spend most of my autumn days.

Tiny blue-winged olives, or Pseudos, give way to the larger *Baetis* around the beginning of October. The size shifts from the #20–24 of the Trico and Pseudo periods to the #18 or even #16 of the season's last mayfly hatch. *Baetis* hatch profusely in October and into November. I have read that in some spring creeks and rivers *Baetis* will sputter along during the rest of winter, too, when the weather allows. Where I fish, *Baetis* last throughout October and November and will trickle into December unless a harsh winter starts early. Midges add greatly to the surface load, with some caddis continuing as late as early November.

The angle of the sun is lower in autumn. *Baetis* will hatch to some degree on all autumn afternoons, generally between 1:00 and 5:00 P.M. The

Autumn's Baetis *mayfly hatch is one of the year's best. Steady-rising and often less-picky fish are found across the West.*

trout aren't so sun-shy as they were in spring, having risen to daylight hatches all summer. It's those overcast, humid, rainy, and snowy days that prompt the best hatches, though. Tremendous numbers of *Baetis* will pop. The cold weather and water means that these flies will float long distances on the water before even attempting to take off. It's easy pickings for the trout, with thousands of duns, cripples, and midges sailing downstream. Steady-rising fish are the end result, an afternoon's or evening's fishing that can hardly be topped. Even on sunny, breezy days, wind-free slicks along lee banks can show numerous trout noses. This fishing is too good to pass up!

    Baetis nymphs are very prominent and active come late summer and fall. Beadhead and standard Pheasant Tail Nymphs catch lots of fish. I'd start the morning either slinging streamers or fishing a couple Beadhead Pheasant Tails beneath a strike indicator (which could be a hopper or October Caddis dry-fly pattern). I'd keep a second rod rigged with a midge dry in the morning, changing it to a *Baetis* dry after lunch. Morning midge hatches can be excellent, especially on humid days.

This nice rainbow is steadily slurping in the season's last mayfly hatch. Baetis *will hatch into November in many places.*

Baetis duns are olive-bodied with medium gray wings and two flimsy curling tails. Their overall appearance on the water is a medium to dark gray. The spinners are tan to reddish brown with clear wings. Their habit of crawling down rocks or logs to lay eggs seems to take them out of the general fishing realm. *Baetis* spinner falls rarely live up to their promise, considering the number of duns, at least in my experience. Duns, crippled duns, and spinners can all be seen on the water at once, though, as spinner falls overlap with late-afternoon hatch activity.

The nice thing about this last and very important mayfly hatch is that the trout seem to get less selective as autumn wears on. I feel confident going out with only one or two dry-fly patterns, though the odd fish might require something more. Skilled down-and-across casting to flat-water fish can be more important than exacting patterns. Repetitive presentations can be the order of the day when the number of flies is high and the trout are gulping. Fish in ripple lines might take upstream presentations just fine.

This *Baetis* and midge scenario offers dry-fly sport much later than

The Parachute Adams remains my favorite fall Baetis *pattern, in #14–18. It's a premium year-round producer whenever trout are looking up.*

many anglers traditionally took notice of. Prime match-the-hatch adventures carry on until the end of November or until premature subzero cold fronts roll down out of Canada. In coastally influenced areas and in spring creeks such fishing can carry on throughout the winter, at least in spurts. There is no doubt that this last bit of seasonal mayfly action (actually about two months worth) is among the best of the entire year when it comes to ideal water conditions, profuse flies, and steady-rising fish. If the ice doesn't come too soon, the fishing will be great.

Baetis, Autumn Olives

MATCHING FLY PATTERN SIZE: #16–20

COLOR: NYMPH—OLIVE TO AMBER TO BROWN, THREE TAILS

DUN—MEDIUM GRAY WINGS (CAN LOOK DARKER ON WATER), OLIVE-GRAY BODY, TWO WISPY TAILS

SPINNER—CLEAR WINGS, TANNISH TO REDDISH BROWN BODY, TWO TAILS

Many *Baetis* spinners crawl under water to lay eggs and will do so on your waders should you be standing in a riffle when a spinner flight suddenly appears. The females pause before descending to carefully roll their wings over their backs. This captures a silvery bubble of air that is very noticeable underwater. I'm not sure what the purpose of this act is—whether it's to breathe from or to help buoy them back to the surface after laying their little patch of eggs. The bodies of some male *Baetis* have clear midabdomens, as is seen with male mahogany duns.

Habitat: Most rivers and streams. The best fishing is on slower, richer waters where the duns pile up and the trout can sip at leisure.

Baetis Fly Patterns

NYMPH:

    PHEASANT TAIL #16–20
    BEADHEAD PHEASANT TAIL #14–18
    OLIVE FLOATING NYMPH #16–20
    CDC OLIVE EMERGER #16–20

DUN:

    PARACHUTE ADAMS #16–20 (EVEN #14 IN BROKEN WATER)
    PARACHUTE BAETIS #16–20
    OLIVE THORAX #16–20
    OLIVE SPARKLE DUN #16–20
    H & L VARIANT #14–20 (MANY TROUT SEEM FOND OF THIS ATTRACTOR DRY
        DURING *BAETIS* HATCHES. IT ALSO MAKES A GOOD STRIKE INDICATOR FROM
        WHICH TO DANGLE A PHEASANT TAIL NYMPH.)

SPINNER:

    RUSTY OR TAN SPINNER #16–20
    PARACHUTE PHEASANT TAIL #16–20
    FLASHBACK PHEASANT TAIL NYMPH #16–20 (TO IMITATE A SUBMERGED FEMALE
SPINNER THAT'S GOTTEN WASHED OFF ITS PERCH)

AUTUMN CADDIS

The number of caddisfly species on the water after mid-September drops off quickly. Those that remain continue to be an important element in the day's fishing. Some, like the giant October caddis, are a dramatic addition to the fall fishing scene—big flies bringing up big fish, including steelhead. Although *Baetis* mayflies usually bring up the steadiest-rising fall fish, the following caddis shouldn't be overlooked. Trout in particular times and places could be focused on them when emergences are concentrated.

Spotted Sedge (*Hydropsyche cockerelli*)

This fly was discussed in depth in Chapters 2 and 3. The hatch's strong point is the brown-and-dirty-yellow-colored pupae. These take a long time to emerge at the surface, drifting there for considerable periods. Trout focus on this easy-to-capture stage. (See color plate no. 26.)

The adults and egglayers feature spotted brown wings and tan to dirty yellow abdomens. Trout take spent adults after egglaying is complete. Some drop eggs while bouncing on the surface. Others dive, paste the eggs to the bottom, then drift slowly back up. Egg-laying activity can be sporadic and continue through much of the day. This is the time to fish spotted sedge dry flies and diving patterns.

The emergers hatch in the evening, continuing into darkness. This is when a subsurface pupa is best. A fall day could feature midges early in the morning, good nymphing from then until early afternoon, some blind fishing with caddis drys or divers at the same time, *Baetis* hatches from 1:00 to 4:00 P.M. mixed with midges and caddis egglayers, and possible evening caddis emergences with midges and *Baetis* cripples mixed in. On smaller swift rivers, mahogany duns are likely to be seen in sparse numbers along quiet edge waters. Giant October caddis could be fluttering around and laying eggs from late morning into evening. The white fly could be encountered in impressive numbers in the right silt-bottomed lower-river habitat come dusk.

Spotted sedges can continue hatching as late as mid-November. In many rivers they might finish up by mid-October. Be on the lookout for trout riseforms like bulges and swirls that might separate a caddis pupa–feeding fish from one gulping *Baetis* duns and midges. (Refer to Chapter 3, page 160, for spotted sedge fly patterns.)

Green Sedge (*Rhyacophila coloradensis*)

This caddis was discussed in Chapter 3. The important fishing stages include the bright green #14–16 larvae. These wormlike forms are abundant, crawling freely across the bottom of swift riffles and runs. Bottom-bouncing a Green Caddis Worm is always a good searching technique in the fast-water areas these caddis are limited to. The naturals are most available to trout during dawn and dusk periods of behavioral drift but imitations can work all day when bounced before the noses of trout.

The adults emerge quickly from riffle areas, too, so quickly that trout generally focus on the fast-swimming pupae. Scattered hatching begins in the afternoon, sometimes showing trout that jump completely out of the water in pursuit of surface-bound emergers. Green sedge pupal patterns are good bets from noon on in quick, broken water. The adults lay eggs in riffles, too, from afternoon until dark. They are much more available to trout than when they first emerged. A dry-fly pattern with a pupa or diving caddis dropper is a good idea whether matching this swift-water hatch or fishing blind in choppy water. Green sedge hatches linger into mid- or late October on many rivers of the West. (See Chapter 3, page 158, for green sedge fly patterns.)

October Caddis, or Giant Orange Sedge (*Dicosmoecus* species)

There's a big caddisfly out there, a darn big one. At first glance you could be excused for not thinking it's a caddis at all. It just seems too big when fluttering through the air. But a caddisfly it is—autumn's giant orange sedge, otherwise known as the October caddis. (See color plate no. 27.)

These big caddisflies, a full #4–8, have patterned gray and reddish brown wings and a dirty orange body. They begin hatching in early September, peak in late September through mid-October, and finish up as late as mid-November on some California rivers. Population densities vary from river to river and stretch to stretch. Even in modest populations they're so big and attractive that big fish may focus on them. They're never as numerous as the smaller species, but they can be prevalent enough to add a fresh twist to the already interesting autumn fishing scene. Slamming takes might be experienced on scenic fall rivers all across the West.

Because most fall hatches are afternoon affairs (as is the October caddis itself), I'll usually start an autumn morning either streamer- or nymph-fishing. One successful tactic includes using an October caddis dry-fly pattern, such as a #6–8 Stimulator as a strike indicator with a #16 Beadhead Pheasant Tail fished as a dropper about twenty inches below. The 5X tippet to the nymph is tied off the bend of the Stimulator's hook. The Beadhead Pheasant Tail is a good imitation of the abundant *Baetis* nymphs that will hatch out later in the afternoon. Trout often inhale nymphs freely on a hatchless autumn morning. Some days just as many fish smash the dry fly as take the nymph, including some larger than average rainbows and browns. Should the fish really be on the October caddis dry, I cut off the nymph to reduce tangles and casting complications.

October caddis emerge and lay eggs in the afternoon and evening. It's not unusual to see some flying about in late morning, too. Their mental imprint on trout must be great, because trout in the know might hit these big dry-fly patterns at various times of day. Twitching and skidding them across the surface can solicit thrashing takes. Using one alone or with various dry, pupal, or nymph droppers is a great way to spend a fall day, especially on swift rivers, where *Baetis* and midges don't bring up as many steady-rising fish as they do on tailwaters, slow rivers, and spring creeks. On the latter water types, October caddis tend to be less numerous. Even here, though, there can be just enough to get some trout's attention. Fall fish can be more gung ho anyway and be used to eating some extralarge morsels, especially hoppers. Stimulators and such could be mistaken as either terrestrial or October caddis by the fish. It can be a win-win situation.

October caddis begin their larval lives in cases built from plant material and inhabit slow-water areas, including eddies. In later stages of larval growth they switch to pebble cases. Many move to swifter-running parts of the river, too. In between stages, come June and July, they are known to drift case-free in the currents. These yellow-orange-bodied black-headed larva are then quite easy to see because of their size and color. This happens midafternoons, too, not at dusk through dawn, as is

203

October caddis larvae switch from plant-material to pebble-built cases in the later stages of their larval lives. These cases are frequently seen by wading anglers across the West.

the case with most migrant nymphs. This can add to the big-nymph load in a river that is already churning out some giant stonefly nymphs.

Weeks before their emergence, October caddis larvae seal up their large pebble cases (which approach #4–6 in size) and pupate. These cases are easily seen on streambed boulders across the West. Trout will eat all stages of this big fly, case and all.

October caddis emerge from afternoon to evening, mostly from slower-water zones of the river. They're slow-swimming but active emergers that make big, easy-to-grab targets for trout. Many anglers have mentioned that orange seems to be a good fly color in the fall. It could in part be due to the presence of October caddis, whose large emerging pupa sport bulky brownish orange torsos. (See color plate no. 28.)

This is a hatch that's worth tracking down. The size of the October caddis and its availability to trout in low clear autumn waters offer big-fish opportunities on dry flies. Inland trout relish them, and coastal steel-

Even steelhead go for big October caddis. Dry-fly steelheading has experienced a lot of growth in the last couple of decades. Many steelhead fly patterns have been based on the October caddis.

head take swipes at them, too. Dry-fly steelheading, a growing sport, is best right in the middle of October caddis hatches. These have inspired many fly patterns used for resident and anadromous trout.

October Caddis, Giant Orange Sedge

MATCHING FLY PATTERN SIZE: #6–8

COLOR: LARVA—CASED, MEDIUM-TONED BLACK HEAD AND LEGS, VERY LARGE

PUPA—BROWNISH WING AND THORAX, YELLOWISH ORANGE ABDOMEN

ADULT—PATTERNED REDDISH BROWN AND GRAY WINGS, DIRTY ORANGE BODY

Habitat: A variety of Northwest river types, swift to medium currents

---

MIDGES AND OTHER AUTUMN TROUT FOODS

As hatches fizzle in autumn, midges regain a prominent position in the trout's larder. Between hatches of larger *Baetis*, mahogany duns, and caddisflies, midges can become the focal point of surface and subsurface feeding. Very large food items, including crayfish, sculpins, and bait fish swim at their own risk, for big fish are looking all the harder for a good meal. There are few medium to large nymphs now, especially when compared to the subsurface bounty of late spring and early summer.

In the medium-size range it's sowbugs and even snails that keep trout occupied. Crustaceans tolerate cold water quite well, remaining active through the winter. A sowbug pattern would never go amiss. Egg

Sowbugs become important trout food as aquatic insect hatches wane in late fall and winter.

patterns and pink scuds (which the trout may be taking for eggs) work especially well, too. There are brown trout and, later, whitefish eggs that fish might feed on. Perhaps it's the lack of varied food forms that keeps late fall and winter trout interested in egg fly patterns.

When it comes to midges, a more uniform gray-black color is seen as autumn wanes. Just a few patterns and sizes suffice in most cases to fool midging trout. It may take repetitive casts and a fly change or two, but once you find the trout's meal ticket, it will probably work on a high percentage of fish. Down-and-across casts might be needed to fool flat-water fish. A twitch or skid of the fly can draw a take as well. Midges hover, buzz, and skid across the surface, often holding a general position over the water as the currents slide by. A supply of #18–22 Griffith's Gnats and midge pupa patterns should take plenty of visible trout. It doesn't hurt to keep a few smaller patterns—down to #26—for ultra-picky fish. Tiny Brassies make excellent droppers with, say, a #16 Parachute Adams for blind-fishing known trout habitat. Slower rivers, tailwaters, and spring creeks will have the most consistent midge and

Baetis activity and steady-rising fish, continuing even into December. Midges will hatch all winter, and when it's humid will come out in force. *Baetis* mayflies reportedly hatch all winter, too, in some spring creeks (with waters maintaining a steady temperature) when the weather moderates.

Another autumn trend is the more regular rising appearances of the mighty whitefish. Whitefish rise more often from late fall through winter and into spring than they do in the summer. At least that's my experience—you will see varying fish behavior from river to river. Whitefish do rise to some summer hatches, but on the whole I think they have so much bottom food with the various summer hatches of mayflies and caddis that they have less need to come to the top. Their downturned mouths lead one to believe that the bottom would be their focus as long as food supplies there are ample. Come late fall through winter, though, the active nymph load is way down. Nymphs are immature and much smaller, too, and tend to stay well hidden. It's probably a necessity for whitefish to rise to midges in winter because other food choices are so poor.

Calm, overcast, and humid mornings portend good midge hatches and probable rising trout in autumn before afternoon *Baetis* hatches kick in. Trout still used to summer rising behavior take midges freely. They have to eat a lot of them to fill up. This means they'll rise continuously, sometimes for hours. To the angler this means excellent and extended match-the-hatch fishing opportunities over steady-rising trout.

On swift rivers midges can be of lesser importance. An October caddis makes a great strike indicator. Beadhead and regular Pheasant Tail, Hare's Ear, and Prince Nymphs are productive droppers. Even here, though, midges and *Baetis* can bring up steady-rising fish in quiet pools, tailouts, and eddies. Always be on the lookout for risers in these spots, should you be fishing the water blind.

As the fall world fades into a cold and brittle winter, mountain anglers let out a collective sigh, knowing the best of the dry-fly year is slipping away. Short daylight hours, Arctic cold fronts, and bone-chilling winds keep many fly fishers indoors. The prospect of visible rising trout diminishes more after every severe cold spell. Sure, the nymphs, egg patterns, and streamers keep producing, but the river world is a little more sullen without the spreading wakes of rising trout. When ice constantly

Fall means good fishing almost everywhere. Some big browns, like this one, come to net then.

forms in the rod's guides and it's so cold that I don't really want to get my hands wet is about the time I back off fishing for the year, more so now than when I was younger. The year's memories are often better than the fishing prospects at hand. It will soon be the official start of cabin fever season in the north. Warm days riding gusty chinook winds get many an angler out of the house. There's no telling how far and to what extremes some will go in fulfilling their need to fish!

Autumn Hatch Chart–Mid-September through November

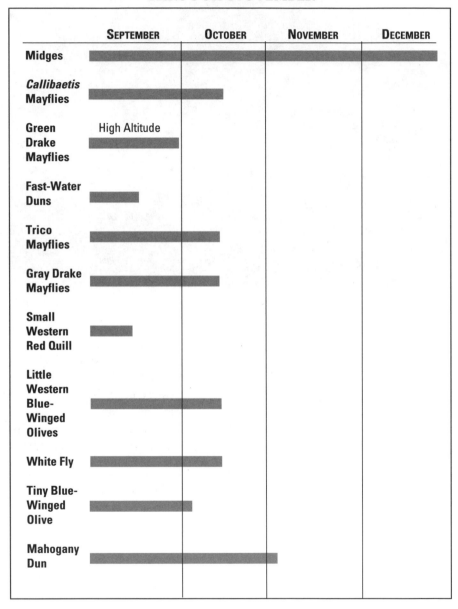

	SEPTEMBER	OCTOBER	NOVEMBER	DECEMBER
Midges				
***Callibaetis* Mayflies**				
Green Drake Mayflies	High Altitude			
Fast-Water Duns				
Trico Mayflies				
Gray Drake Mayflies				
Small Western Red Quill				
Little Western Blue-Winged Olives				
White Fly				
Tiny Blue-Winged Olive				
Mahogany Dun				

Autumn Hatch Chart–Mid-September through November (cont'd)

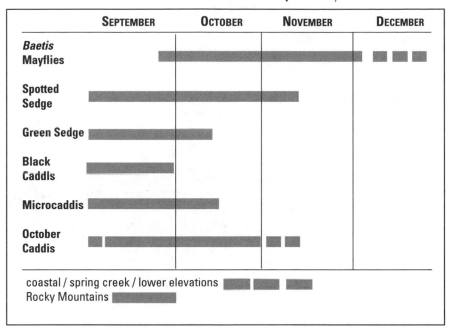

	SEPTEMBER	OCTOBER	NOVEMBER	DECEMBER
Baetis Mayflies				
Spotted Sedge				
Green Sedge				
Black Caddis				
Microcaddis				
October Caddis				

coastal / spring creek / lower elevations
Rocky Mountains

5

WINTER'S CHILL
December through February

FEW ANGLERS look forward to winter as a fishing season unless they're heading to exotic destinations around the globe. I was fortunate enough to spend a number of winters in New Zealand, where one can experience a second spring and summer, linger among spectacular landscapes, and witness a new realm of insect hatches and large rising trout. By comparison, Montana gets pretty bleak come winter. The terrain here is white and dull brown. If it's not too cold, the chinook winds are usually ripping. Some rivers are frozen over. But despite all that, the fishing season remains open and opportunities are still at hand.

The winter temperatures in Montana and other Rocky Mountain states are not as cold on average as many people believe them to be. We have many winter days in the upper thirties, forties, and even fifties. "Extreme" is the word for weather here. It can dip to minus 30 degrees one week only to shift 70 degrees and become 40 degrees overnight. Hardcore anglers have plenty of winter opportunities to get on-stream and catch fish. I know anglers who fish every day they can in winter, mostly with nymphs and pink scuds. They catch fish on a daily basis, including a few in the 20–25-inch range. Whitefish are often part of the by-catch.

Some locals keep these for smoking and eating. Midges can hatch profusely. Rising fish are to be found here and there, though a little selective casting may be in order to separate the whitefish from the trout. Some rivers offer better (or any) hopes of rising fish than others, too. Tailwaters and spring creeks, with their more consistent temperatures, are likely to show some trout noses and swirls across steel gray winter glides.

One advantage of winter fishing is the relative solitude. Whereas past generations had fishing solitude all season, today sees throngs of tourist anglers descend on local rivers just as they come right. Quite a few once-serious resident anglers have given up in disgust, for with crowds comes a lack of courtesy previously unknown, and this is from a group who view themselves as the elite of the fishing world. The fishing experience declines, too. Fishing is certainly a sport where "the less the better" makes for peace of mind and improved catch rates. I know many locals who concentrate on the rivers from late fall through spring, leaving summer waters to those with more competitive instincts. These off-season fishermen catch the biggest fish as a rule, because big trout are more approachable in this time period.

Some spring creeks and tailwaters offer very dependable winter fishing, and the San Juan and Bighorn come immediately to mind. Midging trout might be stalked. Systematic nymphing is usually productive. Ice-free sections of freestone rivers give up winter fish too, though one doesn't expect as high a catch rate as on a banner summer day. The trout's metabolism is down and so are overall results. Each trout may now be a prize, something to be admired as a tough survivor in a harsh winter world. Some winter fisheries do give fairly good catch rates, at least on some days. The best way to find out is to dress warm and get out to fish.

There is a special beauty to a winter river on a calm, warm day. You might be surprised by the activity of the midges, those harmless little flies that seem to know no bounds. A few winter stoneflies might be seen. There is even a caddis species that can make a winter appearance. On the whole, though, the rhythm of systematic nymphing or the slow stripping of streamers sets a working pattern. Your eyes have time to roam over edge-ice designs, mountain terrain, and snow-burdened vegetation. Hardy winter songbirds that look so delicate make you wonder how you would survive in the wild. The rings and tails of surfacing whitefish might inspire you to hunt down a rising trout. It always seems more gratifying to have gone out and tried than to sit home and brood, even if you do come

Midge larvae and pupae are important parts of a winter trout's diet, in many cases dominating it. This brown took a quill-stem midge larva fished near the bottom of a thigh-deep run.

back half frozen. This is really a good time for barbless hooks so that you can do a hemostat release without getting your hands wet and cold!

If nothing else, the winter fishing experience helps you appreciate the abundant aquatic life and active trout of summer. The river is a world of such contrasts that a single run hardly seems like the same place in winter and summer. There are no swallows now, or bats, or nighthawks, no warm evenings and softening greenery. There are no lumbering stoneflies, dancing mayfly spinners, or whirling caddis. No trout are heaving water and splashing in every direction. Sunlight doesn't illuminate the cobbled streambed and summer-green weed beds in the same satisfying way.

Winter fishing is a biding of time with its own cyclic challenges. It sometimes becomes a ritual, a paying of dues, and a maturing of knowledge wherein the balance of nature becomes clearer, like cold winter water.

EFFECTS OF WINTER WEATHER

Little needs to be said about winter weather, at least to those who live in the Rocky Mountain West. Extremes, fluctuation, wind: That's all you need to know. The visitor, however, can be surprised by the mildness of some of our winter periods. We have warming chinook winds blow in from the Pacific, whip over the Rockies, gain in temperature, then pour warming blasts of air across the western edge of the prairie. From Calgary to Great Falls to Denver, chinook winds can ease winter's grasp. It's common with chinooks to have wind forecasts of 40–70 miles per hour. When that wind lets off, and between fronts, is the time to be on the water.

There are mountain areas of the Rockies that fall between the rain-soaked anadromous-fish zones of the West Coast and the wind-battered east slope of the Rockies. River valleys exist where winds are less fierce and temperatures can be mild. For instance, the area from western Montana to eastern Washington and Oregon (including Idaho) has numerous trout rivers that might offer good winter sport. Colorado, Utah, New Mexico, and California have some open water, too. There are even drainages where spring steelhead can be fished for in clear water. The outbound or incoming angler can usually find something to do unless one of those Arctic-express subzero fronts encompasses all.

WINTER RIVER CONDITIONS

Rivers behave in various ways in winter. They might run low, clear, and ice-free at times. Severe winter weather can freeze some rivers. Snow can pile up in massive western drainages one year that will be relatively dry in the next. A warm spell quickly melts lower-altitude snow, causing ice jams, high water, and even serious winter floods. This could easily be followed by another period of open, low, and clear water.

Rivers on the Pacific side of the Rockies see deluges of winter rain. Although added water helps bring in winter and spring runs of steelhead, it's common to have too much of a good thing from northern California on up to the British Columbia coast.

Naturally, it's the tailwaters, smaller drainages, and spring creeks that offer the most consistent fishing conditions. Most tailwater rivers remain ice-free, at least for a number of miles. Spring creeks are ice-free, too, except in the most extreme winter conditions. Smaller drainages are less likely to rise and muddy up during the frequent warm spells that can visit the Rockies, and they clear out more quickly. There is usually clear, ice-free, and fishable water to be found somewhere.

Between above-average warm spells that melt snow and muddy rivers, there are usually long periods when winter freestone rivers flow dependably low and clear. Dam-controlled tailwater rivers usually flow low and clear, too, and stay ice-free for a number of miles. There are some winters when dam releases run higher. This is usually due to high precipitation in the previous year and current heavy snowpack. Room has to be made in impoundments for snowmelt and probable flooding in upstream tributaries. This winter on the Missouri, for instance, the river volume has been flowing at about 8,000 cubic feet per second, twice the normal volume. Western rivers, like others, are governed by natural phenomena, not the whims of human beings.

Although much of the winter sees low, clear, and steady flows, above-average heat triggers high water, ice jams, and floods. Ripping ice jams tear away at banks, trees, and the homes of those who for some reason choose to build in river bottoms. Fish often get dispersed across fields as ice dams up rivers and spreads water before breaking, flooding, and leaving trout stranded. Riverbeds are changed, bridges and cabins relocated, and aquatic life gets battered. The power of a serious ice jam is an awesome thing.

West of the Continental Divide, in the steelhead and salmon coastal realm, high water is the winter norm. Nonflood periods are eagerly awaited by those with big-fish fever. Winter steelheaders hit those rivers hard whenever conditions come right for however brief a time. The combination of overpopulation, overdevelopment, overlogging, and over-damming is making some of those fisheries a thing of the past anyway, at least when it comes to prolific steelhead and salmon runs at historic levels. Some rivers are becoming home to excellent walleye and smallmouth fisheries, which may be the trend of the future.

The Trout, the River, and Feeding Behavior

Now that the big chill is on, trout metabolism slows down. It processes food more slowly, which means trout spend less time and effort feeding. Freestone trout often drop back into deeper and slower pools and runs, and to where spring seepages enter the river. Springs provide warmer water when the main river's temperature can approach 33 degrees. Anchor ice (ice that forms from the bottom of the river up in running water), ice flows, ice jams, and floods can scour shallow positions in a winter river, making these areas potentially dangerous for trout to stay in. This is not to say that all fish will leave shallow to medium-depth riffle dropoffs. Some will want to hold on to productive feeding areas that were their summer and fall homes. Riffles still produce many nymphs, though most are small and immature. A few overwinter a bit closer to their spring hatching size. Sowbugs or cressbugs, snails, and scuds remain active in cold water, too. These are found in a variety of winter water, from eddies to slow glides and pools to riffles.

Tailwater and spring creek trout hold on to summer and fall feeding positions longer. The temperatures in these water types are more constant. Tailwaters drop into the thirties, but at a slower, steadier rate than most freestoners. They can provide some dependable winter action.

Some trout hang in the shallows through much of winter, rising to midges and nymphing as they did in fall. Extreme cold fronts may chase them a bit deeper, especially if repeated fronts maintain a relentless freezing grip. Rather than staying in the shallowest of edge waters, fish are likely to move out a bit to the edges of the main current and just to the slow sides of it. On big rivers, such subtle dropoff zones can be close, or way out from the shore. Eddy lines that peel off points or inside bends can house many fish. Big eddies, some as large as ponds, can show a few sipping trout and whitefish capitalizing on midges. These and inside-bend flats are among the most likely places to stalk rising winter fish. Midging trout will favor zones where they don't have to fight much or any current.

Elsewhere, nymphing will be the best bet. Small to medium-size naturals are what winter trout are eating most. Similar-sized nymphs, sowbugs, and egg patterns should be bounced along the bottom and into trout's faces. The #14–20 patterns are most consistent, with some smaller patterns being necessary to fool midging trout. They are less inclined to chase down large food items in frigid winter water.

Streamers and crayfish patterns can still work but should be retrieved more slowly or even dead-drifted. A sinking-tip line can be used, though I often fish a floating line with lots of added weight on the leader. I might start off fishing weighted streamers with a medium retrieve. If no

Tailwater trout can often be found rising routinely in winter. Midges are likely to be the only surface food then.

takes are forthcoming, I slow the retrieve down. You might even want to add a strike indicator and dead-drift streamers along the bottom with the occasional mend and twitch. Takes on these can be more subtle than usual with streamers, so be alert and quick to strike. In the cold heart of winter, afternoons can give the best fishing as the day reaches maximum warmth.

One strange fish habit seen at this time of year, at least where I fish, is the ingestion by some trout of river weeds. It's common to find trout stomachs either packed with green water weeds and a few insects and crustaceans or to be in various stages of emptiness, where just a scattering of food is found. Typical winter stomach samples here include sowbugs, midge larvae, snails, tiny aquatic worms, and crayfish. Any rising trout will naturally eat midge pupae and adults, and possibly winter stoneflies. On the whole, most food items eaten are on the small side, in the #16–24 size range. This could differ a bit in other rivers and areas of the country, especially in warmer climates and on spring creeks with varied habitat.

Spring creeks can be a little different. They maintain a steady temperature, usually around the mid-forties to fifties. On some, *Baetis* mayfly hatches might come off every winter month. Mature *Baetis* nymphs and larger free-roaming caddis larvae can figure more into a spring-creek trout's diet. Midges, sowbugs, and the like will still be important, too. Trout feed with more regularity in spring creeks because their metabolism isn't as depressed as it is on rivers running in the 33–35-degree range.

Not only fish inhabit such spring creeks. Waterfowl by the hundreds can pack into them when all other waters are frozen. Those with access to private spring creeks, of which there are many scattered across western landscapes, can find some exceptional winter wing shooting. It's not a bad idea to take a rod along, too, wetting a line in the midafternoon period. Nymphs, sowbugs, egg patterns, streamers, and midge drys could all produce some action. It may even be possible to do some sight-fishing, though the low angle of the winter sun makes seeing deep trout more difficult.

Where spring creeks run into larger colder rivers is always a potential hot spot. River fish will gravitate to these spots, which are often good-sized eddies. A large fish might dominate this position, and if one leaves or is removed, another one will soon take its place. Steam or fog over the creek, open water, and weed beds are good signs that this is a spring creek. A flock of ducks might take off, too. This could deserve an exploratory side trip, as long as one is not trespassing.

On many freestone rivers in my area, big trout are often caught whenever rivers become ice-free. This may be at intervals during the winter but is especially true in March and April, when winter relinquishes its brutal grip. Many a big brown is caught just after ice-out, mostly on large streamers, crayfish, and nymphs. The fish are hungry and hit at midday. It seems to be a better trophy scenario than does fall fishing, though many specimens can be a little snakier, having lost weight and condition during winter. Big fish are caught during winter, too, by those who stoically cover the long slow pools in a mechanical and systematic fashion.

WINTER HATCHES AND FLY PATTERNS

When it comes to hatches, winter is the model of simplicity. Midges, midges, and more midges, that's the general rule. Little winter

Large browns are often caught when rivers become ice-free. Their postspawning winter lives make them eager to grab an occasional big bite to eat.

stoneflies add to the scene, and there's even a winter-hatching caddisfly. We'll explore these possibilities in a moment.

As December begins, you might find some lingering afternoon *Baetis* mayfly hatches mixed with midges. Tailwaters (either dam releases or natural lake outflows), spring creeks, and southern or coastal drainages will be best bets for this. If you really like to fish with dry flies, you may want to take the occasional road trip to rivers where rising trout are routinely encountered.

In Montana, *Baetis* will carry into early December on larger warmer rivers and spring creeks if winter doesn't pay a serious visit too soon. Many years witness a mild November and early December, with daytime temperatures in the midforties. Winter generally goes into high gear around Christmas. By then the *Baetis* will have completely fizzled, but fish in rivers like the Kootenai, Bighorn, Clark Fork, and Missouri can still be found sipping midges. Trout can be found midging the rest of winter, too, but in fewer overall numbers in most cases.

Slow-water areas are the best bet. Walk or float and look for risers, or fish blind with nymphs keeping one eye open for spreading rings. Eddies and flats deserve a second look. Take your time with whatever rising fish are found, if for no other reason than to savor the limited sport. Long light tippets and small patterns are a must. A twelve-foot 6X leader with a #18–22 Griffith's Gnat is a good starting point. I'll often hang a midge pupa twelve inches below the Gnat for added fish incentive. Trout can see and will move over just a bit farther for the pupa than for the dry.

Trout have to eat a lot of midges to get full. Some days the fish don't spook much, either, giving long periods of sport. With the right gear, they can be easy to catch. The necessity to capitalize on the food at hand is upon them. A reasonable pattern and delicate cast can be all that's needed for success. Other fish can be pickier or may even have learned to avoid anything attached to a leader. There's only one way to find out, though, and that is to be there. Let's take a closer look at winter's few emerging insects.

Midges

Midges are so plentiful and important to trout that they deserve another close look. They hatch just about every day of the year, providing a key food element to trout between and during hatches of other aquatic insects. From November through April midges can be the trout's food

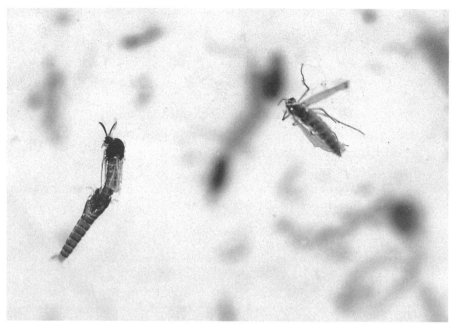

Emerging midge pupae are often the focus of winter trout. Fish taking them just beneath the surface can appear to anglers like rising fish.

mainstay, especially in tailwaters and spring creeks where trout might rise much of the winter.

Midges begin their gregarious lives as wormlike larvae. These can be counted in the millions. Groups of them are seen attached to streambed rocks year-round. Trout may pick them off the cobble when food is limited, also nabbing sowbugs, snails, and the like. Most of these little midge larvae are black to shades of olive and brown in color and #18–24 in size. Simple larva imitations can be fished alone, deep and in front of where trout are known or thought to be, with added weight and a strike indicator. Midge larvae may be even more productive when fished as droppers ten to eighteen inches below a San Juan Worm, Pink Scud, or Beadhead Sowbug. The bigger fly can draw a trout's attention from a little farther away, but it's often the midge larva that's eaten.

Midges seal themselves up in little spun tunnel homes to pupate. Upon emerging, the pupae drift and wiggle to the surface to hatch. Ascending midge pupae are easy targets for trout due to their numbers and

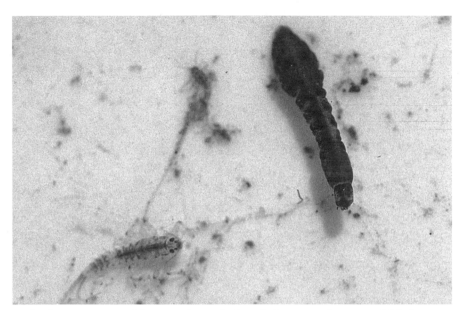

Midge larvae are wormlike, usually in shades of olive, gray, brown, and black. Trout will eat them along with sowbugs and even snails when hatch activity is nil.

defenseless upward drift. They're numerous in the same water types trout choose to hold in, calm zones to the sides of main currents. Trout can fin at leisure, tilting this way and that, to intercept midge pupae through much of the day. They're obviously a godsend to the fish, and because midges don't bite, they're not much of a distraction to flinching humans, either. Midge pupal patterns are almost as simple as larval ones. I usually fish pupa patterns as droppers off a small Parachute Adams or Griffith's Gnat, using the dry fly as a strike indicator. The dry fly is often eaten as well.

Midges escape their pupal shucks at the surface. Traditional illustrations always show them hanging vertically from the surface while emerging. Closer observation has shown me that the difference in current speed between the surface film and the more quickly moving water just below it shoves the emerging pupae up in a horizontal position. A small point, but one with applications to fly tying and fishing over pickier trout.

Some midges get out of their shucks quick and clean. Others have a bit of a struggle, buzzing and dragging their shucks around for a while. This makes them look twice as big as either the adults or pupae by themselves. The struggling motion and added size can get trout to single them out. Fly

CHAPTER FIVE

patterns like the Palomino Midge and even a traditional Adams can imitate a stuck-in-the-shuck struggling midge. (See color plate no. 29.)

Once safely out of the shuck, midges can ride the surface for some distance. Others hover and skate on the surface, zigzagging over the water as the river slides on downstream beneath them. Dead-drifted, twitched, and skidded presentations can all take fish. A subtle twitch just as your fly approaches a steady-rising fish can draw its attention. Griffith's Gnats and traditional Black Gnats and Adamses are midge dry-fly standards. It can be the size that matters most.

Mating midges often cluster into little balls that seem to roll down the river's surface. I've seen some clusters that were actually as big as meatballs. And that's just what midge clusters can be to trout on a surface that's otherwise devoid of crunchy insect life. Anglers get away with using larger Griffith's Gnats on such occasions. Even tiny Royal Wulffs and H & L Variants can work when fished in the #16–20 size range. If you are out on the river in winter, have a fair midge selection along and look for lips, as opposed to the tails of whitefish. Steadily fish smaller nymphs or slow streamers until you see fish. Some luck is sure to come your way.

Griffith's Gnats have become the standard midge dry pattern across the country. This one has a little Z-lon wing for better visibility.

Winter Midges

MATCHING FLY PATTERN SIZE: #18–26, EVEN #16 FOR MIDGE CLUSTERS
COLORS: LARVA AND PUPA—BLACK, OLIVES, BROWNS, REDDISH BROWNS
ADULTS—MOSTLY BLACKS AND GRAYS, WITH SOME OF THE ABOVE HUES

Habitat: All rivers and lakes. Most important to anglers on slower waters where trout can dine at leisure, without burning much energy.

Midge Fly Patterns

LARVA:
MIDGE LARVA #16–22, BLACK, OLIVE, BROWN, TAN, RED
BRASSIE #16–22, COPPER AND GREEN
BEADHEAD MIDGE WORM #16–20, VARIOUS COLORS AS ABOVE

PUPA:
BRASSIE #16–22
CHIRONOMID PUPA #16–24
DISCO MIDGE #18–24
BEADHEAD SERENDIPITY #16–20, VARIOUS COLORS AS ABOVE

EMERGING PUPA:
PALOMINO MIDGE #16–22, VARIOUS COLORS
SERENDIPITY #16–22, VARIOUS COLORS
PARACHUTE MIDGE #16–22
FOAM HEAD FLOATING MIDGE PUPA #16–22
SPARKLE DUN #18–24, VARIOUS COLORS

MIDGE ADULTS:
GRIFFITH'S GNAT #16–24
PARACHUTE MIDGE #16–24
BLACK GNAT #18–24

MIDGE ADULTS (CONTINUED):
    ADAMS #18–24
    ROYAL WULFF #18–22
    ELKHAIR CADDIS #18–22
    CDC MIDGE #16–24

Having midge dry flies that show up well against a variety of backlighting helps you in seeing your fly and in striking on time. For instance, black midges and dry flies show up better on sky-reflecting gray water. Light-hued flies and white-wing parachutes are more visible where dark bank reflections are found. Seeing is an important part of this small-fly game.

The size of the fly can be critical. Fish may take a wide variety of patterns, from #20 Royal Wulffs to Parachute Adamses (you can cut the tail off to reduce apparent size) to more exacting midge emergers, *if* they're small enough.

Sowbugs, Snails, and Scuds

Trout love crustaceans. These remain active and available to trout, making up for the lack of medium to large aquatic insect nymphs over the winter. In my experience, sowbugs are most commonly taken by river trout. Snails come in second. Scuds are a distant third, at least where I fish. Scuds in lakes and spring-fed ponds are another matter. They are exceedingly numerous in those water types. Trout there grow fat, sucking them in like vacuum cleaners. I know of many anglers who've drifted away from rivers and their crowded scenes to focus on lakes with their much bigger average fish.

On rich rivers, it's sowbugs that are most available. These are seen to the sides of heavier currents and in eddies, the same places trout fin. Winter and spring stomach samples reveal many a sowbug, along with midge pupae, snails, tubifex worms, the odd *Baetis* nymph, caddisfly larvae, and scuds. Crayfish, sculpins, leeches, and bait fish are occasionally seen, too, when winter trout summon the energy to tackle bigger meals. Of these, crayfish are usually the most numerous. Pink scud patterns, San Juan Worms, egg flies, and Beadheads produce well in winter, too, and can act as attractor nymphs. Fishing a realistic sowbug or midge larva dropper off one of these more colorful fancies is a good way to go. Additional

Scuds are most plentiful and available to trout in spring-fed lakes, where trout grow fat inhaling them at leisure.

weight might be needed on the leader, with a strike indicator or two above. It's not the prettiest rig to cast, especially in the wind. If results are your goal, though, such winter nymph regalia is likely to be the most consistent producer. Keep an eye open for rising fish in flats and eddies, even while you're hypnotized by the downriver glide of that little orange ball!

General Winter Nymph and Wet-Fly Patterns

SOWBUGS #12–18, GRAYS, TANS, OLIVES
SCUDS #12–18, ABOVE COLORS PLUS PINKS AND ORANGES
SAN JUAN WORMS #6–12, REDS, ORANGES, PURPLES, BROWNS
PHEASANT TAIL NYMPHS #14–20
GREEN CADDIS WORMS #12–18
CASED CADDIS #8–16
BRASSIES #16–22
CRAYFISH #4–10, GREENISH BROWNS, REDDISH BROWNS, WITH HUES OF
    BLUE AND TAN
WOOLLY BUGGERS #4–12, BLACK, BROWN, OLIVE, EGG AND FLASHABOU MODELS
(MOST CAN BE FISHED AS BEADHEAD VERSIONS)

Just about any small to medium nymph might work if it's fished deep and systematically—right in the trout's faces. Smaller Beadheads are an obvious choice. Pink Scuds have become winter standards. The occasional big trout will grab crayfish and Buggers, too. Stomach samples show more crayfish than bait fish, or maybe the claws just don't digest as fast! Fish the bottom slowly, but watch for risers. That's the rule of thumb to go by in the winter.

Little Winter Stoneflies (*Capnia* and *Nemoura* species)

These little black and dark brown stoneflies can hatch all winter. The *Capnia* species, also known as winter stones or little black stoneflies, might hatch anytime over the winter when days are warm. The *Nemoura* species, or little brown stoneflies, are more common from February into early summer. Both like small to medium-sized swift rivers but live in larger medium-paced ones as well. For instance, Montana rivers as divergent as the Boulder, Bitterroot, and Missouri have *Nemoura* populations, but in varying densities. The smaller swift rivers are where populations are highest and where they're most likely to play a role in actual fishing results. Here, midge fishing is less consistent; winter and spring stonefly action can actually be more important. On the wide Missouri winter

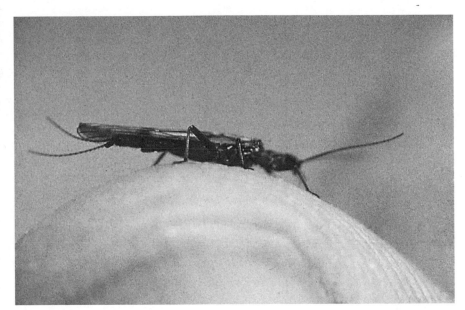

Little winter stoneflies are likely to be seen along ice-free freestone rivers. They can be just numerous enough on warm days to coax a few trout to the surface.

stoneflies are present, but this large mellow flow breeds tons more midges. It's these that get the trout's attention here. Every river flows to its own inner rhythm.

Warm afternoons are the times to find winter stonefly activity. This is nothing like a salmon fly or golden stone blitz, though. Winter stones are a meager #16–18 in size. Hatches and egg-laying flights are semiconcentrated or sporadic. As spring approaches, the little brown stoneflies will get up to the #14–18 size range. Their populations will be modest, too. But when a sunbeam is gracious enough to warm winter earth, they might suddenly be seen flying this way and that, dipping to the water to lay eggs then scuttling in sundry directions. Should a cloud obliterate the sun, all activity might cease. Pick the most pleasant of winter days to look up such hatch scenarios.

One river where this type of fishing has become popular is Montana's Bitterroot. It flows on the mild-weather side of the Continental Divide. Reasonable to good dry-fly experiences are had there, even though trout populations are lower than on many of the more famous rivers east of the Divide. Other medium-size rivers have this type of fishing, too. They tend to fit into the clean, cold, and well-oxygenated-water pattern these little stoneflies require. One just needs to get out and explore the possibilities on a sunny winter afternoon (or a warm and hazy one).

These little stoneflies crawl out of the water to emerge, as do their larger brethren. This occurs sporadically throughout the day. Egg-laying flights are sporadic daytime affairs, too. Neither activity is as synchronized as with the larger summer-hatching species. Winter hatches sputter along for a much longer but less concentrated duration.

The whole game plays to a lazy presence on stream on the nicest of winter days. You can get up late, eat your last pancake, and guzzle one more cup of that earthy brown stimulant. You then check your layering and do the neoprene shuffle up the river at leisure. The sun will feel good as it basks you and the cold cobble. The bugs will like it, too. It's a good idea to prerig a nymph setup in the warmth of your home, but be alert to little stonefly egg-laying flights and the odd rising fish. Don't expect miracles, or to see pods of slurping trout. Any riser or good action is to be savored. There are days, however, when a sufficient level of sport and a dreamlike winter setting make an afternoon along a little freestone river memorable.

Little Winter Stoneflies

MATCHING FLY PATTERN SIZE: #14–18
COLOR: BLACK AND DARK BROWN IN BOTH NYMPHS AND ADULTS

Habitat: Small to large freestone rivers, medium to swift flows

Little Winter Stonefly Patterns

NYMPH:

    MONTANA NYMPH #14–16, BLACK OR DARK BROWN
    BLACK BEADHEAD HARE'S EAR #14–18, BLACK BEAD AND DUBBING
    BEADHEAD PRINCE NYMPH #14–18

Winter Caddis, Snow Sedge
(*Psychoglypha subborealis* and *P. alascensis*)

This entry may be more a matter of interest than a fishable hatch. These two species of large, #6–8, caddis do hatch in winter, though, from a variety of rivers and streams. They could be a sporadic addition to winter midge and stonefly fishing on warmer afternoons.

The cased larvae favor slower-water areas, as do winter trout. Pupae emerge on warm afternoons. The larvae's size helps catch the trout's eye in low clear water—if they're not too suspicious of eating such a big item. Like many large caddis, these species can run across the river to the banks rather than make an airborne getaway.

The color of the adult's wing is reddish brown, and there is a silverish stripe running the length of the center of the wing. The body is brown. The larval stage is cased, on a big scale. A variety of pebbles and plant material are used in constructing the case.

It's probably clear by now that cased caddis in various sizes make good year-round searching patterns. Try blind-fishing a #8 brown caddis pupa on a warm winter afternoon. Start it dead-drifting deep, then let it slowly swing into the shallows. This might turn a few fish while allowing you to look for risers or to gaze at winter land- and waterscapes.

Because there are so few aquatic insect possibilities in winter, it's easy enough to keep your mind and eyes open to those that might exist. The winter caddis and snow sedge could provide a chance encounter for the watchful.

Winter Caddis, Snow Sedge

MATCHING FLY PATTERN SIZE: #6–8

COLOR: LARVA—MEDIUM BROWN CASE, BLACK HEAD

PUPA—BROWN

ADULT—PATTERNED REDDISH BROWN WINGS WITH LATERAL SILVERISH STRIPE, BROWN BODY

Habitat: A variety of river and stream types

Winter Caddis, Snow Sedge Fly Patterns

LARVA:

CASED CADDIS #6–8

BLACK BEADHEAD HARE'S EAR #6–10 (NATURAL HARE'S EAR DUBBING; CUT OFF TAIL FOR MORE REALISTIC LOOK)

PUPA:

BROWN SPARKLE PUPA #6–10 (FISH DEEP AND SUBSURFACE)

PARTRIDGE AND BROWN SOFT HACKLE #8–10

ADULT:

BROWN STIMULATOR #6–10

BUCKTAIL CADDIS #6–10

BROWN ELKHAIR CADDIS #6–10 (USING A LITTLE TWITCH OR SKID ACTION WON'T HURT. THESE FLIES WOULD ALSO MAKE GOOD STRIKE INDICATORS WITH A CADDIS PUPA OR WINTER STONEFLY NYMPH AS A DROPPER, AND EVEN A MIDGE LARVA DROPPER BELOW THAT!)

And so the winter passes. Fly fishers ply the water between killer cold fronts. Daytime temperatures vary from 35 degrees below to 45 above, and warm periods are usually ushered in by chinook winds. Plenty of nymphing, "scudding," and streamer fishing goes on. Encounters with rising fish might be happenstance except on a few rivers like the Bighorn, where trout are steadier risers.

As late winter melts into early spring, renewed fishing possibilities energize many an angler.

Winter will break soon, though. Then there'll be a lot of making up to do. Rivers and hatches are waiting to be explored before runoff (which could come fast and hard). I've got new rods and flies to try. My drift boat needs some fixing, but it still floats. I feel obligated to put in some "research and development" time on-stream before the guide season gets in full swing! If only I had a mammoth RV with a satellite dish—I'd never come home!

Now we have come full circle. Another full year's fishing begins scrolling through the imagination: the *Baetis* and little stoneflies of spring, the march browns and early grannoms, greenery, high water, and salmon flies; clearing, golden stones, and the blitz of summer hatches, the Trico and PMD summer of steady-rising fish, evening caddis action; autumn streamers, *Baetis* fishing, and October caddis . . .

There are so many waters to fish in the West, so many vast and intimate landscapes, that every sunrise and sunset could be spent along a different watery setting. Creek, small river, beaver pond, big river, lake, there's no end to western fishing possibilities.

Each season has its own appeal, hatches, and challenges. And each seems to change just about the time you figured the last one out. That's what keeps fishing, and fly fishing in particular, such a stimulating game. There are so many variations in conditions, hatches, and fish behavior that a lifetime's experience will still leave riddles unsolved. The human brain is just a tiny satellite in a universe full of primitive aquatic insects and persnickety rising trout. You can sure have fun trying to figure the game out, though. The places, settings, and people are all memorable. Individual rising fish, rivers, mountain vistas, boat-ramp scenes, and watering holes all vie for mental cataloguing. When it comes to fishing, this is the season, and now is the time!

WINTER HATCH CHART–DECEMBER THROUGH FEBRUARY

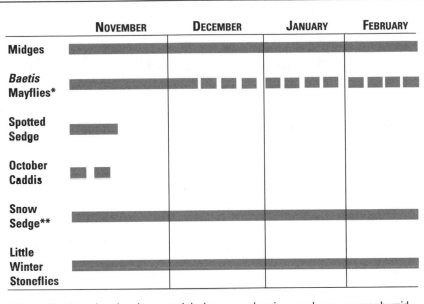

	NOVEMBER	DECEMBER	JANUARY	FEBRUARY
Midges				
Baetis* Mayflies				
Spotted Sedge				
October Caddis				
Snow Sedge**				
Little Winter Stoneflies				

*Sporadic winter hatches in coastal drainages and spring creeks on warmer humid days.

**Probably not as important to anglers as the lengthy hatch period of these two species would imply.

Other Important winter trout foods:

Aquatic Worms	Sculpins
Cased Caddis	Small Nymphs
Crayfish	Snails
Midge Larvae	Sowbugs
Scuds	Whitefish eggs

coastal / spring creek / lower elevations

Rocky Mountains

APPENDIX:
YEAR-ROUND TROUT FOODS

THIS IS a list of some primary year-round food sources available to trout in most rivers. These can be imitated any time, usually with some success. When there's no hatch activity in evidence, patterns imitating these trout foods can be relied on. Sometimes it's nice just to tie a weighted Woolly Bugger on the end of a stout leader, toss it out, slowly strip it in, and gaze off at some spectacular bit of landscape. Daydreaming has resulted in some of my best fish!

SCULPIN

These three- to five-inch-long bottom-hugging fish live in swift trout rivers and forage on nymphs. Broad heads, prominent pectoral fins, and dark mottled pigmentation (designed to camouflage them on the streambed) are their trademark features. They look a bit like a small bullhead catfish at first glance, but a closer inspection will make evident the differences, including the sculpin's lack of barbels.

Trout seem to love sculpins when they can get them. Trout stomach samples often reveal sculpin remains. Sculpin fly patterns from Muddler Minnows to Woolly Buggers to Woolhead Sculpins all catch fish, especially if they are fished deep along the bottom, where the real thing is always found. Sculpins dart and hide along streambeds. A stripping retrieve with a well-weighted fly, leader, and perhaps a sinking line is your best bet. Big trout like sculpin, too. Imitating one is always worthwhile for trophy-hunting anglers. Ignoring the hatch and fishing a sculpin imitation can result in bigger than average catches.

Sculpins are numerous in swift, clean trout rivers, and they feed on nymphs while hugging the bottom. Trout love them.

Sculpin

LENGTH: 3–5 INCHES IS A GOOD WORKING SIZE. SMALLER AND LARGER NATURALS ARE FOUND IN RIVERS AND STREAMS.

MATCHING FLY PATTERN SIZE: #2–8

COLOR: MOTTLED BROWNS TO ALMOST BLACK. SOME HAVE REDDISH ORANGE HUES IN THEIR FINS WHEN SPAWNING

Habitat: Swift, clean, well-oxygenated rivers and streams

CRAYFISH

This crustacean is familiar to everybody who's ever played in creeks and rivers. Trout and particularly large trout love them. In my experience trout consume more crayfish than they do small fish. The crayfish are either easier for them to catch or tastier. The naturals feature shades of olive, reddish brown, and have tinges of blue. Three- to four-inch specimens show up in many a trout stomach. They crawl and hide on the river bottom, often digging in and out of sight, but they can swim backwards with quick darting motions or continuous speed. Strip-and-pause fishing with a well-weighted fly and line works well. One could also crawl flies more slowly along the bottom if blessed with patience.

Trout tend to hit crayfish hard, aiming to disable this claw-wielding prey before eating it. This makes for some exciting action when fish are in the mood. I fish crayfish patterns the most while I'm drifting rivers in boats. I cast toward the shore, let the fly sink, then strip back out into deeper water.

This brown fell for a large crayfish imitation. In my experience, trout often eat more crayfish than small bait fish.

Crayfish

LENGTH: 3–5 INCHES
MATCHING FLY PATTERN SIZE: #2–8
COLOR: OLIVE-BROWN WITH SOME BLUE

Habitat: Most rivers and lakes, in most kinds of shallow water

OTHER SMALL FISH AND MINNOWS

A variety of "minnows," or small fish, including long-nosed dace, young mountain suckers, young trout and whitefish, true minnows, and shiners, show up periodically in trout stomachs, depending on the river's location. Many of these smaller fish feature olive to black backs and white to silver undersides. Some are mottled. A few have orange-red fins or stripes during spawning. One can experiment with color combinations, though fishing olive, gray, and black Woolly Buggers will fool plenty of fish. Mylar-piping bodies combined with fur or feather backs and tails are other popular options, including such flies as Zonkers.

Trout cohabitate with many a small fish but seldom get predacious until they see an injured one that's easy to catch. Therefore, it's best to fish streamers in a manner that imitates wounded fish. Healthy minnows face upstream, often in shallow warm water. They dart and swim quickly. Therefore, fishing a streamer sideways or slightly downstream with an erratic motion is likely to bring success. Fishing from a drift boat and casting to the banks, then stripping the fly out over deeper dropoff water, is an effective technique. Floating lines can be used, though weight added to the fly or leader can improve catch rates, especially if the trout are a little lethargic. The rate of retrieve can be altered to match the fish's mood: a quick retrieve for aggressive fish, a very slow one for sluggish fish.

Wade fishers can do better with sinking, sinking-tip, or shooting-head lines. Getting to the bottom of deeper runs and pools can pay dividends, because most other anglers don't get their flies deep enough to be effective in many situations. Lead- or chrome-eye streamers, which are essentially jigs, work especially well. They drop like stones in the water, getting to where deep-holding stream trout are. Their eye-catching up-and-down motion when being stripped attracts fish, too. The bright chrome-eye models effectively imitate the eyes of bait fish, something trout are thought to zero in on.

Fishing streamers effectively requires thought and the right equipment. It's as challenging as any other style of fishing and tends to produce some bigger fish. Spring is a prime streamer time.

Minnows

LENGTH: 2–6 INCHES
MATCHING FLY PATTERN SIZE: #2–10
COLOR: OLIVE, GRAY, BLACK, MOTTLED OLIVE WITH WHITE OR SILVER UNDERSIDES

Habitat: Most stream locations. Some minnows prefer warmer edge waters and slow-water locations

---

Minnow Fly Patterns

WOOLLY BUGGERS, ALL COLORS, #2–10
ZONKERS #2–10
MATUKA STREAMERS, ALL COLORS, #2–10
THREADFIN SHAD AND OTHER MYLAR-PIPING-BODIED FLIES #2–10
CHROME-EYE STREAMERS, VARIOUS COLORS, #2–6
EGG HEAD WOOLLY BUGGER #2–8 (EGG-HEAD STREAMER PATTERNS SEEM TO
DO A GREAT JOB OF CATCHING A TROUT'S EYE AND INTEREST, FOR WHATEVER
REASON)

LEECHES

Leeches live in most if not all rivers and lakes. In rivers, they seem to stay well hidden under rocks most of the time. I'm not sure how often stream trout really get to eat them. I've only found a few in stomach samples. Maybe they digest too quickly. In lakes (where I don't spend much time) they show up more often, or so I understand.

When swimming, leeches are 2–5 inches long. Colors are mostly dull and dark and designed for camouflage on stream- or lake beds colors. Many are mottled. Olives, browns, grays, and black are common colors. Trout probably don't catch too many leeches unless the leeches are swimming. Leeches swim steadily with an up-and-down undulation. They don't dart quickly, as a minnow, sculpin, or crayfish can. A more continuous hand-twist retrieve or slow, very short strips imitates a leech's swimming action well. Let the fly sink to the bottom before stripping for the best results. A black beadhead or plenty of weight on the leader helps get the fly down and also helps imitate the up-and-down swimming motion of the natural. A sinking line in lakes is recommended.

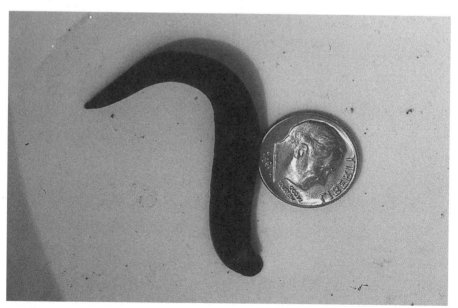

Leeches are of more interest to lake anglers than to river fishers. Although rivers do have leeches, they seem to stay hidden under rocks, rarely showing up in stomach samples.

Leeches are smooth, slimy, and thin when swimming. Many fly imitations are hackled or fuzzy, something that doesn't seem to make sense. Perhaps the answer here is that a trout that would eat a passing leech would also eat a distressed small fish, crayfish, or sculpin. In England, a fly known as a Dog Nobbler features the essential Woolly Bugger arrangement but without the hackle. This chenille-marabou creation, when kept thin, does look plenty leechlike in the water.

Leeches

LENGTH: 2–5 INCHES
MATCHING FLY PATTERN SIZE: #4–10
COLOR: OLIVE, GRAY, BROWN, PURPLE, BLACK, MOTTLED

Habitat: Most rivers and lakes

Leech Fly Patterns

MARABOU LEECH #2–10

You might find leech patterns tied with marabou, or strips of rabbit fur as commercial options. Many people just use black, olive, or purple Woolly Buggers, though they should be tied on the thin side. Dave Whitlock used strips of chamois leather, among other things. The idea is to get a thin profile with plenty of up-and-down wiggle when fished slowly. The addition of a black beadhead isn't a bad idea. River-based fly shops may not have many leech patterns. Shops with productive lakes nearby should have this base covered.

AQUATIC WORMS

There are as many as two hundred species of aquatic earthworms, many of which look like our more familiar land-based robin-feeding variety. Few anglers by now have not heard of the San Juan Worm imitation and its fish-catching ways. A trout hunkered down on the bottom in a rising, possibly muddying, spring flow is unlikely to let an easy-to-inhale worm drift on by! Imitations must be fished on weighted leaders and bounced down near the bottom. In heavier, deeper flows, weight should be built into the fly, too. Strike indicators are generally used, because takes by the fish are easy and subtle. A quick strike upon detection is necessary, because trout can blow a discovered fraud out rather quickly. By the time you feel a trout on a nymph or worm, it's probably trying as hard as possible to let go.

Hanging a small nymph off a San Juan Worm is a good idea, too, particularly on clear-flowing tailwater rivers where there's a lot of fishing pressure and the trout have seen it all. Fish can see the worm from a little farther away, swing over to look, and often take the small nymph instead.

On rivers that see heavy fishing pressure, like the San Juan and Bighorn, San Juan Worms show great diversity and modification. Trout in these rivers learn by experience to dodge patterns they've been repeatedly deceived by in the past. One can almost picture them raising an eyebrow and leaning over to take something entirely new. An ongoing evolution of patterns seems necessary to fool jaded trout in destination waters.

San Juan Worms seem to work well most everywhere. I've even used them with success on a variety of New Zealand rivers. As a good no-brainer rig for blind-fishing freestone rivers, a San Juan Worm with a #10–16 Beadhead nymph dropper is a productive way to go. Watch out for tangles, though, and cast smoothly. A strike indicator, weight on the leader, and two wet flies makes for a self-tangling rig!

Aquatic Worms

LENGTH: 1–4 INCHES
MATCHING FLY PATTERN SIZE: #6–10
COLOR: REDS, ORANGES, PURPLES, BROWNS, TANS

Habitat: All waters, but used primarily on rivers where they're dead-drifted to waiting fish.

Worm Fly Patterns

SAN JUAN WORM, RED, TAN, PURPLE, BROWN #6–10
MICROWORMS, RED, TAN, PURPLE, BROWN #12–16

SOWBUGS, CRESSBUGS

These crustaceans are numerous in rivers, especially in oxygen-rich, hard limestone-type waters. They're abundant in shallow zones, around rocks, in leaf matter, and in aquatic vegetation. They crawl along the bottom mostly, but if washed free are rather helpless and inept swimmers. Trout may break them free from weed beds or pick them off the bottom at times, as well as take them in the drift. Dead-drift, bottom-bouncing, strike-indicator fishing is the ticket to fairly steady success with them. The naturals remain active in very cold seasonal waters. This makes them a good winter and spring option where they are found to be numerous.

Sowbugs are mottled gray or tannish brown in color. They're flattened in shape and segmented, with seven pairs of legs. Due to the naturals' great numbers and year-round availability to fish, sowbug or cressbug imitations make excellent standby patterns in any fly box.

Crustaceans, including sowbugs, are plentiful in rivers and are favorites of trout. They remain active in winter and can be important food items for trout when hatches and nymphs are few. This is especially true from late fall through spring.

Sowbugs, Cressbugs

LENGTH: 5–20 MM
MATCHING FLY PATTERN SIZE: #12–16
COLOR: MOTTLED GRAYISH OR TANNISH BROWN

Habitat: Shallow to medium-depth zones of rivers

Sowbug and Cressbug Fly Patterns

SOWBUG #10–16
TAILLESS HARE'S EAR #10–16 (CUT THE TAIL OFF A SCRUFFY HARE'S EAR NYMPH AND LET HER FLY!)

SCUDS

Often called freshwater shrimp, scuds are numerous, widespread, and especially important in lakes. Some rivers have a lot of scuds, too, primarily spring creek and tailwater river types. Scuds are hunchbacked, somewhat flattened crustaceans with fourteen pairs of variously shaped legs. They rest in weed beds, under rocks, and in soft bottoms. Their active swimming and scavenging lifestyle makes them easy prey for trout. Lake-dwelling trout can grow very large at a rapid rate by devouring scuds. A trout's flesh and exterior coloration is changed by eating crustaceans. The flesh turns pink-orange and skin patterning can be brighter, too, with more reds.

Scuds can and do swim forward, backward, right side up, and upside down. They're quite active but not particularly fast. They prefer dim periods for active feeding, including evening, night, and cloudy days. Their general coloration is olive-gray, and some are paler and others are darker. Upon molting, the color is temporarily tan or grayish pink. Trout eat scuds in all sizes and color variations. If you want big trout, fish lakes and ponds with good scud populations!

Freshwater shrimp, or scuds, can attain spectacular populations in spring-rich lakes. Big trout are the end result of this food chain. Spring-fed rivers can have them, too, though sowbugs are usually a more prominent moving-water crustacean.

NYMPHS IN GENERAL

It is often heard that nymphs make up about 80 percent of the average trout's diet. Nymphs are available to trout year-round to one degree or another. Some species, like the giant salmon fly nymph, take two to three years to mature. There are always some fairly large ones around, though they can stay well hidden from trout. Most mayfly, stonefly, and caddisfly species produce one generation a year. Some, like the widespread *Baetis* and *Callibaetis* mayflies, produce two generations a year, or even three. Midges are plentiful year-round and are of particular importance in winter, when they are often the only aquatic insect hatching in magnitude and readily available.

As a general rule, the largest, most diverse, and most active nymphs are most abundant and available to trout in early summer (late May to mid-July). As the various species hatch from spring through fall, mate, and lay eggs, it's only natural that the available nymphs of late fall, winter, and early spring are smaller early-instar specimens, most of which hide and are harder for trout to eat. Nonetheless, nymphs and midge larvae and pupae are the year-round staple for most river trout. This diet is augmented with crustaceans (sowbugs, scuds, snails, crayfish), small fish, terrestrial insects (from spring into fall), young fish, and even plankton.

If in doubt, fishing one to three nymphs deep and using a strike indicator is usually the best starting point for those wishing to catch fish, especially in nonhatch periods. In low and clear spring waters, a medium and small nymph would be a good combination, say a #10 Beadhead Hare's Ear or Prince Nymph with a #14–18 Green Caddis Worm or Serendipity

Medium to large nymphs become most available to trout in early summer. Numerous hatches and the largest aquatic insects hatch in this time period, particularly on swifter rivers. Trout can be quite happy hugging the bottom and nymphing while this food source is peaking.

dropper. As spring waters rise and muddy up a bit with rising air temperatures and snowmelt, larger nymphs come into play. A #4–8 salmon fly nymph, perhaps with a #10–12 Beadhead Hare's Ear dropper, would be a good searching rig, if you don't mind casting the extra weight. As rivers continue to rise, more weight on the leader and large flies are commonly used to get the trout's attention in murky flows. I often fish two-fly rigs for added water coverage. A dozen different nymph patterns in a few varying sizes can catch most of the river's fish.

One Dozen Productive Nymph Patterns

Kaufmann Stone, black #2–8
Bitch Creek #4–10
Rubber Legs (George's Stone and Girdle Bugs) #4–8
Beadhead Prince Nymph #8–14
Beadhead Hare's Ear #8–16
Beadhead Pheasant Tail #12–18
Pheasant Tail #14–20
San Juan Worm #6–10
Sowbug #12–16
Serendipity #16–20
Brassie #16–22
Peacock and Partridge Soft Hackle #12–18

This selection of nymphs will catch trout most anywhere. Three other top runners I can't leave unmentioned include:

Montana Nymph #4–10
Zug Bug #10–16
Beadhead Green Caddis Worm #10–14

BIBLIOGRAPHY

Most OF THE information in this book results from time I spent on-stream, but there is plenty that I had to substantiate with reference material from the following books. Information for some hatches with which I don't have much personal experience are described in the text by comparing and whittling down usable material from as many sources as possible. We can all be grateful to these authors who have provided a foundation on which we can build our own experiences.

Arbona, Fred, Jr. *Mayflies, the Angler, and the Trout.* Tulsa, OK: Winchester Press, 1980.

Caucci, Al, and Robert Nastasi. *Hatches II.* Piscataway, NJ: Comparahatch, Ltd., 1986

Hafele, Richard, and David Hughes. *The Complete Book of Western Hatches.* Portland, OR: Frank Amato Publications, 1981.

Juracek, John, and Craig Matthews. *Fishing Yellowstone Hatches.* West Yellowstone, MT: Blue Ribbon Flies, 1992.

Knopp, Malcolm, and Robert Cormier. *Mayflies.* Helena, MT: Greycliff Publishing Company, 1997.

La Fontaine, Gary. *Caddisflies.* New York, NY: Nick Lyons/Winchester Press, 1981.

McCafferty, W. Patrick. *Aquatic Entemology.* Boston, MA: Jones & Bartlett, Inc., 1981.

Richards, Carl, and Robert Braendle. *Caddis Super Hatches.* Portland, OR: Frank Amato Publications, 1997.

Scammell, Robert. *The Phenological Fly.* Red Deer, Alberta, Canada: Blue Ribbon Books, 1995.

Schollmeyer, James. *Hatch Guide for the Lower Deschutes River.* Portland, OR: Frank Amato Publications, 1994.

———. *Hatch Guide for Western Streams.* Portland, OR: Frank Amato Publications, 1997.

Stolz, Judith, and Judith Schnell. *The Wildlife Series—Trout.* Harrisburg, PA: Stackpole Books, 1991.

Streeks, Neale. *Small Fly Adventures in the West: Angling for Larger Trout.* Boulder, CO: Pruett Publishing Company, 1996.

Swisher, Doug, and Carl Richards. *Emergers.* New York, NY: Lyons & Burford, 1991.

———. *Selective Trout.* Piscataway, NJ: Nick Lyons/Winchester Press, 1971.

Walinchus, Rod. *Fly Fishing the North Platte River: An Angler's Guide.* Boulder, CO: Pruett Publishing Company, 1994.

Walinchus, Rod, and Tom Travis. *Fly Fishing the Yellowstone River: An Angler's Guide.* Boulder, CO: Pruett Publishing Company, 1995.

Whitlock, Dave. *Dave Whitlock's Guide to Aquatic Trout Foods.* New York, NY: Nick Lyons Books, 1982.

INDEX

Eddies: fishing in, 122; nymphs in, 53
Edge waters, fishing in, 122, 181
Egg patterns, fishing with, 16, 187, 208, 219, 226
Elkhair Caddis: fishing with, 86, 93, 104–5, 110, 127; olive-bodied, 104–5; photo of, 88
Emergers, 2, 83, 86, 156; color of, 102; fishing with, 29 (fig.), 36, 110, 137; imitating, 45
Epeorus species, 61, 78, 80 (photo)
Ephoron, 178, 187; hatches of, 188 (photo), 189
Eye of the pool, fishing in, 11, 11 (fig.)

Fast-water mayflies (*Heptagenia* species), 61, 115, 134, 145; fishing with, 78–80, 82, 118, 124, 145; pattern for, 82, 83
Feeding behavior: autumn, 181; early-spring, 10–15; early-summer, 47–51; high-summer, 122–26; temperature and, 116, 118, 119, 124winter, 216–19
Firehole River, speckled Peter on, 98
"Fishing the water" strategy, 50
Flav (*Drunella flavilinea*), 134, 149; fishing with, 68–69; hatches of, 69; pattern for, 69
Float fishing, 12, 47, 114, 115 photo of, 90
Fluttering Stones, fishing with, 128
Fly patterns, 1, 2; autumn, 185, 187–89, 191–99; early-spring, 16–39; early-summer, 51–58, 60–61, 64–71, 73–74, 76, 78–80, 82–86, 88–89, 91–106; high summer, 126–28, 130–32, 134–4, 149–50, 152; realistic, 125 (photo); winter, 221–24, 226–34
Forage fish, fishing with, 173
Freestone rivers: *Baetis* in, 26; blind-fishing, 244; cased caddis on, 152; fishing in, 16–17, 51, 106, 109, 110, 119, 119 (photo), 216, 219, 230; green sedge in, 156; hatches in, 47, 50, 54, 126; levels of, 42; midge fishing in, 169; summer on, 114; temperatures in, 123, 181

Freshwater shrimp: fishing with, 247; photo of, 247

Gallatin River: runoff in, 115; stone flies in, 43
George's Stone, 250
Giant orange sedge (*Dicosmoecus* species), 166; fishing with, 202–3; pattern for, 205
Ginger quills (*Heptagenia simplicioides*), 78, 134
Girdle Bugs, 250
Golden stoneflies (*Calineuria californica, Claasenia sabulosa, Hesperoperla pacifica*), 22, 100, 122, 126, 130; fishing with, 60–61, 124, 128, 129 (photo); hatches of, 54, 58, 59, 61, 116; pattern for, 63; salmon flies and, 60
Golden stonefly nymphs, 44, 65, 109, 128, 233; photo of, 62
Grannom, 36, 44, 51, 84, 103, 233; hatch of, 41; photo of, 35
Gray drakes (*Siphlonurus occidentalis*): fishing with, 124, 143–44; pattern for, 144, 145
Great gray spotted sedge (*Arctopsyche grandis*): fishing with, 100; pattern for, 101
Green caddis worm, 36, 156, 202; fishing with, 23, 249
Green drakes (*Drunella grandis, D. doddsi, D. coloradensis*), 41, 44, 48, 69, 70, 134, 149, 191; fishing with, 66–67, 110; hatches of, 66, 67; pattern for, 68; photo of, 66
Green sedge (*Rhyacophila bifila, Rhyacophila coloradensis*): fishing with, 156–58, 202; hatches of, 158; pattern for, 158, 159; photo of, 157
Griffith's Gnat, 224; fishing with, 18, 207, 221, 223; photo of, 224
Grizzly Wulffs, fishing with, 82

H & L Variants, 31, 49, 224
Hare's Ear, 53, 80, 91; fishing with, 82, 131, 185, 208